Think to Win

The New Approach to Fast Driving

By Don Alexander

Foreword by Mark Martin

RB

ROBERT BENTLEY, INC.
AUTOMOTIVE PUBLISHERS

RB ROBERT BENTLEY, INC. AUTOMOTIVE PUBLISHERS

Information that makes
the difference.®

1033 Massachusetts Avenue
Cambridge, MA 02138
USA
800-423-4595 / 617-547-4170
e-mail: sales@rb.com

Copies of this book may be purchased from selected booksellers, or directly from the publisher by mail. The publisher encourages comments from the reader of this book. These communications have been and will be considered in the preparation of this and other manuals. Please write to Robert Bentley, Inc., Publishers at the address listed on the top of this page.

Since this page cannot legibly accommodate all the copyright notices, the Art Credits page at the back of this book listing the source of the photographs used constitutes an extension of the copyright page.

Library of Congress Cataloging-in-Publication Data

Alexander, Don
    Think to win/by Don Alexander.
        p.   cm.
    Includes index.
    ISBN 0-8376-0070-7 (pbk. : alk. paper) : $19.95
    1. Automobile racing--Psychological aspects. I. Title
    GV1029.A44 1994
769.7′2′019--dc20

Bentley Stock No. GDAL

Ford SVO Part No. M-1832-Z3

97 96 95 10 9 8 7 6 5 4 3 2 1

The paper used in this publication is acid free and meets the requirements of the National Standard for Information Sciences-Permanence of Paper for Printed Library Materials. ∞

Think to Win: The New Approach to Fast Driving, by Don Alexander

Front cover: From the top: a) Photo by Earl Yamagami; b) Photo by Kenny Kane; c) Photo of Mark Martin by Kenny Kane

Back cover: From the top: a) Photo courtesy Sutton Photographic; b) Photo courtesy Sutton Photographic; c) Photo by Don Grassmann; d) Photo by Don Grassmann

Think to Win

The New Approach to Fast Driving

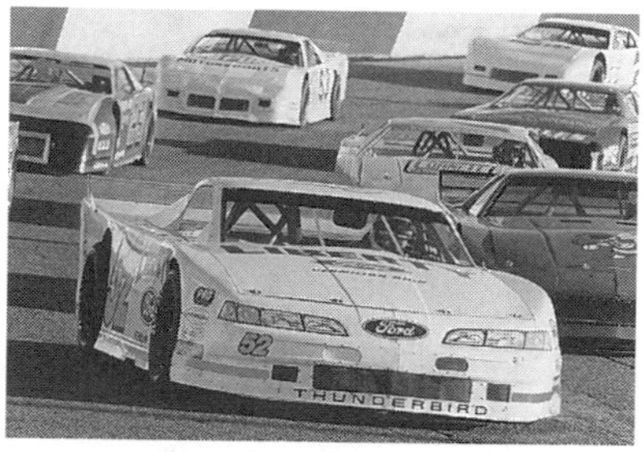

Fundamental concepts for the winning driver, see Chapter 1.

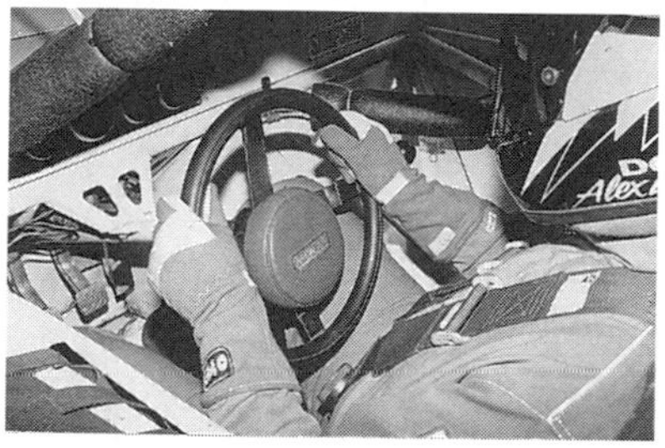

Set-up for maximum performance, see Chapter 5.

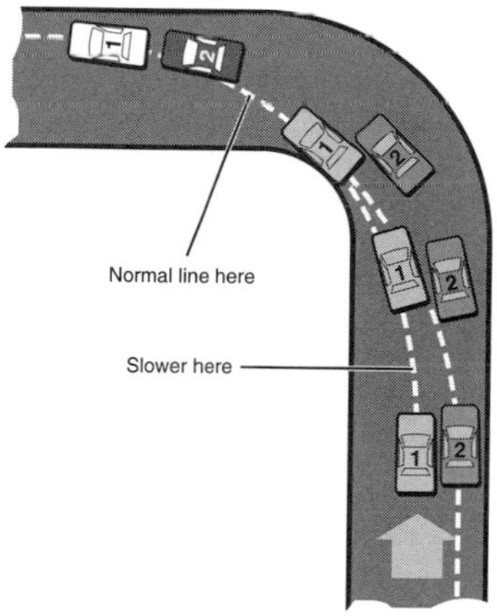
Normal line here
Slower here

Techniques for specific race situations, see Chapter 11.

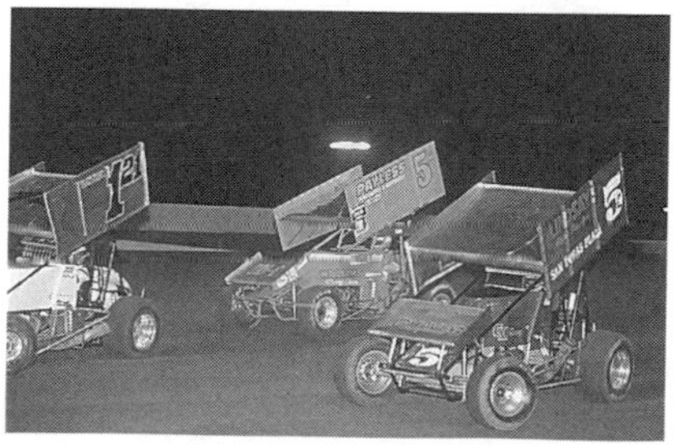

Tips for racing on different track layouts and surfaces, see Chapter 13.

Contents

FOREWORD

by Mark Martin

Short of going out and getting in a car, where else are you going to get the experience it takes to be a winning race car driver? This book is a great place to start. Don Alexander offers lots of practical advice in *Think To Win* about things experienced racers do unconsciously after years of practice, things like car control skills, race plans and tactics.

A big part of planning my tactics, and knowing when to attack and how to defend, is knowing who I'm dealing with and what their personality is—their driving personality. You need to store up this knowledge of who you're driving against. Don calls it keeping a 'Drivers Book'. Every driver has a driving personality. You watch him drive, and after a while, you can anticipate how his car will move. If you don't know a driver, you better be more defensive than if you do know him. But once you do know them, you can just go right to the limit all the time with those guys. And that's what we do out here. We mostly all know each other and we always race each other right to the edge of one another's threshold on everything from beatin' and bangin' to going four wide through a turn.

Then there's the importance of what Don calls 'visual fields', and how to use your eyes during a race. You have to train yourself to use your eyes through turns and to protect yourself. I might be looking straight ahead, but if something unnatural happens— smoke starts happening, a car starts spinning off to the side—I detect it out of the corner of my eye. If I'm doing my job, I've already seen it coming. I can see and know what's going on without looking directly at it.

Peripheral vision is a major, major factor in being an effective driver, especially in avoiding crashes. I stay on top of what's going on, otherwise, I'll wreck. Or be wrecked.

When I'm racing I use the sense of smell a lot with the engine. When you get into tuning an engine to the max you do your share of burning pistons, and a lot of times I'll smell that, and catch it before it goes bad. This is just one aspect of knowing your car, what Don calls 'Mechanical Empathy', and it's the kind of skill that wins races.

Don also talks about the importance of having a plan when you go into a race, and then to modify that plan as the race develops. When people ask me what my strategy is for a race, I tell them, simply, to win. The strategy is to *win*! But it's not that simple. Now that I've been racing for twenty years I just don't think about it—for me, my initial racing plan is almost unconscious. Here's what I do. I try to make sure that I have a reasonably fast race car with a balanced set-up. Then when the race starts, all that preparation becomes a given, and I look at what's in front of me, see what's happening, and watch how the race develops.

Until the race starts you don't really know what kinds of advantages or disadvantages your competitors are going to have. You don't know for sure what the tire wear is going to be like, who's going to truly whup you on fuel mileage, who's car is going to be stronger in traffic, or whatever.

As the race wears on, you see what becomes important, really important: this guy's got us on handling in the turns, this guy's got us on tire wear. You start building up all these observations, a bunch of data that you collect. Your crew chief is critical because he's gathering this data too, and you put it all together, and if you've got good communication, you come up with a plan, that even if you don't have the strongest package to start, you can still do something really smart and gain the advantage. So you develop your plan and make your decisions quickly. Bam! I'm going to pass him high here. Bam! I'm going to defend my lead by running lower there.

Communication figures into all kinds of strategy, from racecar preparation and set-up to organizing travel to the races. Good communication is critical, as Don points out, because without it you're only going to be as good as you are. But if you have a smart crew around you, and you have good communication with them, you can combine their strengths with your own, and you're that much stronger than you would be on your own. You're out there trying to beat some other people that are probably pretty good at it. The only way you can beat them is to try to pull more strength in.

I had to learn what questions to ask. Jack Roush had to teach me what it was that I wanted in my race car. He had to kind of shake me a few times and look me straight in the eye and say, "Listen to what I'm asking you." Now I have the ability to drive the car three laps, two laps, and come in and tell my crew what it needs. That's learning, and I had a good teacher. Jack Roush didn't ask me a bunch of questions about things that didn't matter. He had the experience, he knew what questions needed answering, and pretty soon it all came together.

Now it's hard to paint a perfect picture for fans so that they can understand what it's like to drive a race car. Every time that I go to the stands and watch a race I'm overwhelmed, because it looks totally different from what I see from behind the wheel.

One thing that you can do is watch the in-car camera. Another is read this book. To me, they both give great insight to what goes through a driver's mind at a hundred and eighty miles an hour. Don helps you understand the challenges we face out there so you can answer your friend when he turns to you and says, "Man, why doesn't he just *pass* that guy?"

One thing that fans and beginning drivers don't fully understand or realize about racing is the amount focus it takes to be good. I have absolutely mind-boggling focus. For years I had tunnel vision like you wouldn't believe. I could not see anything but that racing mass in front of me, and that's all there was in my whole life. I blocked the whole rest of the world out, and just went after that thing, full-focus. I'd have to say that was certainly one of my biggest assets. I didn't have any other interest in anything. All I did was work. Eighteen hours a day, seven days a week, trying to win. That's all it is. I had natural abilities, but no one would ever have known that if it hadn't been for my focus and dedication. I had a scary amount of focus and the same kind of dedication.

It's like the way physical fitness has been a big, big part in my recent success—and I say that in life, not just in racing. If you work hard enough and care enough to do it, then you will be better than the other guys, 'cause that means that you *want* it. You make the commitment. It isn't whether or not you lift the weights, it's whether or not you *will* lift the weights, for no apparent payoff or no guaranteed payoff.

If you've got the dedication, *Think To Win* will help you train and direct your focus.

Author's Introduction

When I started racing go carts in 1960, little information was available about the art of driving a race car, even less about the science. Everyone learned by trial and error and observation. In a sense, it was much easier back then. I guess ignorance is bliss.

About ten years later, I was still racing. I then began a career as a racing instructor. A few years later, I began writing about racing. *Think to Win* contains most of what I learned about the art and science of this sport over a three decade period.

What is most different is my perspective. Much has been written about driving race cars; most offers good information. My goal with this work is to offer insights and perspectives that have, up to now, been overlooked.

Whether you agree or not, you need to think about the issues presented here. For, while *Think to Win* covers the art of driving a race, it is really about creating a PLAN to become a winning race driver, choosing directions, strategies, approaches. The plan is not mine, it is yours. So when I refer to the plan, keep in mind that the information presented is for you to use in *your plan*.

As you develop your plan, you establish priorities. I offer many suggestions concerning priorities, but decide for yourself what your priorities are. You can use the information in this book in any way you choose. The important point is that the plan you create allows you to get where you want to be.

To insure that key ideas are easy to find and review, several sidebars titled *The Winning Driver* are spread throughout the book. While each of these concepts is presented in the main text, each of them offers an idea worth further emphasizing for your consideration.

For you to reach your goals, you must be willing to make a commitment to yourself. You also must deal in reality. In the world of driving a race car, there is no right or wrong, good or bad, only reality. While you may perceive that something is bad or wrong, you still must deal with it as a real situation. Judging it only delays dealing with it. In a race car, you have precious little time for any judgements.

Think to Win is a tool intended to help you reach personal goals. It is nothing more, nothing less. As with any tool, it must be used to be helpful. I hope you find it helpful in your personal quest to become a winning race driver.

1 THE ART OF RACING

Automobile racing is arguably the most scientific of all sports. Yet the skills required to win races transcend science and become art; the strategies and tactics even more so. Unlike most sports participants, the race driver works within the tool, the entire time facing the life-threatening consequences of misuse or poor execution. The art of driving a race car would compare to the art of chess only if the chess player actually rode the figures at high speed, approaching the limits of physics and having less than a micro-second in which to make tactical and strategic decisions. All of this in an environment detrimental to concentration. Art indeed!

A race driver is anyone who drives a car to its limits in a competition. And while the point of the competition is to win, the winning race driver is not necessarily the fastest or the first to finish. A winning race driver pushes personal performance to new limits. True victory is very personal. In a sense, driving race cars involves two art forms: driving a car to its physical limits, and competing wheel to wheel on the race track in an attempt to win.

The Art of Fast Driving

The art of fast driving entails driving a car to its limits of performance. This requires that you explore personal limits, and constantly redefine them as experience leads to new understanding.

The Art of Race Driving

The art of race driving requires the same skills necessary to master the art of fast driving. But the art of racing requires additional skills. The strategy

Fig. 1-1. The moment of truth begins when the green flag drops. Pictured is start of 1992 Indianapolis 500.

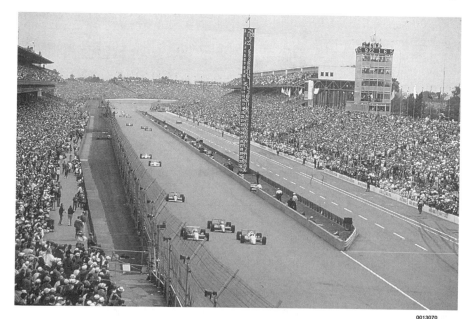

0013070

THE WINNING DRIVER

To become a fast, winning race driver, you must develop all of the necessary skills.

Natural ability is not enough.

Tools: All of the tools in this book, used to the best of your ability.

Game Plan: Create a plan; implement the plan; check its effectiveness; identify strong and weak points; develop the strong points and work on weak points; alter the plan as you gain new knowledge and insights.

Priorities: Create a flexible plan; know your goal.

Practice: Write the plan; write a plan for change.

---

and tactics of wheel-to-wheel racing include, but clearly go beyond, the art of driving to the limits of physics.

The Qualities of a Winning Race Driver

A winning race driver possesses several characteristics. I list the most important:

Perception: The ability to perceive reality, both emotional and physical.

Anticipation: The ability to "see" the future by looking ahead on the track and by recognizing subtle clues in the actions of other drivers.

Judgement: The ability to determine accurately the relative effects of time, speed, and distance as well as forces, both on and off the race track; additionally, the ability to determine when a plan is effective or changes are needed.

Patience: The ability to delay immediate gains for more important gains later, both on and off the race track.

Discipline: The ability to stand by a commitment and stick to a plan.

Commitment: The bridge between dreams and reality.

Planning: The conceptualizing, implementation and refinement of the blueprints and construction process for your bridge.

Fig. 1-2. The goal for most race drivers is to reach victory lane. Sterling Marlin celebrates his 1994 Daytona 500 win.

0013071

THE WINNING DRIVER

The skilled race driver has complete confidence because he has done his homework, developed a plan and honed his skills.

This requires practice, insight and personal honesty. True confidence lies in the personal knowledge that you are working to reach your internal goals.

Tools: Setting goals that will allow you to reach your external goals; doing the work to develop and hone skills.

Game Plan: Recognize needed skills; develop a training plan; create a positive belief system.

Priorities: Understand belief systems; develop visualization skills; practice, practice and more practice of techniques.

Practice: Learn visualization techniques; time mental laps; practice all driving skills every time you drive a car anywhere.

Self-evaluation: The ability to evaluate in complete honesty where you are and what you need in order to maintain your commitment.

Concentration: The ability to focus attention *right now* on the most important priorities.

Understanding: Knowing the most important priorities.

Knowledge: The internalization of information which allows all else to occur.

Car Control: The ability to make a car do what you want it to; knowing and understanding how to direct it.

Mental Attitude: The development of honest self-confidence based on the reality that the work has been done or is in progress to keep the commitment. This creates a truly Positive Mental Attitude.

You have the ability to develop these and other attributes. Each of these is an internal goal, since you have complete control over reaching the goal.

Winning

Winning has two elements. The first is winning by being the fastest or the first to take the checkered flag. This is an external goal, requiring many factors outside of individual control. The second is winning by committing to turn a dream into reality. Every step you take in this quest is a winning step. Winning on the race track is simply the outcome. The journey to reach that level requires the development of skills and attributes, and the courage to face fears and meet a commitment.

Setting Goals

Presumably, since you are reading this book, you have a dream or goal to become a race driver, or improve your skills if you already are racing. Whatever your goal may be, one factor is crucial to achieve success.

Creating a Plan

Creating a plan is fundamental to success in any endeavor. And in a real sense, any plan, even a poorly conceived one, is better than no plan at all. *Think to Win* is not a plan for you. You must create that for yourself, in the same way that you must set your own goals based on your own dreams and desires. *Think to Win* is, however, a source of information. It is a compilation of ideas, concepts, principles, techniques and experience integrated over a 30-plus-year career. I present them here for you to consider. I also offer them as a tool to help you create a plan to become a winning race driver.

Fig. 1-3. Marlin takes the checkered flag at the Daytona 500.

0013072

THE WINNING DRIVER

The skilled race driver creates a plan, determines its effectiveness and improves the plan as needed.

The plan is crucial; even a bad one is better than none. The plan must be dynamic allowing for instantaneous as well as long term alteration. This is crucial in all aspects of racing, both on the race track and in promotional/business activities.

Tools: Write the plan, put the plan into action, make evaluations, and be ready for change.

Game Plan: Implement the plan, analyze it, and make changes as needed.

Priorities: Use the plan dynamically; don't write it, then ignore it. Determine what you want, and establish priorities to get it. If progress is sluggish, be patient. If some part of the plan is not working as expected, try a change.

Practice: Create plans for simple activities, check their effectiveness and try making changes.

THE WINNING DRIVER

The race winner is a driver who best accomplishes the following five goals:

1. Creates the best car set-up for the race conditions. It is difficult, usually impossible, to overcome an inferior set-up.

2. Achieves the most consistently fast laps. Consistently fast laps, as opposed to a few quick laps followed by breeches of concentration or focus, is a key to winning.

3. Spends the least attention on driving fast and the most attention on tactics and strategy. With well-developed skills for driving fast, you will spend less attention on driving and more attention on strategy and tactics.

4. Manages the vehicle platform best. Mechanical empathy is crucial, as well as smooth control of the throttle and brake and minimal steering to save tires.

5. Expends the least energy during a race. A relaxed driver in a calm mental state expends less energy. This improves endurance, concentration, and the ability to determine priorities and stay focused.

Tools: This book.

Game Plan: This book.

Priorities: Relaxation, concentration, sensitivity, practice, mental attitude.

Practice: Visualization, meditation, yoga, video games.

Fig. 1-4. Here, at Columbus Motor Raceway in 1993, Butch Miller runs the only V-6 powered Ford in a field of V-8 powered cars. The first element in being competitive and winning races is a good car set-up.

0012813

2 MENTAL SKILLS

Driving a race car is primarily a mental exercise. Mental skills are the most important to develop and the most difficult to comprehend. Your brain works very much like a computer, taking in data, processing it, organizing it, making a decision, and directing the actions needed to implement the decision. To do this, the computer (your brain) must be programmed. This requires experience so that you can choose, accurately and with lightning speed, a course of action.

Part of brain programming involves human emotion, and that can have an effect on the quality of your decisions. Emotions will be covered in the next chapter. For now, we will look at the intake of sensory inputs, mental focus, concentration, anticipation, outcomes and maintaining focus. The goal is to help you take in data (inputs), process it quickly, make the correct decisions (outputs), and have all of this based in reality, not on hopes or desires.

DRIVER INPUTS

Driver inputs are any information that flows to you from outside. This information gives you the data you need to make decisions during a race. Inputs include the status of your car, other drivers and their cars, race circumstances, the track, the environment, and you. It is best to just let inputs flow, and spend no time consciously analyzing the information. If you

Fig. 2-1. Not all your preparation takes place on the track. Mental preparedness is as important as car set-up. Bobby Gill takes a break to meditate on his performance in the 1992 All American 400 for the NASCAR Winston All Pro Series.

0012814

start paying attention to the "voice" of your conscious mind, the input data stream is slowed and your capacity for analysis is lessened. This costs time and increases risk.

Visual Input

The most common data input is visual. Your eyes take in more information more quickly than any other human sense. Visual inputs are well-suited to certain types of data acquisition, and less effective for others. The most important areas for visual inputs are those requiring action at some point in the near future, where *anticipation* is needed.

The Most Effective Uses of Visual Inputs

VEHICLE PATH. To plan vehicle paths you must look ahead to determine the optimum path. Then you must "see" the path once you make the decision.

DETERMINING HAZARDS OR POTENTIAL PROBLEMS. Visual inputs, if taken in early enough, allow you to take positive action to change your plan and avoid the problem.

PLANNING STRATEGIES. Visual inputs give you the data you need to plan passes, defense and other strategies and tactics.

SPEED JUDGEMENT. Combined with other sensory inputs, the eyes offer effective data for judging speed.

JUDGING CHANGES IN TRACTION. While visual inputs are not effective for Traction Sampling (more on that later), they can offer data about possible changes in traction that require immediate or future action.

TIMING. Any action requiring timing must be anticipated, by seeing what is happening.

Ineffective Uses of Visual Inputs

TRACTION SAMPLING. This relies mostly on feel and balance.

MECHANICAL PROBLEMS. Feel and noise offer the best inputs here.

How Visual Input Works

Without lengthy explanations about the physiology of sight and how the brain processes visual inputs, the process occurs nearly instantaneously and with incredible accuracy. This information flow can be disrupted or slowed due to emotions. Information quality can also suffer if you focus attention on less important areas. Finally, information can flow without di-

Fig. 2-2. Many hazards, like a car spinning or crashing in front of you, present themselves on the race track. How well you analyze the data available determines your safety and success on the race track. Cars tangle at the Winston Classic 100.

0012815

rect visual contact, given adequate prior experience. Let's look more closely at each of these factors.

Disruption of Visual Data Flow

This can be caused by other inputs that interfere with data flow, or which alter your perception of the data. Emotional responses to track events—fear, anxiety, anger, joy, etc.—are good examples. Additionally, emotions not related to current situations can have the same effect. Examples include crew personnel problems, business or family situations, etc. These emotional responses can be either positive or negative in nature, but the effect is the same: visual concentration on NOW is diverted to past or future events, and your ability to "see" reality diminishes; the level of risk increases.

Focusing Visual Attention

You must constantly decide where to focus visual attention. Advance planning is crucial, or attention can easily be diverted away from the highest priority areas. For example, looking at the bumper of a leading car in the braking zone takes away the full visual picture, making the ideal visual path difficult to find and follow. Visual attention is constantly shifting. You must frequently make decisions about priorities. Your plan must include a basic idea of the visual priorities, as well as ways to deal with unexpected visual inputs. If you are ready to take in unexpected occurrences, the response to those situations will be judged on reality, and not biased by fear-triggered emotional responses.

Flying Blind

In racing situations, due to other cars, terrain and weather conditions, you often cannot see far enough ahead to plan vehicle paths or avoid hazardous situations. Fortunately, the mind has the capacity to "see" when the eyes cannot. The art of "visualization" is very powerful. In fact the mind does not really know the difference between real visual data and imagined visual data. We will cover this topic in greater depth later in this chapter.

THE WINNING DRIVER

To drive at the limit, a race driver must assimilate (process) inputs instantly, precisely and free of judgement.

To process data, you must understand the information, have a plan that allows using the information, and have the ability to respond to the data free from value judgement. A narrow mental focus can cause, at worst, an improper response or, at best, a less than effective response. The open mind can take in more information, process it more quickly and respond more accurately. To keep your mind "open," focus on the reality of the current situation. If your thoughts become judgemental, you lose time and clarity, leaving the door open for further errors.

Tools: Positive mental attitude, meditation, visualization, an understanding of the limits of tire adhesion, experience driving a vehicle to the limit, a fluid plan.

Game Plan: Maintain a clear mind, sense inputs, and focus on the desired outcome based upon your plan.

Priorities: Accepting reality; fine-tuning your plan; learning to make corrections, not judgements.

Practice Exercises: In any activity, make errors without making judgements; practice driving any vehicle to the limits of the tire adhesion, especially your race car on a skid pad or other area where errors have minor consequences.

Fig. 2-3. Where do you look? At the bumper of the car in front? The driver's hands? The car three lengths ahead? Four? Make visual priorities for each situation and constantly shift your visual focus.

Two elements must be present for the mind to "see" clearly. First, you must have enough data inputs to create an accurate mental picture and define the situation. Second, you must believe the mental picture for it to be effective. If the belief is not there, the emotions will take over, creating doubts and altering the desired outcome to suit what is actually "believed." Here is an example of the process. On a blind corner on a race track, after, say 100 laps, you have a "clear" mental picture of the portion of the corner that is not visible. If the visual inputs are accurate based upon the 100 experiences of driving through the section, the mental picture will be equally clear. This allows you to "see" through the blind area as it is being approached as if the area were completely visible.

If, however, you do not "believe" that what you have experienced is what is really there, your brain will act accordingly. The path will change, you will reduce speed, lose time, because your actions are based largely on fear and tentativeness. It requires both experience and trust in your perception of reality to take a blind section of track "at the limit."

If you had zero data points, if you had never driven this section before, you would not have even a fuzzy image of the terrain, let alone a clear image of the best or fastest vehicle path. In this circumstance, not only will your mind be unable to see the path, but your belief system cannot believe that you will complete the section of track safely. In this case, your belief system would be very much correct.

As experience increases (more data points), not only does your mind have the information to see, but you begin to trust that what the mind sees is real. The combination of inadequate data points and lack of complete trust will cause you to make incorrect decisions about vehicle paths and vehicle speed, and divert attention to less desirable areas. Correct decisions require adequate data and trust in your ability to perceive reality.

Remember! Visual inputs are your primary source of data for situations requiring *anticipation* as opposed to *reaction*.

Fig. 2-4. Blind corners present unique problems and opportunities. To be an effective race driver, you must "see" through the corner in your mind's eye, and believe in what you "see."

0012817

Auditory Input

Noise can be very helpful, but is much less important than vision, "feel," and balance inputs. The primary noise input is mechanical, in monitoring engine speed and overall mechanical condition. In some cases, traction sampling can be enhanced by the sound of tire squeal.

HOW AUDITORY INPUT WORKS. Sounds usually require reaction, especially for response to possible mechanical problems. Some sounds lend themselves to anticipation, such as engine speed for shifting, especially when visual monitoring of the tachometer is not possible or desirable.

As with visual inputs, you must create a plan for response to auditory inputs. Experience is crucial for accurate response, and planning responses to unexpected auditory inputs allows more accurate and quicker responses to problems.

"Feel" and Balance

The sense of feel and balance is used primarily in circumstances that require reaction. It is through feel and balance that we sense accelerations (lateral and longitudinal) due to braking, steering, throttle applications, and weight transfer (a by-product of traction). Traction sampling is a parameter of acceleration. Vehicle speed sensing combines elements of feel and visual inputs.

HOW "FEEL" AND BALANCE INPUTS WORK. Feel and balance inputs are based on what is occurring *now*. The sense of touch, which is very sensitive to forces, works in unison with the balance mechanism of the inner ear to analyze forces caused by accelerations. Sensing the effects of these forces gives you clues about the vehicle relative to the limits of tire adhesion and to differences between front and rear tire traction.

As with other sensory inputs, you must have sufficient data points to know what the traction limit "feels" like. The more experience, the more likely you can stay near the limits. And, again, your belief system must believe that the senses are telling the truth.

Literally millions of nerve endings accumulate data. The body is so sensitive to accelerations that accelerations are probably the most important source of data for you. It is important that as much accurate data as possible be transmitted. This requires the minimum compliance in the sensory system. In exactly the same manner that soft suspension bushings, soft shocks, and flexible tire sidewalls slow feedback, so too does a compliant seating environment. If you can slide around in the cockpit, valuable inputs are slowed or lost. Excessive padding in the seat has the same effect. So do loose-fitting harnesses and belts. To optimize this crucial input, you need to minimize compliance in all vehicle systems. The limit (i.e., how "harsh" the environment is) is up to you, and should not cause discomfort or adversely affect your endurance.

How Sensory Input Is Used

Sensory inputs should accomplish three objectives:

- Acquire information for current analysis and future reference
- Provide data relative to the analysis of your plan
- Initiate your response

Four factors can alter or block the data:

- Belief systems founded on false assumptions or inadequate data
- Belief systems modified by emotions
- Excessive significance placed on low priority information
- Judgement of the information

If you collect the wrong information, it is not useful. If you analyze the data improperly, you may have faulty outputs. If you judge the information as right or wrong, good or bad, you waste valuable processing time *and* are unable to assess the reality of the information. Information must be accepted as reality, and not tainted by hopes, desires, fears, or false beliefs.

Regardless of the reason, when you misuse data there is always one consequence: lost time. Often, the level of risk increases as well. A winning race driver creates the best plan to take in data without judgement or bias, establishes the best priorities for data acquisition, and is most open to using the data to implement the plan. Additional data requires evaluation of the plan, and possible modification to the plan.

Fig. 2-5. Reality is your race car on a race track and what happens during the race. All that occurs during the race is input—visual, auditory, and "feel"—that you must process, without making judgements, to make decisions and car control choices.

Turning Input into Output

All of the senses work together to gather pertinent data. The data is nothing more than information based on the reality of a situation. The data is neither good nor bad, right nor wrong. It merely *is*! You determine what you do with the information, and that is determined by how your brain has been programed. The more you are based in reality, the more accurate your response. While the system of data processing is highly complex, only three factors determine the nature of your brain's program:

- The number of data points (experience)
- The understanding of the parameters (what the data means and what the effect of outputs is)
- The degree of filtering and modification of the data by emotions and beliefs

We have already explored the importance of experience. The importance of understanding concepts is paramount.

What about emotions and beliefs? They are very powerful. Entire cultures are controlled by beliefs. Emotions can create false beliefs. If the very first time you drove a car, you spun on the very first turn, it would be very difficult to drive a second time. One data point has created a belief.

If, as a child, you were told that you are uncoordinated, it would be difficult to be coordinated until you believe that you are coordinated. This can happen from one data point. Why? The basics relate to survival. If you perceive that an action or feeling threatens your survival, either physical or emotional, one data point, or experience, is enough to create a belief system. It is important to have this belief system in order to survive *if the perception is based in reality*! If the perception is based on incorrect assumptions, then the belief is false and will lead to either no action, ineffective action, or the wrong action. A positive mental attitude fits in here, but only if it is not used to distort reality. No matter how much we would like reality to fit our needs, desires, and instincts, reality often counters them. Reality will not change. To be effective as a race driver, your perceptions must fit reality.

In order for you to transform inputs into outputs, experience, understanding, and reality must be present. The best experience begins at a level that minimizes emotional factors by minimizing negative consequences. In the early stages of development, it is important to gain experience with low-stress, high-quality inputs that give maximum data to allow you to build a reality-based belief system.

For example, if you buy a new race car that performs to a much higher level than anything you have previously driven, should you immediately take the car to a high-speed race track where errors usually mean crashes? Or should you drive the car on a skid pad with lots of run-off so that errors do not cause major traumas? Learning the limits where the consequences of a mistake are minor will give you positive data points, which build confidence. But if you crash in a high-speed corner on your first lap in the car, you will have difficulty recovering from the trauma.

Understanding the concepts of driving a race car allows you to create a plan to process the data and act on the information with the best possible driver outputs. Lack of knowledge, or misunderstanding of the concepts, leads to ineffective action and builds false belief systems, and beliefs can be very difficult to alter, once established.

Dealing in reality is crucial to assimilation. Altering the reality of data for any reason clouds driver outputs, causing them to be slow and ineffective.

Most drivers should look to this process when they encounter problems, or when progress bogs down.

PAYING ATTENTION

How many times in your life have you been told to pay attention? Many, no doubt! Whoever told you that was right. Little did you know, as a kid, that they were talking about driving race cars. If only *they* had known!

Webster says that attention is "the act or state of applying the mind to an object of sense or thought, involving a selective narrowing or focusing of consciousness and receptivity." Attention is concentration in the conscious portion of the mind. It is where you take in data *and* make decisions about the data and your outputs. Many aspects of driving a race car require attention. Some require more; and more than one priority at a time usually requires some amount of attention.

How Much Attention Do You Have? Attention is a commodity. You have a supply of attention which can be apportioned any way you choose. It can be used on one priority, several, or on extraneous "stuff." Most likely, the total amount of available attention varies from one individual to another, or even within a given individual from day to day, but the amount is substantial. The difference is primarily in how one chooses to use attention.

THE WINNING DRIVER

The fast, effective race driver spends most of his attention on the priorities that will reap the greatest rewards.

Everyone possesses a given capacity to pay attention. It is important to establish priorities to assure that attention is spent in the best possible ways. Attention on the wrong areas is as ineffective as losing focus altogether. Being able to shift attention to a new top priority quickly is an important skill.

Tools: Understanding the important priorities. Creating an attention plan for different scenarios.

Game Plan: Create a priority list for several different areas of driving, including on the track where conditions and situations change rapidly.

Priorities: It's your list.

Practice Exercises: Create priority lists in other areas of your life. Test the effectiveness of the plan, and change as needed. As your knowledge and experience increase, your plan will become more sophisticated.

Establishing Attention Priorities

Every aspect of driving requires some level of attention; some require more than others. The need for attention changes as situations change. Different portions of a track and various segments of a corner require altering attention priorities. Most of the time, you will need some percentage of attention for several different priorities. How do you determine attention priorities?

The selection process is based on several criteria:

- Driver experience in given areas
- Weather and track conditions
- Vehicle performance
- Strategy
- Tactical considerations
- Traction sampling

DRIVER EXPERIENCE. If you know a track layout thoroughly, less attention is needed on driving the course. A driver new to the track will need a larger percentage of attention on the track layout. This applies to a given car, or type of car. The greater the number of data points of experience in a given area, and the more based on reality those data points are, the less attention you require to deal with those areas.

WEATHER AND TRACK CONDITIONS. When conditions change, especially when they deteriorate, a larger percentage of attention is needed for monitoring conditions.

VEHICLE PERFORMANCE. If mechanical or handling problems occur, more attention is diverted to this.

STRATEGY. Strategy is the creation of a game plan prior to an event based on one's best estimates of the probable occurrences. Strategic considerations require the use of considerable attention. In qualifying, more attention is spent on traction and paths than in a race situation. Race starts require attention on other cars more than on the fastest path.

TACTICS. Tactics involve the judgement and reaction to situations unfolding during an event. When planning and executing tactics, more attention is diverted away from driving.

TRACTION SAMPLING. Traction sampling is a crucial part of driving at the limit, and requires attention whenever the limits of traction are approached.

Throughout this book you will find recommendations concerning attention and priorities to assist you in making attention decisions. This is part of the plan. And the plan must include a way to shift attention to other priorities as needed.

Shifting Attention

As situations change, some percentage of attention must be shifted from one priority to another. As you approach the end of a straightaway, attention will shift from such things as gauge monitoring, checking mirrors, etc., to the turn-in point and braking. Paths and traction sampling become higher priorities. If the situation is a tactical one, where defensive or offensive considerations must be made, attention will shift more to those areas as they become a higher priority.

In order to quickly shift attention, you must have a clear mental picture of the priorities at any given moment on the track, and under any given set of circumstances. This requires that attention priorities become part of the plan.

Fig. 2-6. Shift attention from the apex to exit of a turn before you reach the apex.

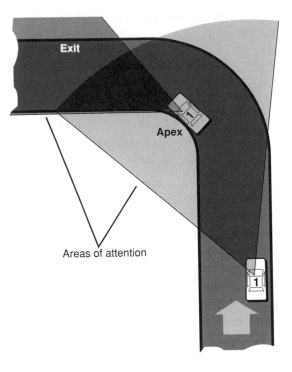

Attention Reserves

As experience increases for you in a given area, you will need less attention in that area to effectively handle it. This creates an attention reserve, allowing you to focus more attention on other important priorities. For example, as you learn a car and track combination, less attention is needed to drive at the limit, leaving greater attention for tactics. Should conditions change, such as rain, more attention will be required for driving, since the new situation has caused a change in overall priorities.

Regaining Lost Focus

Possibly the most difficult job during a race is to maintain concentration and focus. If your attention is diverted to extraneous areas, focus is taken from important priorities. It is important to regain focus on the important priorities as quickly as possible. The longer the process takes, the more time is likely to be lost, and the greater the risk of errors.

There are several tools that help regain lost focus. The most important is simply recognizing that focus of attention has faltered. In many cases this is enough to regain focus of attention.

Some drivers use an external stimulus to regain focus. This can be anything from a word painted on the dashboard to a mental image that helps you find lost focus. This is highly effective, but does require mental practice beforehand.

A good time to initiate this method, and to practice it, is during visualization exercises. It can be very difficult to maintain concentration and focus during visualization. Using this technique to re-establish focus is very effective, and will minimize the time needed to accomplish the task during real driving conditions.

Fig. 2-7. Losing focus is easy. Getting it back is more difficult. Often a word or phrase can trigger the mind back to right now. Some drivers paint a word on the dash to help with this. Here, Brian Ross loops it in Turn 2 of the 1992 Winchester 400.

0012820

THE WINNING DRIVER

The effective, fast race driver maintains acute focus on all aspects of driving.
Corollary: When focus is lost, the effective race driver will recognize the distraction and re-establish focus immediately.

Focus is the point of concentration, and requires the ability to establish the important priorities, create the plan, and maintain focus on the plan. To maintain focus, the race driver must live in the present. The past does not exist, the future is only as far as visual inputs allow for anticipation of immediate events.

Tools: Creating the plan; practicing focus through visualization, meditation, or some other means; mental rehearsal.

Game Plan: Recognizing skill needs and priorities.

Priorities: Concentration.

Practice Exercises: Visualization, video games, mental rehearsal.

Avoiding Distractions

The best way to maintain focus is to avoid distractions. Several techniques and exercises can help you accomplish this:

- Create a routine that helps you to establish a clear focus before going onto the track
- Ignore inputs not related to your job at hand
- Use visualization, meditation, and other mental exercises to practice maintaining focus
- Participate in activities where it is necessary to keep focus for long periods of time, like video games, fast-paced sports activities, and technically difficult sports like skiing and shooting

Like most mental aspects of racing, attention requires a plan for priorities and focus.

CONCENTRATION

Webster's says that to concentrate is "to bring or direct toward a common center or objective." Concentration is paying attention. Concentration is maintaining focus. How do you know when you are concentrating? Time will pass unnoticed. Thoughts extraneous to the activity in which you are involved do not pop into your mind. Concentration is broken when focus shifts to areas unintended or extraneous to the current activity.

There are two elements to concentration. First, you must "do it." Second, you must focus on the "right stuff." The ability to utilize these elements is crucial. Breaches in concentration on the most important priorities cost time on the track and can be very dangerous.

One clear sign of a lack of concentration is inconsistent lap times. One fast lap requires anywhere from 20 seconds to two minutes of intense concentration; most drivers can muster this level of focus. The best drivers can maintain this level of concentration for the duration of a race, up to five hours of intense focus on pre-determined priorities.

Almost all errors stem from ineffective concentration. Either you lack the necessary intensity of focus, or you focus attention in areas other than the most important ones on the priority list. For example, concentration on braking in the braking zone, when concentration should be shifted to speed and vehicle path, will not allow you to be fast and consistent. The degree of concentration may be high, but is misplaced. You may as well be focusing on the post-race party; either way, you will not be taking home the trophy for first place. The driver who focused on the important priorities during the race can focus attention on the party at the appropriate time. Chances are the driver who was thinking about the party in Turn 2, is thinking about Turn 2 at the party.

Fig. 2-8. By the time you are in the braking zone of the corner, your attention must be focused on the turn-in, vehicle speed, and the path through the entire corner.

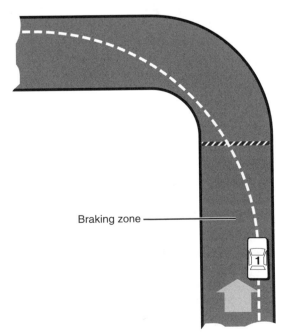

Braking zone

0012821

The biggest key to maintaining concentration is living *now*. The past is over; the future, beyond your field of vision and only a concept. If your goal is to win a race, you must set aside the goal during the event, and focus attention on the job you must do *right now* to win the race. Focusing on the goal is the wrong priority if you want to reach the goal.

Focus of Concentration

You must continually make decisions concerning priorities. At any given moment, you have the option of focusing on several important areas and hundreds of meaningless things. It is important to create the plan in advance to address specifically the issues of concentration priorities. Just where do you focus concentration? Your game plan must be created by you. Most of this book is devoted to the issues that will assist you in creating this plan.

Practicing Concentration

Concentration comes naturally for some people; others must work at maintaining high levels of concentration for long periods. Fortunately, many forms of exercise will enhance anyone's ability to concentrate. Practicing any of these methods will help elevate your ability to maintain focus on anything you choose. Here are some ways to improve concentration:

DRIVING. This is probably the best practice exercise of all.

VISUALIZATION. Run laps mentally (see the section later in this chapter).

MEDITATION. Teaches you to clear your mind by focusing on nothing; possibly the most difficult of all concentration exercises, and therefore, the most valuable.

VIDEO GAMES. Video games require a high level of concentration.

OTHER SPORTS ACTIVITIES. You can combine physical training with mental training; fast-paced sports are the best, especially those enhancing hand-eye coordination.

OTHER ACTIVITIES. Any activity requiring complete focus of attention, such as work and hobbies.

It is difficult to practice concentration to become more proficient at it. It is something that must happen more naturally; it must flow because you are completely content participating in an activity. Concentration is very difficult when you would rather be doing some other thing, or when emotions, like anger, fear, or self-doubt cause the mind to focus on them instead of the activity. To truly reach the necessary level of concentration to become a winning race driver, you must be totally absorbed in the activity, living in the present, and loving every second of it!

OUTCOME CONDITIONING

The old adage "What you see is what you get" is especially true in auto racing. And you can see with either the physical eye or the mind's eye. Outcome conditioning is nothing more than training your "eye" to see where you want to be or what you want to have.

There are two sides to outcome conditioning. The first is mental/emotional and helps you to reach goals. Your plan is your definition of what you want! Once you know what that is, it is much easier to accomplish. Vague ideas don't cut it. Precise plans do. The second is physical, and allows you to do what you have in mind. The mechanism is identical for both.

Fig. 2-9. Look where you want to go, not at what you want to avoid.

0012822

This principle, as applied to the physical side, is often called "pot-holism;" look at a pot hole when you're driving and you'll hit it every time. I call it the "Bott's Dots Principle." Bott's Dots are those lane separator markers that allow you to hear and feel when a lane change takes place. They are often used to mark crosswalks. My favorite form of training is bicycling. Near my home are crosswalks marked with rows of Bott's Dots. My wife and I ride a tandem bicycle some of the time. A few years ago, in a moment of frustration, she asked me how, while she usually hit the Bott's Dots, I always managed to ride perfectly between them. I asked her what she looked at as she approached the dots. She answered that she looked at the dots. I then told her that I look *between* the Bott's Dots. I look where I want to go, not at what I want to avoid.

THE WINNING DRIVER

The effective, fast race driver is oriented to a positive outcome. Corollary: Negative perspectives create negative outcomes.

This affects all areas of life, especially driving a race car to the limit. For precise vehicle placement , focus on where you want to go, not where you don't want to go. Additionally, mental focus should always be on the desired outcome, not on the fear of an undesirable outcome. What you envision is most likely what you will get.

Tools: Living in the present; positive attitude; focus on outcomes you want.

Game Plan: Live in the present; make no judgements of good/bad or right/wrong.

Priorities: Keep focused; be positive.

Practice Exercises: Visualization, video games.

After relating this story to a class, a student asked if you could look at the dots, but tell yourself to miss them. I figured that it was possible, but it seemed to me like traveling north on a street, needing to turn to the west, and making three right turns instead of a single left turn. You end up in the same place, but the path is longer and takes more time.

Subsequent to this, I tried an experiment. You can miss the dots by looking at them and telling yourself to miss the dots. It takes maybe five times more attention to do this, however. The part of the brain that controls these things takes messages very literally. If you are in motion, and gathering visual data concerning your path, the brain knows the purpose of the data. If you look somewhere, you go there. The brain interprets the data as "he is looking there, so that must be where he wants to go." During the learning phase for an exercise requiring movement, you can literally look at where you want to go, say "Go there" and that's where you go. With experience (data points), the mental command can be eliminated, saving one step in the process.

On the other hand, if you take the negative approach, that is, look where you do not want to go and give the command "Do not go there," the brain is confused. You must convince the brain that is what you really want. It is an unnatural reaction, taking a finite amount of time to undertake—time and attention which could be spent on more productive matters.

The mental/emotional side is similar in function. If the mind's eye clearly sees where you want to be, and the path to get there, then you will get there if action can be taken effectively. The plan of action must be based on reality, must consist of clear, manageable steps, and requires a complete commitment from you.

Practice   The physical side of outcome conditioning is very easy to practice. In fact, you do it all the time. The trick is to focus on the outcome you want. Try this experiment right now. From a short distance, throw a wad of paper into a waste basket. Did it go in? What were you looking at? Look at the center of the opening and try a few shots. Now look at the closest edge of the rim and try a few more. Look behind the waste basket. Look at the clock on the wall and try to hit the basket. Where does the paper land each time in each scenario? You have just been practicing outcome conditioning. Every time you drive, work on this principle. Just be sure to look where you want to go.

Finally, be positive. This is crucial in two senses of the word. First, look where you *want* to go, not where you *do not* want to go. Second, be positive about your direction. Don't guess or be indecisive. In some cases, indecision has minor consequences; on the race track, the consequences can be much more serious.

I sincerely hope that this paragraph is unnecessary. Drugs and alcohol have a serious negative effect on concentration, as well as on reactions and judgement. If you feel that you must partake in any substance in order to control your emotional state on the race track, you have a serious problem. You should seek professional help. And you should also stay off the race track, especially if I happen to be racing. Pilots have a rule: 24 hours from bottle to throttle. In reality, alcohol can affect the system for much longer periods of time. The effects of alcohol and drugs are so detrimental to performance, there is no place for them in this sport.

ANTICIPATION

In racing, looking ahead is paramount for both speed and safety. Anticipation is nothing more than taking a look into the future, and making at least an educated guess, or at best a precise evaluation, about what will occur.

How far you can look into the future depends upon the conditions and your skills. If at a speed of 100 miles per hour you look at a point 100 yards ahead, the future (between you and that point) is 2.04 seconds long. How well you can predict what will occur in that 2.04 seconds is determined by the quality of the inputs, how you perceive them, and the scope of the judgements. If you are only looking 20 feet ahead at 100 mph, the future is only .136 seconds long. This is not even enough time to react, let alone anticipate what is going to happen.

When the range of visual input, either real or perceived, is this short, fear grows and little attention can be spent on any activity other than survival. It is no wonder that the driver with a short field of vision is driving over his limits, but usually well below the limits of the vehicle. Conversely, when a driver learns to expand the field of vision, the environment slows down, and the process is simplified.

Try an experiment. As a passenger in a car on a highway at 60 mph, look straight down at the passing dashed lines. They are blurred, and if you did not know in advance that they were dashed, you would probably assume that the line was solid, but lighter in color. Should the line change direction, it would be impossible to follow with any precision.

If you look ahead at the oncoming dashes, they are easy to distinguish. If you look too far ahead, the line again looks solid, but its direction and actual path are clearly seen until an obstruction or the horizon interferes. The ability to look ahead allows you to *anticipate* the direction changes of the line and make precise steering outputs to follow the path of the line.

Fig. 2-10. Eyes up, visual attention far down the track, gives you a longer "look into the future."

0012823

Managing Fear   Another element is important here. The ability to anticipate reduces your level of fear. In a very real sense, fear is based upon a lack of information, especially concerning future events. Using our dashed line experiment again, if you are looking straight down at the line and suddenly a 1000-foot drop-off appears in place of the line, a rush of adrenaline, induced by fear, would flood your system, elevating your heart rate and resulting in some level of trauma.

If you're looking ahead, however, you would have more time to take in data, process it, and draw a conclusion about what you may expect. If the "look into the future" is adequately long, it is less likely fear will result. This is a major component of anticipation. You would never drive looking out the side window at the passing dashed line, unless fog reduced visibility to a few feet. By the same token, you should not drive with your visual focus just in front of your hood. A broad visual field is crucial for good powers of anticipation.

Of course, if something unexpected happens, fear will occur. For example, as you crest the rise of the blind turn you see a stalled car in the road. Fear is a normal reaction. One way to minimize the effects of fear in this instance is to anticipate the *possibility* of an unexpected occurrence. By visualizing such possibilities, and plotting a course of action to avoid the problem, you can reduce the response time and to some degree the fear.

This occurs in much the same way that anticipation based on real visual input takes place. The mind does not know the difference between the real visual input and the visualized, practiced inputs. If you believe that the road goes to the left over the rise, your mind will anticipate that the road does in fact go to the left over the rise.

Anticipation transcends all aspects of racing, from driving at the limit to tactical decisions, from judging track conditions to setting up the suspension.

Anticipation   To most spectators or outsiders, it appears that the successful race driver
vs. Reaction   has lightning-fast reflexes. While some do, and it is most useful to have quick reactions, it is anticipation that sets apart the truly great driver. If you rely only on reactions, not only will you be slower and encounter serious tactical disadvantages, but sooner or later you'll encounter big problems.

An interesting example of this appeared in a pre-1991 Indy 500 newspaper story. A former Formula One driver and Indy star compared driving a Grand Prix Formula One car to driving at Indy. In an F1 car, he felt that he could react to any situation, but at Indy, since speeds are so fast, he felt that anticipation was mandatory. Everything happens too quickly to rely on reactions alone.

This individual is an excellent race driver, among the world's elite. But to date, he has never won an F1 or Indy car race. Semantic differences in his statements aside, part of the reason he has not won in these categories is probably his lack of anticipation. Had he been less gifted with quick reflexes, he might have developed the powers of anticipation sooner, and possibly achieved more success.

Often, my students get by on reactions. As they learn to anticipate, the environment begins to slow down, and the processing time to take inputs and turn them into outputs is reduced. This allows more time to work on more intricate details and to plan tactics. As the student learns to take in a broader visual field, and to pinpoint specific, high-priority portions of the visual

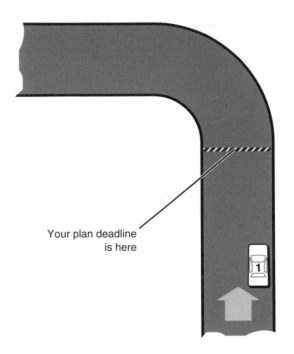

Fig. 2-11. At the corner entry, by the turn-in point, you must have a plan for vehicle path and speed. The planning zone for speed and path occurs during the approach to the corner, often while braking. Anticipation is the key.

Your plan deadline is here

0012824

field, the more easily anticipation becomes second nature. Developing the skills of anticipation is crucial, and surprisingly simple. It just takes effort.

Developing and Practicing Anticipation

Anticipation has many elements, as well as uses. To fully develop this skill, the uses and elements must be understood and practiced.

ANTICIPATE YOUR RESPONSES. The first element of anticipation is the ability to anticipate your own outputs to the vehicle. Anticipating each movement of the steering, brakes, and throttle will allow you to act, smoothly and accurately, at the precise instant intended. There are specific points on the track, like the turn-in zone, that require planning and accurate outputs to the controls. Anticipating these outputs allows you to complete them with the minimum of attention, freeing attention for use on other priorities. As experience increases, even less attention is needed on outputs.

ANTICIPATING YOUR CAR'S RESPONSES. The second element of anticipation relates to vehicle response. Most often you will rely on reactions and car control skills to respond to the vehicle. If you use anticipation to "know" what the car will do given specific driver outputs, you can save valuable tenths of seconds. This also allows you to time the outputs more accurately, and frees attention to focus on other important priorities.

The other side of this coin can create problems, if you only anticipate the expected vehicle response. Part of your plan should include *unexpected* vehicle response. Unexpected reactions to your outputs will scare you silly. Anticipating unexpected responses reduces the potential level of fear. It also allows you to analyze what caused the unexpected reaction. Have the track conditions changed? Did you make a mistake? Is there a mechanical problem with the car or tires? Was the cause aerodynamic turbulence from another car? Or did you expect the wrong response? Something caused the unexpected response. The more quickly you can analyze the cause, the more quickly you can correct the problem.

Without anticipating unexpected responses, most of your attention will be instantaneously shifted to correct the problem. That leaves little attention to analyze the cause of the problem, let alone to deal with other important priorities.

ANTICIPATING EXTERNAL FACTORS. In racing situations, the key to success and survival is your ability to anticipate what occurs outside your vehicle. The more input you receive from outside, the easier it is to anticipate dangerous situations and avoid them. By selecting specific portions of the visual input, you can make tactical decisions based upon the interpretation of the data. A broad field of vision is required. Selecting and processing that information requires experience, both real and visualized. Here is an example:

You come around the apex of a blind corner, ready to hit the throttle hard. Suddenly you see that there is an accident right in the middle of your line. Now you are in trouble. Many clues may have presented themselves if you had an adequate field of vision and the ability to "see" the possible clues. A waving yellow flag is probably the most obvious, but others exist also. Skid marks entering the turn that were not there on the previous lap; smoke; spectators looking or running to a spot around the track; these are all clues that something has occurred, with possible danger to you.

You can also anticipate changing track and weather conditions in many cases. Wind can cause problems, and if the wind shifts, it can affect the balance of the car. For example, at Willow Springs International Raceway the wind usually blows diagonally across the front straight. This helps keep the car on the track in Turn 9, which leads onto the straight. Occasionally, the wind shifts, blowing up the straight. In this case, the wind tries to blow the car off the outside of Turn 9, requiring a reduction in cornering speed. Unless this is anticipated, the car can literally get blown off the track. Being aware of the direction of the flags or blowing dust to see changes in the wind direction can give you time to alter your plan and stay on the race track.

Sometimes changes occur so quickly that anticipation is impossible. Another car dumping oil in front of you is an example. But if that same car was smoking for the previous 5 laps, expecting a blown engine would be reasonable, and that expectation would allow you to anticipate a potential problem.

Fig. 2-12. A waving flag is just one important visual clue to external factors on the race track.

0012825

It is also very easy to get lulled into a false sense of security, especially when everything is going smoothly. I once proved this in an endurance race. We were leading in class by a comfortable margin. Late in my stint, I noticed a car off course on the inside of a long sweeper. Assuming a mechanical problem, I failed to anticipate that the mechanical problem could affect me. There was no oil flag displayed, but as I turned into the sweeper, I quickly spun, even though I had slowed slightly. I had failed to anticipate that the disabled car may have dropped fluids on the track. The anti-freeze which caused the spin was difficult to see, due to the angle of the sun, at least until I was going backwards; then it was clearly visible. I recovered without losing a position, but this slight mental lapse could have cost us a victory.

Anticipation As a Tactical Tool

In passing situations, the ability to anticipate what the other driver will do can aid immensely. Developing this ability requires practice and experience, which can be obtained any time you drive. The key is to watch what the other driver does. Head movements, looking in the mirrors, hand movements on the steering wheel, brake lights, attitude changes of the car, consistent driving mistakes, inconsistent lines, braking points, can all offer clues. Previous experience with the other driver can enhance your anticipation.

Another valuable input is to watch the interaction of a group of cars. Often, the interaction is predictable, and creates passing opportunities in unlikely places. This is especially true if the group has slowed behind traffic, but has not "seen" that options exist. When a car is well below the limits in a turn, many optional lines are possible, and anticipating the possibilities of off-line passes when traffic has slowed gives you many opportunities.

The Process of Anticipation

The process of anticipation involves the creation of a visual field, the selection of specific visual inputs which require increased attention, the processing of the acquired data, and a decision to take specific action.

When creating a visual field, keep in mind that the larger the field, the more potentially useful information there is in it. A larger visual field allows you to look farther into the future, and gives more time to effectively select and process information and choose a course of action.

Using Anticipation

Anticipation must be used in every aspect of race driving to achieve success. The process must become automatic. In addition to on-track experience, anticipation skills can be developed and honed in everyday driving.

Work first on your visual field; change its length and direction, including the mirrors. Take in as much information as possible. As this process develops, you will begin to notice that some of the information is more pertinent than the rest. This will allow you to focus more attention on the pertinent areas, less on the less important ones.

As an example, seeing brake lights a quarter mile ahead is more pertinent than checking the billboard 200 yards down the road on the right shoulder. What course of action should you take? Should you slam on the brakes to slow? Or swerve? Maybe slowing gently is the best course of action until more information is received. Was the cause of the brake lights an accident? Or did traffic slow due to congestion or a slow driver in the left lane?

As more information becomes available, you can modify your plan of action and avoid a dangerous situation, before evasive action or a panic stop is required. If your field of vision was only 100 feet ahead, you would receive the information very late, leaving little time for anticipation. Same thing if

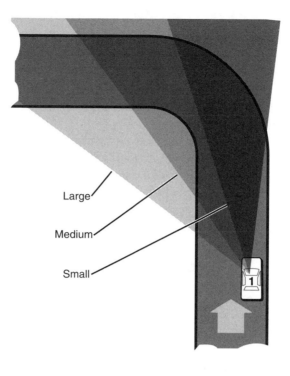

Fig. 2-13. Small, medium, and large visual fields determine the anticipation time available to you.

your attention was focused on the billboard. The payoff is increased aware-ness, strong powers of anticipation, and a safer driving experience, on and off the track.

To become an expert at anticipation try this exercise: analyze the actions of other drivers on the highway. Can you predict their moves? This becomes a challenging pastime, and you will be surprised at how easy it is to predict most of their actions. As you improve this skill, you will find it much easier to anticipate the actions of other drivers on the track. The more you prac-tice and develop this skill, the easier it will become to drive at the limit on the race track, to make decisions that allow you to race with a higher degree of safety, and to gain a tactical advantage.

VISUALIZATION

Visualization is defined as the formation of mental visual images. The con-cept is quite simple: visualization is structured daydreaming. To visualize requires clear mental images, sharp mental focus, and considerable con-centration. To become adept at visualization requires mental discipline and substantial effort.

Visualization can be used in many ways to reach goals, improve perfor-mance, program the brain, and practice most any activity. In a very real sense, the brain cannot differentiate between real visual experiences and those which are visualized mentally. For that reason, it is crucial to use vi-sualization in a very positive way. If you practice something physically, what you practice is what you learn to do. If you practice the wrong things, you learn the wrong things. In the same way, keep your visualization prac-tice positive. Otherwise you will become proficient at the wrong stuff.

How to Practice Visualization

The most powerful and entertaining visualization exercise I have tried uses practice laps. The idea is to mentally run a series of laps around a track, timing the laps with a stop watch as you visualize them. Here's how to do it:

Sit in a comfortable chair, in a position similar to the car you will be "driving" during visualization exercise. The car should be one in which you have experience driving. The environment should be quiet, with no distractions to interfere with your concentration. The track you will drive should be one which you are completely familiar with from actual experience.

Before you begin driving laps, close your eyes, develop a clear picture of the environment, including the pit area, landscaping, etc., at the facility. Go through the process of entering the car, strapping in, and the start-up procedure. Many people actually move their hands and feet to operate the controls while visualizing. The entire process is undertaken with eyes closed. Use a stop watch in one hand for timing your laps. A watch with memory and recall is best for consecutive laps.

After the preliminaries, exit the pits mentally, just as you would in a real practice session. Build up to speed, shift gears, etc., for the warm-up lap. As you approach the starting line, prepare to start the watch. As you cross the line, start the watch. The first time you try this, run only two or three laps. Look at the times. How close are they to real laps around the track in that car?

This exercise is tremendous for practice around a given track. It is crucial to have a clear mental picture of vehicle paths, apexes, visual reference points, and any other physical features of the environment. Deviations from reality will reduce the usefulness of the exercise.

This exercise is a great way to practice concentration. Make a notation of breaches of concentration. How often does your "voice" try to break concentration? Do the images become fuzzy? Does your mind wander to things unconnected with driving? The accuracy of your lap times is a good indicator of the level of concentration you can maintain. If you can run 10 laps consecutively, within one percent of each other, your consistency in the car will be very good, and you have shown excellent powers of concentration.

Once you have become proficient at lapping with visual mental images, try to develop mental images of how the car feels and the forces acting on the car. This requires a much higher level of concentration and more sophistication, but is a logical progression of the exercise, and can prove helpful in developing more precise force sensing and traction sampling skills.

Use visualization only when you have clear mental images of the complete environment. Unclear or distorted images will cause your practice to be less effective or force you to practice inappropriate things.

Diligent use of visualization techniques with clear, precise mental pictures can pay big dividends on the race track. There are a number of on-track scenarios where the use of visualization can be useful.

DEVELOPING A PLAN FOR FAST LAPS. The above exercise works well for this. Remember to pay attention to priorities as you develop your plan.

DEVELOPING A PLAN FOR RACE STRATEGY VARIABLES. How are you going to alter vehicle paths in traffic? How will you defend position? How and where will you try passes? How will you deal with changing conditions? What will you change for more effective tire management? Check your plan by visualizing how it will work.

DEVELOPING A PLAN FOR EMERGENCY SITUATIONS. Emergency situations occur frequently on the track. The time to learn the correct responses is not during a real situation. Since race drivers do not have "situation simulators" like aircraft pilots (though they are being developed), you must plan how to respond in emergencies. A planned response carries two benefits. First, it reduces response time; second, it reduces emotional alterations of reality, i.e., fear is less likely to cloud response outputs.

How will you react if a car spins in front of you? Or drops oil on the track in front of you? How will react in your own spin? Or in a crash situation?

I have had some people say they do not want to even consider mental practice for these situations, fearing that thinking about them will cause them to occur. You must decide your own course of action, but I believe that mental practice in these areas can save your life. No one likes to think about the worst case, but it is better to have a plan and never use it than to hope you never needed it, but did. Let's look at an example of a possible response to the worst case scenario.

In a crash, we know that certain reactions will maximize the chances for survival and minimize risks. If a collision is imminent, relaxing the body, releasing the steering, and moving the feet off the pedals at the last possible instant will reduce the possibility of injury. Mentally practicing when to activate the fire system can save precious time when a fire erupts. Mental practice to use all of the controls, especially the kill switch, can be helpful. And when do you release the belts to exit the car? Drivers have suffered serious, even fatal injuries because they unfastened the belts too soon. It is crucial that the car is stopped, *and* that no other cars are going to collide before your belts are released. And what is the quickest way to exit your car? Mental and physical practice are important in creating an exit plan.

PROBLEM SOLVING TO REDUCE LAP TIMES

When something is not going according to plan, a problem exists. The first step towards solving the problem is to identify it. On the surface, this process seems simple. In reality, it can be tricky. The trick lies in how you define the problem.

Let's say you're practicing for a race and your lap times are a second and a half slow. You define the problem as being too slow. Certainly, this is a problem, but this definition does not offer a framework for a solution. Nor does the "obvious" solution to drive faster. The problem and its solution are so broadly defined that no plan is possible. In reality, the fact that your lap times are 1.5 seconds too slow is not a problem at all. It is a *symptom* of a problem that exists elsewhere.

Now comes detective work. The first step is to identify the problem causing the symptom. In the broadest sense, two things could be the cause of the slow laps: the car and/or you. (This assumes that the slow laps are relative to other cars, so that track conditions are not a factor, which they could be!) Without knowing the answer to this question, moving to the next step is difficult, if not impossible.

Three options exist here:

- Is either system a known quantity? For example, is the car a lap record holder with a new driver, or vice versa. If one system is a known quantity, then the problem mostly likely, but not necessarily, lies with the other
- Can you honestly and clearly determine the problem? Do you possess the insight and self-evaluation capacity to identify driver errors? Can you pinpoint car problems?
- Put a driver of proven skills in the car for comparisons. Or put yourself in a car of known capability. This is probably the most accurate system, but the most damaging to the ego. Can you handle a major dose of reality?

Since this book is for race drivers, let's assume the car is a rocket ship, and that you're a rookie with insufficient experience to analyze the cause of the problem. Now we need to know *where* the problem occurs. Is it all around the track? In one turn? Or one type of turn? There are several tools you can use to evaluate this.

- Have an experienced driver follow you for subjective evaluation
- Take segment times compared to segments of an experienced driver in the same car
- Use an in-car video or data acquisition system for analysis
- Have someone observe you at selected points around the track watching for speed relative to similar cars, and especially, vehicle paths

The best case uses all of these tools. With this information, you can more clearly define the real problem. Based on this new information, you can plan a solution to the problem.

Continuing with our example, let's assume you are slow everywhere around the track, but mostly due to cornering below the limit of tire traction. The problem is then best defined as an inability to keep the car at its cornering limits.

One of two situations exists. First, you may lack adequate traction sampling skills. Or, second, the sensory inputs you receive may not be fully recognized, or they may be distorted due to emotional inputs (most likely fear) altering real perceptions.

In both cases, a lack of experience is a major factor. You need more seat time. The seat time needs to clearly address the relevant issues. Since fear is often caused by inexperience, and driver errors can cause an increase in the level of fear, the solution should allow for the elimination of fear. This also allows you to focus on the other part of the problem, traction sampling, and gives you the opportunity to develop that important skill.

The best course of action is to create a low-speed situation that reduces fear, and which allows you to focus maximum attention on traction sampling, and reaching the limit of tire traction. Skid pad time, autocrosses, or low-speed corners are ideal. Trying to learn the limits in high-speed corners is not only intimidating, but dangerous. It is perfectly reasonable for you as a rookie driver to experience fear in high-speed corners when you have not yet developed good traction senses. Now is the time to take a step back and work on developing the skills and controlling the emotional reactions, i.e., the fear. Taking the time and exercising the discipline to do

Fig. 2-14. Practice on a skid pad is a low-risk situation that allows you to learn more quickly.

this will integrate the solution with the real problem, while *dis*-integrating the problem itself.

This problem solving system works on virtually any problem. Just follow the steps with insight, honesty, and a little logic.

1. Realize that a problem exists
2. Define the area causing the problem
3. Define the true problem
4. Develop a plan to solve the problem
5. Take action to integrate the solution and dis-integrate the real problem
6. Evaluate progress towards the solution, and alter your plan as needed to continue the progress towards a real solution

The most important step requires the realization that the problem exists. In racing, since lap times are concrete indicators of reality, problems relating to lap times are the easiest to see. Other problems can be much more difficult to recognize and evaluate. Since problems of all sorts will

Fig. 2-15. Autocrossing is another low-risk environment in which to learn the limits of a car.

continually present themselves, insight and honesty on all levels are your most important tools for problem solving.

Errors

Part of problem solving for a race driver is recognizing errors. Errors cost time. Smaller errors cost less time. Naturally, we want to commit the smallest errors. Even the best race drivers commit many errors on any given lap. The reason they are good is twofold: their errors are very small and they rapidly correct. The least amount of time is lost. The number of possible errors is almost endless. Let's isolate an example to illustrate the way to approach errors and corrections.

One of the most common errors occurs at the corner turn-in zone. If turn-in occurs too early, the exit will either be wide or slow; both cost time. The question is, how much time? The first factor is to recognize the error. The sooner it is acknowledged, the sooner the correction can take place. If the error is not recognized until the exit zone, it is too late to correct. But if the error is recognized just after turn-in, you can make a correction to speed and/or vehicle path allowing nearly maximum cornering speed and early acceleration, as if no error were made. Handled in this fashion, it is virtually impossible for anyone other than the driver to detect the error.

Self-education

To minimize the effect of errors, experience and self-education are required. In the above example, the first time the error is made, you will need more time to recognize the situation, and will probably be unable to make an effective correction on the spot. If you realize the error, and understand the necessary action to make a correction, the next time the same error occurs, the recognition will take place more quickly. It is during this process where it is easy to make serious mistakes.

THE WINNING DRIVER

The effective race driver never makes mistakes; he commits errors. Corollary: The fastest and safest race driver commits the smallest errors. The number of errors is much less important.

Mistakes imply judgement as in doing something "wrong." Errors are unintentional deviations from the desired path. In motorsports, committing an error is the failure to execute an output in order to achieve a desired result. Committing an error is not judgemental and allows for correction instead of judgement. Making errors is not the issue; everyone does. By developing driving skills, and creating the right mental attitude, you keep errors small and recognize them quickly, minimizing their effect. Lingering on an error makes it worse, and causes other, larger errors. Recognizing the error, filing it for future reference, and staying in the present allow the most effective analysis of inputs and the most precise outputs by the race driver.

Tools: Skills development; no judgements; precise corrections.

Game Plan: Judging errors causes mistakes. Stay in the present.

Priorities: File away the information about the error and get on with driving.

Practice Exercises: Keep a log of errors and your reaction to them. After a session or a race, use the errors you make to evaluate your plan, and to implement changes to the plan.

Fig. 2-16. If you make a turn-in error, and recognize it quickly, you can make a correction to your line to help minimize the effect of the error.

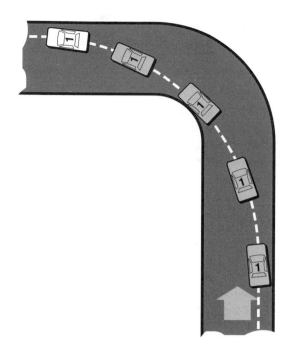

0012829

If you take even an instant to be self-critical about the error, the error has escalated into a mistake. It is virtually impossible to make corrections, or learn from the error, if time is spent beating-up on yourself. It is crucial to recognize the error, evaluate a change in the plan to correct or minimize the error, and get on with driving. The change to the plan may have to wait until that error is repeated, but with evaluations based on reality and without self-judgement, the error will be effortlessly corrected, minimizing its effect.

THE WINNING DRIVER

The fast, effective race driver eliminates the judge.

When you commit errors, file them away for future analysis; spend no attention on judgement. The errors are neither good nor bad; they simply exist. Spend attention to minimize the effect of the error, not to self-criticize. It is appropriate to learn from the error in order to minimize its effects when the error occurs later. Time spent on self-criticism not only diverts attention to the wrong area, but also exacerbates the error into a larger, more costly one.

Tools: Focus, concentration, attention priorities.

Game Plan: Watch for the judge and turn it off. Re-establish focus on pertinent priorities.

Priorities: Learn from errors, but don't make the BIG mistake by judging the error as good or bad, right or wrong.

Practice Exercises: Make your errors fun, laugh at the them and learn. Errors are simply a part of life, not a problem or disaster. Lingering on them is a problem.

Storing Data Input

When you commit an error, it is important to store the data so you can correct the error more quickly on the next occurrence. To accomplish this, you must first recognize the error, understand the consequences of the error, and create a plan (or alter an existing plan) to compensate for the error.

In many racing situations, time is not available to evaluate errors on the track. It is important for you to store the information for evaluation and planning after the session on the track. Driver debriefings are crucial, whether they are conducted by you alone taking notes, or with a team manager/crew chief or coach. Note specific references to each error, along with a plan to correct the error, or recognize it earlier, and take action to minimize its effect.

Using Errors to Go Faster

Every time you commit an error, you also create an opportunity to learn from that error. If you learn from errors, you are learning to go faster. In most cases, you will learn that the scenario created by the error costs time on the track. Sometimes, you may learn that the unintended scenario is actually faster. Additionally, you have learned a new approach which could be used in circumstances requiring a different method, such as a passing situation, a defensive move, or evasion of a hazardous situation. No matter what is learned from the error, that knowledge will become useful to you sooner or later.

THE WINNING DRIVER

Skilled race drivers create opportunities by becoming effective problem solvers.

Errors are a constant part of driving at the limit. Using errors to learn about your vehicle can lead to opportunities later, but the mind must be open to opportunity, and your plan must allow for changes to take advantage of your own errors or those of others. When errors are committed, create opportunities by learning something new from the error, even if it is to avoid the same error. If you are open to change, and non-judgemental about what you do, learning and improvements will happen.

Tools: Develop problem solving skills in all areas; create room for change in your plan.

Game Plan: Racing is dynamic with changing situations; plan for change, and be open to it. Use change to create opportunity; don't be crippled by the prospect of change.

Priorities: Use errors to improve skills, insight, and tactical position with other drivers.

Practice Exercises: Turn errors into advantages by learning from them.

GAME PLANS FOR CHANGE

The Dynamic Nature of Racing

The most consistent aspect of racing is the constant change. Technology, rules, competitors, tracks, track conditions, weather, and vehicles seem to be in a constant state of flux. Some of these changes occur over a season or several years; others occur almost instantly on the race track. The possibility that the situation will change must be part of your plan.

You must be able to shift gears in more ways than one. If your plan does not allow for change, the plan will create situations void of flexibility. Opportunities will be lost, surprises will occur, and adapting to the new circumstances will be slow and cumbersome. The ability to succeed will be reduced greatly.

Being flexible is an acquired skill for most individuals. An open mind, the ability to face the reality of the situation, and the understanding that everything is subject to change, like it or not, are prerequisites to effectively be flexible.

These are the parameters for hitting a moving target. When the target moves, you must be prepared to move with it; it will never move to suit you, except through blind luck. To meet this challenge, you must be prepared to adapt.

Alternate Game Plans

Planning ahead for change, since it's safe to assume that everything will change, is the best way to adapt to a new reality. Recognize the areas where changes are most likely to occur. Gather information about those areas. Prior to an event, keeping tabs on the weather reports will give you insights concerning one area of probable changes. Knowing that you will have to drive off-line to make a pass gives you the opportunity to find which path change will cost you the least amount of time. Practicing this in advance

THE WINNING DRIVER

The winning race driver never quits.

By living in the present, and refraining from judgement, the winning driver is always at peak performance, and creates opportunities to win or improve position. At the 1991 Marlboro Challenge Race at Laguna Seca, Michael Andretti had little chance to beat Rick Mears to the line for a win. But he maintained constant pressure, never giving up, for if the one-in-a-million opportunity arose, Andretti would be in a position to take advantage. It did; he won, but only because he stayed close. If he had accepted 2nd place earlier, Mears's bobble at Turn 11 on the last lap would not have made a difference. Andretti's desire gave him a big payday.

Tools: Concentration, focus, desire.

Game Plan: Maintain peak performance at all times.

Priorities: Achieving the best now; the past and future do not exist.

Practice Exercises: In any activity, keep performing to 100% even when chances look dim. It's more fun and more rewarding that way anyway.

eliminates one of the unknowns from the equation; this makes the solution much easier to find.

Every area of possible change offers resources for information that will give you some idea of the effect that change will have on you. Knowing the possible effects will allow you to create and add to your basic plan ways to adapt to changes, and to minimize their effect. The need for change is universal; without it no new knowledge would surface.

CONCLUSION

The mental skills needed for racing require considerable insight, planning, and practice. Many elements of racing rely on clear, accurate data inputs which you process into appropriate control outputs. A great number of factors covered in depth in this chapter must be fine-tuned by you to reach the Winner's Circle. Careful self-analysis of skills and weaknesses will allow you to work on and develop techniques that will help reach specific goals, whether on the race track or in other areas of life. A plan for mental skills which are created, implemented, evaluated, and modified will become the road map for reaching important goals. To become a winning race driver requires a complete commitment to learn and refine mental skills.

3

EMOTIONAL SKILLS

Sam has never driven a car. As he gets into the car, he eagerly anticipates that he will have an exciting adventure. He drives away, feeling a little apprehensive, but good. Sam starts to drive a little faster. After all, all those guys on TV drive fast. Why not! As Sam approaches a corner, he turns the steering wheel, but the car starts to slide straight on. He misses the turn and plows head-on into a fence, fortunately at low speed. Sam is uninjured, but very shaken. He has just terrified himself.

In the instant that Sam shot through the fence, an emotional program was created. The primary element of the program is fear. The next time Sam encounters a related stimulus, which could be an offer for a car ride, or even the sight of a car, Sam will feel fear. He has no choice in the matter. The fear will be there; it is part of a program burned into his psyche. The fear is very healthy. It is signalling to Sam that danger may be present. Some form of action is needed.

The only question now is: what will Sam do about the fear? He has two options. He can ignore it or he can acknowledge it.

Let's say Sam acknowledges the fear. A few days later he encounters the same stimulus. He may say to himself "this is a scary situation!" He now has a choice to make. He could flee the scary situation, or confront it. If he chooses to flee, he will likely continue to flee similar situations when the

Fig. 3-1. What do you feel when you get behind the wheel of a race car? Fear, elation, anger— and more—are all emotions that arise before, during, and after a race. Do not ignore your feelings. Deal with them in a rational, planned way.

stimulus is present. At least it is his choice. At some future date, he may decide to confront the fear.

Sam, however, showed some courage and decided to confront the fear. The thought of being able to drive is most appealing. Sam now has several options to drive a car without scaring himself. He can start out more slowly, having learned from the previous disaster. He could even take a driving lesson. In both cases, Sam is applying logic to create a solution allowing him to acquire what he desires while minimizing the risk of another disaster. Sam is taking positive action based on conscious decision-making.

At the same time, Sam has modified the emotional program created when he crashed the car the first time he tried to drive. He has learned from the process, and devised a plan to reach his objective successfully, in spite of the fear he felt. Since he now knows that his plan works, the next incident will be less fearful, further modifying the emotional program and adding to his positive experience data bank.

Sam feels great. He is proud that he confronted the fear. He feels satisfied that he created and implemented a plan. And he is happy that his plan worked. His confidence and self-esteem are high.

But what would have happened if Sam had taken the other path, ignoring the fear the next time he encountered the stimulus? It is possible that he would have had the same painful experience, but far more likely is a different scenario. He could have walked away from the car without a conscious decision. The fear is still there, but goes unacknowledged. Sam probably walked away mumbling one of the following to himself: "I don't like to drive anyway," "cars are dumb," or "I hate to drive; I'll take a taxi."

When Sam ignored the feeling, it did not go away. He had no choice but to respond to the fear. His subconscious took over the decision-making. The subconscious mind is notorious for making irrational decisions, and creating a very believable defense for them. Sam now believes that cars are dumb and to be avoided. This irrational process is keeping the benefits of a valuable tool away from Sam. Additionally, Sam's self-esteem and confidence plummet. Sam will never confront the fear if it goes unacknowledged. The longer it takes to feel the fear, the more difficult it will be to acknowledge; and once acknowledged, it will take longer to confront.

In this scenario, the feeling of fear is exactly the same. Sam's response, or lack of response, to the feeling is the only variable. If the feeling is acknowledged, the action is based on conscious decisions and the behavior following is typically rational. After several experiences confronting the fear, Sam will no longer feel fear from this stimulus. That's because he has learned a positive way to cope with the situation which allows him to get what he wants while minimizing the risk.

Let's take Sam into another situation. Suppose Sam is a curious fifteen year old whose mother told him to keep away from the car since he might hurt himself if he drives. Sam will explore the forbidden car given the chance. In this scenario, Sam already feels fear; this time he fears disappointing his mother, possibly losing her love and care. Undaunted by the fear, and with little or no concept of consequences, Sam proceeds to drive the car, crashing as in the last episode. His mother, in a moment of sheer terror, unloads her anger and fear on poor Sam, adding some insult to the injury.

Now Sam has a litany of feelings to confront. The possibility of pain from another wreck is not at the top of the list. Several emotional programs have been created. It will become much more difficult for Sam to sort out the variety of feelings, acknowledge them, and act consciously on them. Sam has now been pushed onto a difficult road, with many obstacles to self-esteem and confidence.

This little story illustrates the important nature of emotions and coping skills.

- Emotions exist in everyone. Emotions happen. We cannot control the presence of an emotion
- The human organism will respond to emotion, *always*
- The control we have over emotions is in how we deal with emotions, in other words, how we *cope*
- In order to cope, we must acknowledge the feeling, check out the meaning of the feeling, create a plan of action and implement the plan
- Ignoring the feeling, regardless of *why*, triggers a subconscious action plan, which is most often irrational

Every emotion works in a similar fashion. Like it or not, emotions are there. It is much more effective to feel and cope than to ignore. While this applies to all aspects of life, it is particularly true for the race driver.

EMOTIONS IN RACING

If you were to ask most anyone on the street about fear and race drivers, most would say that race drivers are fearless. They are not fearless! The issue is not whether emotions of any sort are desirable or undesirable in racing. Emotions are neither good or bad, right or wrong. Emotions are part of human reality. They exist whether we want them to or not. Without emotions, racing would become exceedingly dangerous. In fact, racing involves extreme emotions of all types.

The goal in racing is to use emotions as tools in a positive way to enhance performance and understand risks, not to eliminate the feelings. Since the feelings cannot be eliminated, it is counter-productive to try. Feelings only go away when they have been effectively dealt with in a logical and rational manner.

Pleasant Emotions

Pleasant emotions, such as satisfaction, happiness, and joy are usually triggered by a positive outcome. These emotions are more easily recognized because they are associated with good. There is one downside to specific reactions to these feelings.

When things are "going well," it is dangerous to become overly confident, especially in mid-stream. When the inner voice starts making statements such as "It's in the bag now!" or "I've got this handled!", watch out. The situation is likely going to change.

My friend and trainer, Dr. Jeff Spencer, one of the world's leading motorsports trainers, calls those statements or thoughts "Cosmic Boomerangs." Once they are placed in motion in the cosmos, they will come back to nail you upside the head, usually when you least expect it.

A while back I was testing a ZR-1 Corvette on a quarter-mile drag strip. As I was returning from lunch, I thought how easy the process of driving the quarter mile is, even though it had been several years since I had done this. That thought was a classic "cosmic boomerang." On the first run after lunch, I missed the second to third gear shift, going into first instead. Luckily, I caught the error before releasing the clutch fully, avoiding a crash or scattered transmission parts, not to mention extreme embarrassment.

The process is simple. Attention shifts from the job that needs to be done. If the thought occurs during the event, not only will immediate attention be diverted, but later focus could be affected. In my example above, the thought was prior to the event. But my attention was diverted because I lost focus on an important priority by thinking that it was not very important. It turned out to be crucial.

Cosmic boomerangs are impossible to pull back once released. When I now have such thoughts, I try to catch them before they "take off." I usually ask myself "What am I thinking about? Nothing is in the bag!" Then I refocus attention on the important stuff. Watch out for cosmic boomerangs!

Fear

For most race drivers, the most frightening undertaking is high-speed corners driven at the limits of tire traction. The faster the car, and the faster the corner, the more likely the fear level will increase. The fear will be there, which is fortunate. The situation *should* be scary; the risks to the driver are at their highest level in this situation. A complete lack of fear would be irrational. Since fear will be present, the only variable is how we cope with the fear. Several factors determine the level of fear *and* the driver's ability to cope with the fear.

DRIVER EXPERIENCE. This includes experience in the car, at a given track, overall experience driving at the limit, overall experience at speed, and experiences such as previous crashes, injuries, etc.

TRACK CONFIGURATION AND PERCEIVED DANGER LEVEL. Some race tracks look more dangerous than others; some are more dangerous. Whether imagined or real, if you perceive that a track is dangerous fear will be present.

Fig. 3-2. Fear of crashing is normal.

0012831

SPEED POTENTIAL OF THE CAR. Faster cars are more risky and have the potential for reaching the limits in more corners.

DRIVER CONFIDENCE. This includes confidence in the car, safety equipment, safety personnel, the driver's own skill, other drivers on the track.

Let's illustrate how these factors come into play with some examples. Let's say you intend to race a Trans Am car, but you have no experience in the car at all. Also, your first time in the car you go out on a high-speed road course on which you have never driven.

Would it be rational for you to feel extreme fear? Not only is it rational, but you would be foolish not to. This scenario shows poor coping skills because you are asking for trouble by placing yourself in this environment. You will either be very slow for quite some time (best case), fall off the track (which will elevate the level of fear, for good reason), or crash (which will probably keep you out of a race car, one way or another). The level of fear should be so high that you have little hope of reaching your potential, let alone the car's potential.

Many would blame the speed potential of the car as the problem. This is not necessarily true. A strong case can be made for learning in the type of car you plan to race. One important element of coping is learning. The problem is more the approach.

It is very difficult to learn under extreme stress caused by the high speeds and a selection of factors unknown to you. The very real sense of danger combined with a fear of the unknown create extreme stress and impede coping skills.

Instead of jumping into a high-speed racing situation, let's assume you take the car to a skid pad and low-speed track for a day. You drive laps on the skid pad, learning the feel of the car and the traction limits of the tires. You can also learn about the car set-up from this exercise. You drive the car through a row of traffic cones in a straight line slalom to learn about the car's transitional characteristics. You practice acceleration, shifting, and limit braking from a variety of speeds. Finally, you drive several laps on a low-speed track to learn the limits of the car.

Fig. 3-3. A GTP car can be an intimidating ride. Starting in a slower car, and creating a plan to build up to speed, is the key to learning the limits of a very fast car.

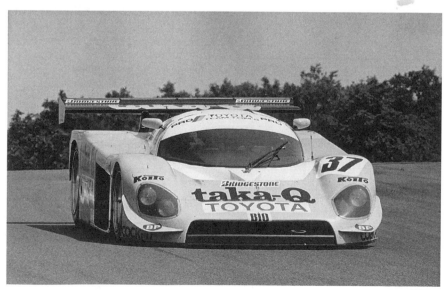

0012832

THE WINNING DRIVER

The skilled, fast race driver feels fear, and is faster because of it.

Fear is an integral part of life; ignoring it can be dangerous, often leading to irrational decisions. Facing fear (or any feeling) and choosing to proceed anyway can open the mind and spirit to new horizons. Being prepared with developed skills, knowledge, and experience helps you to cope with situations which trigger feelings. Lack of preparation is more likely to trigger strong feelings, and cause irrational reactions to those feelings.

Tools: Being in touch with feelings. Understanding what the feelings mean. Creating a plan to cope with situations that trigger feelings. Gaining knowledge and experience in a low-stress environment lays the groundwork to better cope with situations which are likely to trigger emotional responses.

Game Plan: Feel fear, recognize its purpose, understand the stimulus that triggered the feeling, create a conscious plan for action, and implement the plan.

Priorities: Putting fear, and other emotions, in the proper perspective. Develop skills and gain experience in a way that minimizes stress.

Practice Exercises: Learn to recognize those things which cause fear, such as public speaking, etc., and do them in spite of the fear.

By using discipline and patience, you have undertaken a systematic approach to learning in a low-stress environment. You have developed an understanding of the car and personal skill level. Acquired experience allows you to deal with new situations as they occur on the track. You have created a program which will assist you in coping with fear effectively when pushing the performance envelope on a high-speed track. All of these factors will increase the level of confidence, and you will learn more quickly in a new situation because you have established a solid groundwork.

Do you suppose you will feel fear when you venture out on the high-speed track? Of course you will! It is still a threatening situation. But this time,

Fig. 3-4. Practice driving through a row of cones to learn the limits of a car in transition.

0012833

Fig. 3-5. Learning is more productive in slow-speed cornering situations with run-off areas. The consequence of errors is smaller and much less intimidating.

0012834

instead of fighting for survival, both literally and figuratively, you have developed a program to gain experience that will allow you to effectively face the fear and continue progressing at a comfortable but rapid pace.

Reducing the stress by learning the limits at low speeds and reducing the number of unknowns enhances the learning process and improves coping skills. To effectively deal with situations, *to cope*, requires the following steps:

1. Recognize the feeling
2. Acknowledge the feeling
3. Understand the stimulus that triggered the feeling
4. Consciously determine a plan of action
5. Implement the plan

In some cases, this can occur in a very brief time frame. This is especially true as experience increases. When facing a new, high-risk situation, such as racing, additional steps will reduce stress and enhance coping abilities.

1. Prior to participation, anticipate your probable feelings, like fear, anxiety, etc.
2. Devise a plan that allows you to learn as much as possible about the activity prior to physical participation. Read books, ask questions, watch videos, attend a racing school, etc.
3. Devise a plan which allows low-stress, low-risk practice that will directly apply to the activity
4. Accept the feelings and choose how to deal with them. Ignoring the feelings leads to irrational action or no action at all

IDEAL EMOTIONAL STATE

Several years ago, a well-known World Champion wrote that the ideal emotional state for a driver in a race car was a state of no emotions at all.

On the surface, that seems very desirable. The job of driving a race car is very demanding. Diverting attention to deal with emotions is not desirable. In reality, however, the "no emotion" state is not very practical.

A more achievable emotional state has two elements. The first requires that any stimulus *outside* the racing environment which could trigger an emotional response be blocked. While driving a race car, if thoughts wander to other areas, like business or relationships, attention is diverted from the job of driving a race car.

Second, you must develop a plan to *cope* with emotional responses triggered by the racing environment. We have already explored some ways to do this. The emotions will be there. The key is to cope with them, not ignore them.

Achieving the Ideal Emotional State

The first element requires focus on the important priorities and complete concentration on the job of driving a race car. The methods to practice this were outlined in Chapter 2.

The second element requires skills specific to coping. Developing coping skills requires all of the elements outlined earlier in this chapter: acknowledge the feelings, understand their purpose, make conscious decisions about acting on the feelings, and take positive action.

Psyching Up

"Psyching up" for a game or activity is common in some sports. Personally, I feel that psyching up is a way to convince yourself to do something that you really would rather avoid. To me, it is a form of ignoring feelings. I have never felt that I needed to psych up to drive a race car. The day I feel that way, I'll quit racing. It is much more effective to deal with feelings directly.

Coping with Pressure

Feeling pressure is actually feeling a form of fear. Pressure comes from feeling inadequate to perform to a given standard. The pressure comes from within, even if the standard is created externally. When the standard is low, or little is expected, pressure is low, or non-existent. But when expectations are high, so is the pressure.

Confidence in your abilities counters the feelings of pressure. Having expectations based on reality also counters the pressure. If you have proven your abilities to yourself, and your expectations match those abilities, the pressure to perform is low. But if your expectations exceed your proven abilities, or are outside the bounds of your control, the pressure is high.

If you have not proven your ability to win races, but *expect* to win, the pressure will be very high. Additionally, if you do not win, self-esteem and confidence will diminish. Even if you have proven your ability to win races, and expect to do so, pressure will still be very high because your expectations are beyond your control. Many *external* factors can keep you from winning. If your expectations are based on the reality of your self-proven skills and are within the bounds of your control, the pressure is very manageable.

For example, if your expectations are simply to drive to your peak performance, then you are dealing in reality in an area where you have complete control. You may be in a position to win if *outside* factors do not interfere, but that is not your aim. You have no control over the car that blows an engine in front of you with no warning, dumping oil on the track. Since you were not expecting to win, the level of disappointment is low. Confidence and self-esteem are not damaged. Pressure is not a factor, and will continue to be manageable as long as expectations match reality.

THE WINNING DRIVER

The fast, effective race driver lives in the present.

Living in the past makes it impossible to be 100% effective right now. Living in the future makes it impossible to make the future the way you really want it to be. Driving a race car requires complete concentration and attention. The future and the past detract from the attention right now!

Tools: Concentration, focus. The ability to refocus on now when attention wavers.

Game Plan: Eliminate judgements; create a method to regain focus when attention is diverted and make that a tool in your plan.

Priorities: Do your best in the present.

Practice Exercises: Meditation, yoga, visualization, video games, driving.

The key elements for managing pressure are:

- Developing skills to a level where you *believe* in your ability
- Having expectations which match your self-proven skill level
- Having expectations only within the boundaries of your control. Expectations relying on external control are not reasonable, and increase pressure
- Maintaining focus on what *you* can do
- Accepting responsibility for where you are now. Have you put in the time and effort to develop your skills and plan?
- Living in the present during the event. No matter how important a single event may be, focusing on the result increases pressure and reduces focus on the job to be done to achieve the desired result. Your attention is on doing the job, not on winning
- Taking control of those areas where you really have control; letting go of the things over which you have no control

All of these areas can build confidence and reduce pressure. The feeling of pressure, or more accurately the fears causing the pressure, can best be coped with consciously. "Yes, this event is very important. I feel very scared about the outcome. But I will focus my energy and concentration on performing to the best of my ability. I have worked hard to develop skills, and now I must implement those skills. The outcome will take care of itself. My best chance is to do what I know I can do. Nothing more, nothing less!"

The alternative: "This event is so important! Everything is riding on this. I have to win it. I hope I'm ready. Did I train enough? Is the car set-up OK?" This leads to a lot of pressure-building second-guessing. Just writing this script ties big knots in my stomach. Which scenario do you believe is most effective?

CONFIDENCE

Confidence is the quality or state of being certain. True self-confidence is the state of being certain of your own abilities. False self-confidence is believing that your abilities are actually greater than reality would dictate. In other words, you lie about your own ability, mostly to yourself.

To acquire true self-confidence requires action. You must actively participate in an activity and reach some level of proficiency to gain this confidence. And you must truly believe that you have reached that level of proficiency.

If you build confidence based on hopes, dreams, and desires, when the moment of truth arrives, you will be wrought with anxiety and fear. It is impossible to perform to the expected level because you do not have the skills to do so. And the underlying fear of failure makes it unlikely to reach even the actual level of performance potential. In auto racing, this situation elevates the risk level as well.

True self-confidence requires the same elements as for managing pressure, plus a couple more:

- Total self-honesty when evaluating your skills and their development. Dealing in reality is a prerequisite for true confidence
- Making, and keeping, a commitment to develop skills to the level necessary to achieve honest goals

By working on these factors, you can build and maintain self-confidence. When it wavers, look at these factors, and those relating to pressure, for clues and methods to rebuild your confidence level.

WINNING AND THE COMFORT ZONE

In his classic book *The Racing Driver*, Denis Jenkinson describes a characteristic of champion race drivers he calls "Tiger." In situations of intense competition, often when it looks as though a driver has little or no chance

Fig. 3-6. One of the great racing books is Denis Jenkinson's **The Racing Driver**. Many of his ideas and observations apply today as much as they did nearly 40 years ago. I see no difference in the next 40 years.

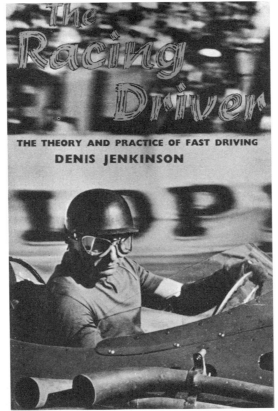

0012835

for victory, some event triggers a Tiger response, allowing the driver to rise to the occasion and perform beyond all expectations.

More than three decades later, it is clear that the Tiger characteristic is still important for a winning race driver. But today, we have a slightly different perspective on this character trait. While the Tiger instinct is still important, it is much less obvious due to modern cars and the driving style they require.

Today, this instinct is better described as exceeding the "comfort zone." The comfort zone is the place most of us live our lives. In a race car, it is determined by the level of your proficiency. If you are comfortable driving at 98 mph in a 99 mph corner, your comfort zone is 98 mph or less in that corner. The stimulus of driving that corner at 98 mph does not cause a negative emotional response. In other words, you will not experience feelings of fear in that corner at 98 mph unless something unexpected occurs. But since you are not completely *convinced* that the corner can be negotiated at 99 mph, and since you have never tried it, to do so will force you beyond your comfort zone.

In order to become a winning race driver, you must, on occasion, break out of your comfort zone. The increased risk, and perception of risk, will trigger fear, which must be dealt with as previously outlined. Staying entrenched in your comfort zone breeds complacency, which stagnates the learning process and increases risks.

To effectively drive beyond the comfort zone requires planning and commitment. For some drivers, especially more experienced ones, the process is very quick. Others must work up to the edge of the envelope in small but distinct steps, analyzing the risks and evaluating the plan.

The best plan to move the comfort zone closer to the limit is the same plan incorporated in the learning process when starting from ground zero:

1. Lay concrete groundwork
2. Understand the feelings triggered by exploring the unknown
3. Create a plan
4. Implement the plan in small steps
5. Evaluate the plan
6. Modify the plan as needed based upon new data

By doing this in a contrived manner under controlled circumstances, it is much easier to "turn up the wick" when the situation calls for action beyond all expectation, while still effectively managing risks. The concept of throwing caution to the wind sounds romantic, but is unnecessary and certainly not desirable. The "Tiger" instinct is the extreme example of feeling fear and doing it anyway, with a sound plan.

BELIEFS

Beliefs of all sorts trigger emotional feelings. If you believe something to be true, occurrences contrary to the belief will elicit an emotional response. Often, perceptions of reality are distorted so that a belief is not threatened.

Beliefs are based upon knowledge and experience. Neither parameter must necessarily be based upon reality. In other words beliefs can be based on false information. Additionally, trauma, such as injury or life-threatening situations, real or perceived, can create intense beliefs which are so strong that they elicit irrational behavior. Phobias and compulsive behavior are often brought about from such instances.

When your beliefs are based upon knowledge and experience gained in controlled, low-stress situations, they are more likely to be reality-based. This allows you to cope more effectively with a given situation.

For example, you should include as part of your plan the possibility that the engine could blow. What would you do in this situation? You may want to prepare for poor visibility from smoke or oil on the windshield/helmet visor. It's a good idea to put in the clutch, since the engine could seize, locking the drive wheels and resulting in a spin or crash. And what about the oil you dumped on the track, or the possibility of an oil fire?

Being prepared for this or any other eventuality allows you to learn and mentally experience the situation. The belief created from this, that you could blow an engine, will allow you to *cope* with the situation (and the emotional response it *will* cause) more quickly and safely.

Beliefs can be changed, given the necessary experience and knowledge. Recognizing that a problem exists is the first step. Creating a new belief that allows a more effective way to cope is the tool needed to accomplish change. There are several ways to accomplish this, and many resources to draw from. Many books, agencies, and therapists offer effective methods to help implement change.

TAKING RESPONSIBILITY

While this is not part of emotional skills, taking responsibility does affect emotions as well as other aspects of racing. If you place responsibility for any situation on external factors, circumstances, or other people, you give up control over your own destiny. When you take responsibility for a situa-

Fig. 3-7. Part of your responsibilities as a race driver is communicating with others in a clear, helpful manner. Driver Randy Porter talks with driver Butch Miller at the 1992 Winchester 400.

0012836

tion, control is in your hands. Accepting personal responsibility places you in a position to take positive action to reach goals and maximize personal performance. Blaming outside factors has a crippling effect. It's easy to make excuses for most anything. It takes courage and conviction, as well as confidence, to face your fears and cope with good or bad situations. Facing reality and accepting responsibility for any circumstance or situation empowers you to take positive action. Like emotions, ignoring responsibility has consequences.

THE WINNING DRIVER

The effective, fast race driver takes responsibility for personal situations and performance.

When you blame your crew, car, other drivers, etc., for problems, you cannot learn from errors, and are destined to continually repeat them.

Tools: Self-assessment and honesty. Making assessments firmly based in reality, not on hopes, dreams, or desires.

Game Plan: Recognize the truth, whether or not the truth is comfortable or desirable.

Priorities: Learn from errors.

Practice Exercises: Reality is neither good nor bad, right or wrong. Reality IS; accept it for just that.

4 PHYSICAL SKILLS

To drive a race car requires specific physical skills; to drive a race car consistently to its limits, including in traffic and extreme conditions, requires the development of those physical skills to a very high level. You must learn how and what to see. Your operation of car controls must be precise, smooth, and quick. You must learn how to read the mechanical signals of your car. Finally, the very high level of concentration needed in the inhospitable environment of a race car demands that you have the physical conditioning of an endurance athlete; anything short of maximum conditioning reduces performance level from the peak, hurts speed and consistency, and increases the level of risk.

Vehicle Placement on the Track

Paramount to success on the race track is your ability to place the race car in the most desirable location. Determining *where* to place the car is an issue we will cover later. Here we must determine *how* to place the car. Ideal car positioning requires that you see effectively (utilize visual fields) and operate the controls to best advantage (maximize driver outputs).

VISUAL FIELDS

Visual fields are both the entire range of vision at any instant, and the primary focal point within that range. Your eyes take in much more than you think you "see." To effectively process all of the data requires that you use some portion of attention on the peripheral areas outside the primary focal point. While it is important that you monitor the entire visual field, the primary focal point is the highest priority on your visual field checklist.

Visual Priorities

As part of your overall plan, you must understand clearly the important areas requiring visual attention. Your plan must account for ever-changing visual requirements and priorities. To haphazardly take in visual data is to assure lost time, reduced performance, and increased risk. Managing the visual field is a crucial task, one most drivers usually overlook and rarely use to best advantage.

Factors Requiring Visual Data

- Monitoring vehicle speed
- Planning vehicle paths
- Developing tactics
- Monitoring track and weather conditions
- Planning race strategies
- Handling traffic situations
- Watching course workers

Fig. 4-1. Your visual field must encompass as much area as possible, especially in a corner, so that the you have the necessary data you need to control speed and vehicle path.

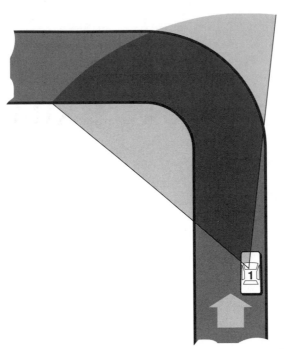

Fig. 4-2. Within the visual field are specific primary focal points which are locations marking upcoming events, like corner turn-in, apexes, etc.

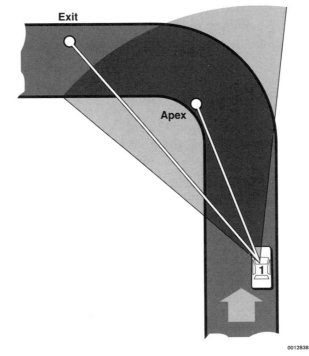

- Assessing hazards
- Monitoring vehicle systems
- Watching crew signals

At various times, each of these items moves to the top of the priority list. Careful planning will allow you to rapidly shift visual attention from one priority to another while still maintaining some attention on all priorities.

Fig. 4-3. The entry zone into a corner is a very important place on the race track. In that area you must judge speed and paths. Seeing well into the corner makes speed judgement more precise.

Some situations may eliminate priorities, but at one time or another in a race each of these will be a top priority.

EXAMPLE. Imagine a section of a track during a race to see how your visual priorities change. As you exit the last turn onto the straightaway, you have little need to plot paths and monitor speed. Checking traffic—in the mirrors, and monitoring any cars you may overtake on the straight—is the first priority. You want to minimize steering to maintain speed on the straight, so the path across the straight is now an important visual priority. As you pass the pit area, checking the crew signals shifts visual attention. Then you monitor the gauges. Next, watch the starter for any signals. If a car is coming up behind, you may need to plan defensive strategy, or minimize the effect of being overtaken. If you are catching slow traffic, you must judge speed to plan a smooth, safe pass. If you are in a heated battle with another competitor, you must plan how to handle the situation, which requires some visual input. As you approach the next turn, you must judge speed and track and weather conditions. When you enter the turn-in zone

Fig. 4-4. Efficient vehicle paths through corners require accurate visual data and prior data based on experience.

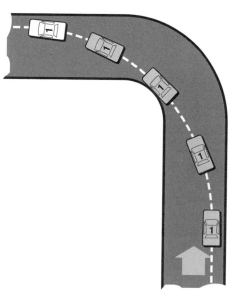

(the area where you turn the car into the corner), your primary visual attention is on the path of the car through the turn. Then you must quickly shift visual attention back to speed and other crucial factors, like corner workers and other cars.

Note how this straightaway and single corner required at least a dozen changes in visual priorities. Visual priorities, and the visual field itself, may change as often as 10 times per *second* on the race track in a traffic or dicing situation. It helps to have a clear understanding of visual priorities for any scenario. Leaving the selection process to chance guarantees that you will lose important visual data.

Fig. 4-5. An instant response in tactical situations can give a driver substantial advantages; effective visual data is a must. Most of your data for a passing situation comes to you through your eyes.

0012841 / 0012842

Fig. 4-6. Monitoring vehicle systems (the gauges) is primarily a visual exercise, though feel and sound also offer important information.

0012844

THE WINNING DRIVER

Tip

A common mistake on the race track is to keep the field of vision too close to the car. Looking farther down the track is important. Try placing a thin strip of tape horizontally across the middle of the windshield if you drive a closed car.

Fig. 4-7. Most drivers have a tendency to look too low. A tape line placed on the windshield will help you become more aware of where you are looking, and make improvements easier.

Notice how often you look above or below the line. Spend more time looking above the line if you find you are looking below it often. Also note the effect it has on your performance. Looking farther ahead increases anticipation time, allows for smoother driver outputs, and reduces anxiety. If you're still not convinced, try riding around town as a passenger, looking out the side window. Attempt to anticipate what the driver is going to do. This should change your perspective, as well as your anxiety level.

Where to Look

The most important concept of visual fields is where to look. Most drivers, especially new race drivers, look in the wrong place, usually too close to the front of the car. Large fields of vision allow the input of more data. Your plan then helps to select the pertinent data, using and storing it as needed, and to dump the extraneous information.

In some cases, the place to look is obvious. For example, when a corner worker waves a flag, your focus is automatically drawn to that point. If the gauges need checking, your eyes go there.

But where is the best place to look when monitoring speed or planning vehicle paths? There are two rules of thumb: 1) Always look where you *want* to go, and 2) Look as far ahead as possible, often even farther ahead than you can actually see (anticipate).

In earlier chapters I explored the concepts of anticipation and looking exactly where you want to go. For now, let's concentrate on the range of your visual field for planning paths. Let's again use an example of areas that become visual priorities when planning vehicle paths.

As mentioned earlier, when you approach a turn, your visual focus must shift to the turn-in zone of the corner.

Fig. 4-8. As you approach a corner, your line of sight and visual field shifts from the braking area to the turn-in zone before you even apply the brakes. Once you brake, shift visual focus to the turn-in and apex so that you can plot vehicle path and use visual data to monitor speed.

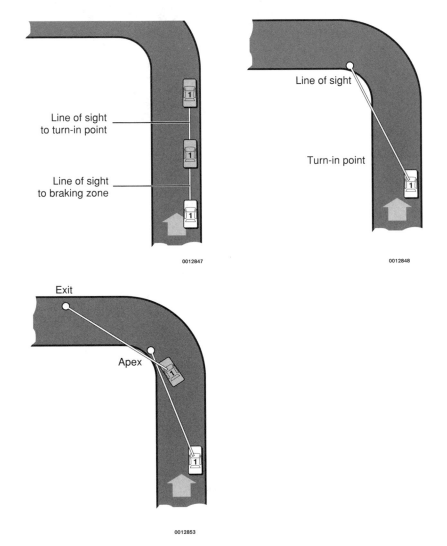

You must attempt to find the optimum turn-in point as early as possible in order to monitor speed immediately and plan a reduction of speed so that corner entry velocity is the highest possible without exceeding the limits of traction through the corner.

Additionally, you want to maximize braking to save even more time. As soon as you find the optimum turn-in point, and monitor your speed, visual focus must move through the entry zone path to the apex of the turn. Your focus continues to move through the entire corner to the exit.

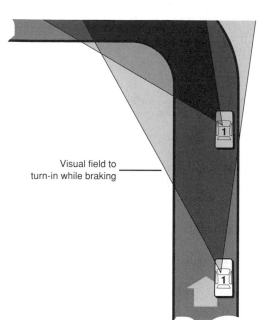

Fig. 4-9. Even before the turn-in, your visual field must be moving ahead to the apex...

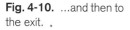

Visual field to
turn-in while braking

0012849

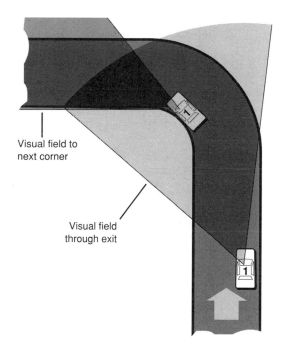

Fig. 4-10. ...and then to the exit.

Visual field to
next corner

Visual field
through exit

0012850

All of this occurs prior to the turn-in, no later than the moment the car is being rotated into the corner.

Keep in mind that once you initiate steering, your concept of the vehicle path is already determined. If the speed is right—not too fast or slow—path changes will be difficult, and will cost time. It is important to have a clear concept of the corner path *before* turning into the corner. This applies *even if the corner is blind*.

In addition to helping you plan the path through a corner, broad visual fields encompassing a large area allow you more anticipation time, as well as more time to react to track events.

Fig. 4-11. Your visual field should take in the entire corner.

0012852

0012851

Large visual fields also help you see how you are doing relative to the cornering path plan. Various spots on or near the track, known as Visual Reference Points (VRPs), trigger action as you approach them, and let you check on progress. The more accurate the VRP, the more quickly you can respond to output errors, making quick corrections. This minimizes the "cost" of the error and allows you to judge the effectiveness of the plan and make changes based on the new data.

Finally, broad visual fields reduce feelings of fear and anxiety by giving you more time to analyze data prior to action, and more time to anticipate your outputs.

To summarize, the best place to look depends upon the circumstance. The visual priority most often at the top of the list is planning cornering paths. This requires looking as far ahead as possible, often through other cars or blind spots on the track, so that you have a clear picture, physical or

Fig. 4-12. The line of sight is your primary source of path information. Peripheral vision allows you to receive other data, such as early warning of a car spinning ahead.

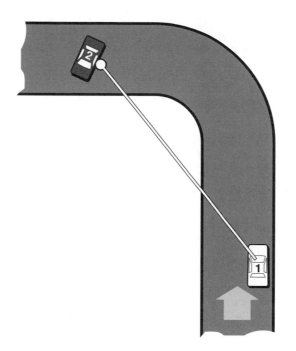

0012843

Fig. 4-13. Visual reference points (VRPs) can be away from the race track. A good VRP here is the valley between the peaks of the hills on the horizon.

0012874

mental, of the track and vehicle path. Constant shifting of the visual field and a priority plan for moving the field of vision are the way to process the maximum amount of pertinent data in the least amount of time.

Eye Movements and Focus

Since a big part of managing visual fields is moving the eyes from place to place, developing eye movement skills and quick focusing capability is crucial. On the surface it may seem unnecessary to practice eye movements and focusing; these are natural, subconscious actions. But these skills can be improved with practice. Combining the exercises listed below improves visual response and creates more effective visual planning.

This series of photos approximates the visual field at several points around the Streets of Willow Springs race track. The course diagram is marked with locations of the photos. The lead car is used for reference only. The actual visual field is wider, since the lens of the camera is more telephoto than the eye.

Entry to Turn 2 braking zone.

Looking through Turn 2 while braking.

Exiting Turn 2, looking down the straight into Turn 3.

Looking through the Turn 3 sweeper.

At the apex of Turn 3, looking through the exit towards Turn 4.

At the exit of Turn 3, looking towards Turn 4.

At the turn-in of Turn 4, looking through the apex to the exit.

At the apex of Turn 4, looking down the straight to the next kink.

Looking through Turn 5 from the apex to the braking zone of Turn 6.

In the braking zone of Turn 6, looking through the apex to the exit.

At the apex of Turn 6, looking past the exit to the next straight.

At the exit of Turn 6, looking at Turn 7.

0012866

Entering Turn 7.

0012867

At the exit of Turn 7, looking into the braking zone of Turn 8.

0012868

Under braking, looking through Turn 8.

0012869

Transition to the skidpad in Turn 9.

0012870

Midpoint in Turn 9, looking through the turn.

0012871

Looking through the exit to the straight entry.

At the apex under power, onto the long straight.

On the straightaway, looking ahead to the high speed sweeping Turn 1.

- While driving on the road, move the focus of visual attention from the car in front to one a quarter mile ahead. Then check the mirrors. Look to the left shoulder, then the right shoulder and try to find clues about what may happen. Move your eyes quickly, and focus quickly. Look through corners and "see" the path you want to drive.
- On roads where you have considerable experience, project your visual sense through cars ahead and blind areas to "see" the unseen road.
- There are several eye exercise books and programs available. Try one, especially if you have eyesight problems.
- Fast-paced games, especially where a wide field of vision and moving objects require constant focal point alterations, are great exercises. Tennis, racquetball, and video games (Super Monaco Grand Prix by Genesis is one of my favorites) are good for this. With time and work, visual skills will improve and visual field priorities will become second-nature.

When to Look   In addition to planning where to look, you must plan when to look to a certain area. Looking at your gauges in the middle of a turn is asking for trouble.

Let's look at the list of visual priorities again, but this time with an emphasis on overriding priorities for specific situations.

- Any time a corner is being approached, the overriding priority is monitoring vehicle speed and planning vehicle path.
- When dealing with traffic, either passing or being passed, defending or attacking for position, all other priorities except #1 are secondary.
- Monitoring course workers takes priority except when #1 & 2 apply.
- All other visual priorities, checking gauges, pit signals, etc., are only considerations when #1, 2, & 3 above are not important.

Many elements of when to change visual fields should be obvious. Remember, though, that under the stress of competition, it is easy to lose sight of important priorities. Pre-planning how best to use visual fields will insure that you do so in the heat of battle. Leaving the plan to chance is risky, with lost time or off-course excursions/crashes the consequence.

Driver Outputs

Any physical command you give to the car is a driver output. There are only three outputs: steering, braking, and using the throttle. Each has a specific purpose, and how well you perform each determines your car control ability, speed, and overall performance. In addition, you must show sensitivity (empathy) for the vehicle in order to maintain its peak performance.

Fig. 4-14. Driver steering outputs determine the path of the vehicle around the track, while influencing speed and car balance.

Fig. 4-15. Your goal for brake usage is to minimize applications.

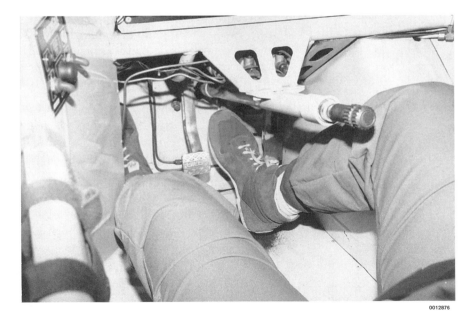

Output Techniques

What you do with car controls is the essence of the art of driving a race car. The steering wheel, brake pedal, and throttle are the tools of the driver's trade. Effective use of those tools is paramount. Misuse, or poorly devel-

Fig. 4-16. The throttle is the speed pedal; the driver who maximizes acceleration will usually be the fastest.

0012877

oped skills, cost time on the track and increase the risk level. The time and effort spent to develop car control skills is among the most important at any level of proficiency.

Steering   The most basic of race driving skills is turning the steering wheel. The effect of steering is so dramatically important that it is crucial to do it correctly.

The steering wheel also provides you with important data, especially concerning traction. The act of steering not only turns the car, but creates feedback.

The steering control factors which you must manage include:

- When to begin steering
- How much steering is needed
- How quickly to steer
- Determining the need for steering corrections
- When to finish steering

The most important concept for you to fully understand concerning steering is this: *Turning the steering wheel is like applying the brakes. It reduces speed.*

With this in mind, the most important goal for the fast race driver is this: *Turn the steering wheel as little as possible for the entire lap, or event.* All else being equal, the driver who turns the steering the least will be fastest around the track.

Any unneeded steering costs speed and time. Making steering corrections falls within this category. While making a steering correction is crucial at the appropriate time, your goal is to eliminate the need to make corrections by planning cornering paths and "seeing" the optimum path before beginning steering. If you begin to plan steering at the turn-in point, there is little chance that the path will be optimum.

In Chapter 6 I will explore the techniques for driving on the desired path, and in Chapter 7 I will examine the decisions that help you choose

Fig. 4-17. The result of too great a steering output is tire scrub. This reduces speed and overheats the tires.

0012878

the best path. Here I will examine the physical steps you need to generate optimum steering.

When to initiate steering depends on your *plan* for the optimum path, as does *how much* to turn the steering wheel. How quickly to turn the wheel is another factor.

Steering speed affects the rate of weight transfer, as you will see in Chapter 6. If you turn the wheel too slowly, the car will not follow the best path, and/or will not reach maximum cornering force quickly enough. On the other hand, steering too quickly can cause overloading of outside tires, which can upset the balance of the car. This causes steering corrections, traction reduction, and overheated tires. The optimum steering speed is as fast as possible *without* causing tire overload, steering corrections, or reduced traction at one end of the car. Several vehicle parameters affect optimum steering speed:

- Car weight
- Tire design (mostly sidewall flex)
- Available traction
- Suspension design
- Shock absorber rates
- Suspension system compliance

The more responsive the overall vehicle system (above parameters) the more quickly you can steer; a slow-responding vehicle requires slower steering.

Steering Response Reflexes

While reflexes, or reaction time, are not as important in racing as the ability to anticipate, steering is one area that proves the exception. Quick reflexes are important in making steering corrections. This is especially true in cars with very responsive steering systems, like open wheel cars and pure-bred race cars. Quick reflexes here can help you maintain car control and minimize the effect of mistakes. While reflexes are mostly natural, you can improve skills with practice. Driving where corrections are needed, like on a skid pad or autocross, provides the best possible training exercise. Other sports where quick reflex reactions are needed are also valuable exercises. Your goal is to minimize or eliminate mistakes, not use lightning-fast reflexes to correct them. Relying on reflexes to "fix" mistakes will ultimately cause lost time and increased risk. The best drivers minimize the need to use reflexes by developing anticipation and driving skills.

Braking   Braking is a necessity, but the least desirable of car control. The basic goal when using the brakes is to minimize their use. To minimize braking is to minimize lap times. Keep in mind that, all else being equal, the fastest driver around a race track is the one who turns the steering wheel the least and who uses full throttle acceleration the most. The only reason to brake is to reduce speed so that the race car can stay on the track into and through a corner; too little braking causes you to fall off the track. The line between the goal and the necessity is very thin. The situation is complicated due to some misunderstandings about braking.

Most cars on most tracks spend about 10% of a lap decelerating. The rest of the time is spent accelerating and/or cornering. It is important to maintain this perspective: little time can be saved during braking, but considerable time can be lost. While some attention must be applied to braking, the greater emphasis should be on vehicle speed for the upcoming corner. The focus of attention is on the speed necessary to negotiate the corner at the limit of traction.

The only other areas where you need to brake are in a tactical situation, where you use braking to initiate a pass, or to avoid a collision. Remember, in a passing situation, the focus of attention is on the tactics; braking is your tool to make the pass.

Braking into a Turn   As you approach a corner where you must reduce speed, you have two priorities. The first is to reduce speed to the optimum to negotiate the corner at the limits of tire traction. The second is to spend the minimal amount of time braking. This allows maximum time on the throttle. Which priority is more important? Hands down, getting the speed correct for the upcoming corner.

Even if you reduce speed too quickly because you began braking too early, simply modulate the brake pedal pressure to reduce braking force. Even though you began braking too early, the speed over that portion of track is

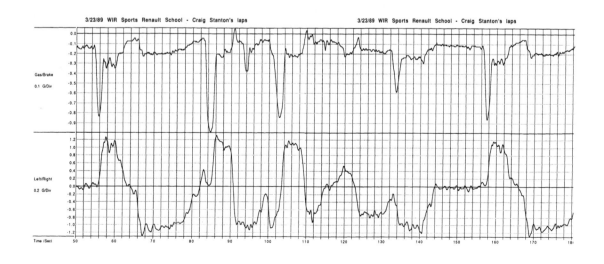

Fig. 4-18. This g.analyst printout shows that braking (any deceleration) is a small percentage of total time around a race track. In most cases only about 10% of a lap is under braking. Even new drivers usually use the brakes to about 90% efficiency. This means that only one second in a 100 second lap can possibly be gained. A better place for most new drivers to gain several seconds is in cornering speed and on corner exits.

Fig. 4-19. In an outbraking situation, attention and priorities shift. The focus becomes the tactical situation, and braking is the tool you use to implement your tactics. Speed requirements are different, and making the pass becomes a higher priority than cornering speed.

Fig. 4-20. Braking is a tool to control vehicle speed when entering a corner. While it is desirable to spend minimum time braking, getting the speed into a corner is much more important and should be a higher priority, even if braking must take longer to accomplish.

nearly as high, on average, as it would be if you had perfectly executed braking. You are much more likely to get the cornering speed correct since that is the primary focus of attention.

The chances are very strong that primary attention on limit braking (braking just to the limit of tire traction) will get the speed wrong at the entry. This will cost time at the entry of the turn and all the way through the turn and down the following straightaway. If you make a braking mistake when focusing on speed, you may lose only hundredths of a second; but if you make a mistake in limit braking, you may lose tenths, even full seconds.

Fig. 4-21. Wheel lock-up is the result of too much pedal pressure for the available traction. This is also one way to sample traction. But, as seen here, wheel lock-up usually causes problems. Rear wheel lock-up, combined with steering lock, will result in a spin.

0012882

Braking Skills

To become a skilled race driver, you must develop specific braking skills. They include:

- Judging the relationship between brake pedal pressure, distance traveled, and velocity reduction
- Braking at the limits of traction
- Modulating brake pedal pressure to control speed reduction *and* avoid wheel lock-up

Finding, and using, braking points is an ineffective method to maximize braking performance. As you saw in the discussion on braking attention above, where the brakes are applied is much less important than vehicle speed at the turn-in; and when to apply brakes is totally a function of getting the entry speed correct.

Brake Pedal Techniques

APPLYING THE BRAKE PEDAL. Applying the brakes effectively requires a quick movement from the throttle pedal to the brake pedal. As the ball of your foot, which is the most sensitive area of the foot, touches the pedal, apply pressure to the pedal smoothly. Jabbing at the brake pedal with an abrupt movement causes excessively fast weight transfer, and possible wheel lock-up. A smooth, but quick, application of foot pressure to the brake pedal likewise generates smooth braking forces, minimizing the chance of wheel lock-up while building pressure to the optimum as fast as possible. It is also important to elevate the heel of the foot used for braking off the floor. This facilitates smoother braking, increases sensitivity to force and traction inputs, and allows improved pedal feel and more accurate pedal modulation.

PEDAL MODULATION. Brake pedal modulation is fine-tuning pressure from the foot to the brake pedal. It is not pumping the brake pedal, which requires complete release of the pedal followed by reapplication of pressure to the pedal. The goal of pedal modulation is to sample traction. Feedback comes from the tire/road interface through the pedal. This allows you to alter pedal pressure so that maximum deceleration occurs without wheel

Fig. 4-22. Use the ball of your foot on the brake pedal, since it has more nerve endings per unit area than any other part of the foot, thus giving you more feedback.

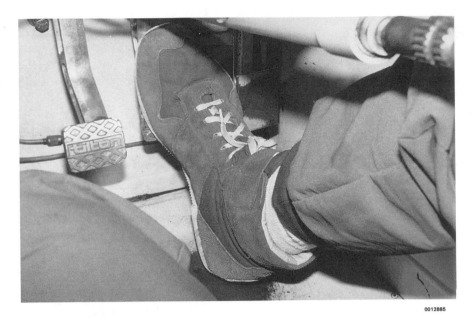

lock-up. Small pedal pressure changes are what you're aiming for. The modulation process usually occurs constantly during braking at the limit.

LEFT-FOOT BRAKING. Left-foot braking is a very important skill. In the modern racing environment, many cars do not require the use of a clutch for shifting. In this instance, using the left foot for braking and the right foot for throttle blipping during downshifts is easier, more accurate, and saves thousandths of seconds on lap times. On any car, when no downshift is needed, you can use left-foot braking to minimize the transition time from throttle to brake and back to the throttle. But be sure that your left foot is completely off the brake pedal when no slowing is intended. The brakes will overheat very fast even with a small amount of pedal pressure. There is no reason, short of some physical impairment, that a race driver cannot learn effective left-foot braking techniques.

Braking Skills Practice Exercises

LIMIT BRAKING. To become proficient at braking to the limits of traction requires practice. To do this exercise on the highway is dangerous, so part of testing or practice sessions on the track or a skid pad should be devoted to this. Autocrossing is very good experience for limit braking. The type of car or tires on the car do not matter. What is important is to experience and learn how the car feels just before and during lock-up. Note the effect of pedal pressure, the pedal sensations, and all forms of visual and auditory data.

At some point, you will need to practice limit braking in you race car. This is best accomplished in a test or practice session where risk factors are low. It is a good idea to use old tires, since they are likely to get flat spots from wheel locking. Testing also creates a good opportunity to tune brake balance and check out the brake system for overall function and feel.

DISTANCE/SPEED REDUCTION JUDGEMENT. The key elements in braking are the relationship between current speed, estimated speed requirements at corner turn-in, available traction, distance required to reduce speed, and the pedal pressure needed to change the speed. To understand this relationship requires practice, but does not require braking at the limit of traction. You can practice this while driving on the street.

Fig. 4-23. These photos show small changes to brake pedal pressure. This is called pedal modulation and is a very effective technique. In most cases, the pressure change is so small, it can be accomplished by slight relaxation of the ankle muscles as opposed to movements of the entire foot.

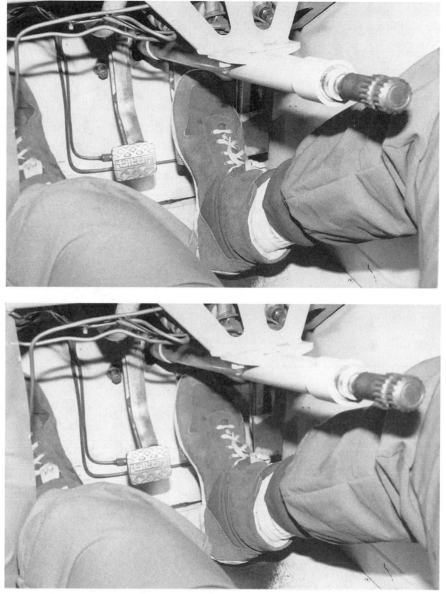

0012883 / 0012884

As you approach a stop sign or light, pick a visual reference point where you want the vehicle to come to rest. Apply the brakes with a quick, but gentle application of pressure. This can occur at any point, as long as braking at the limit is not needed to stop. Do not modulate or change foot pressure on the brake pedal until you are close to zero velocity. Now, where are you in relation to your reference point? To reach it, do you need to increase or decrease pedal pressure? Practice this until you can make perfectly judged stops at your reference point without altering pedal pressure.

Exercise extreme caution if doing this on the street. Do not brake at the limit since following drivers may be taken by surprise and run into you. Additionally, limit braking leaves no room for error if you misjudge speed and distance; you could end up in the middle of the intersection or the side of someone's car.

Fig. 4-24. Left-foot braking is a very effective tool, but requires practice in order to gain adequate sensitivity. Some cars do not lend themselves to left-foot braking.

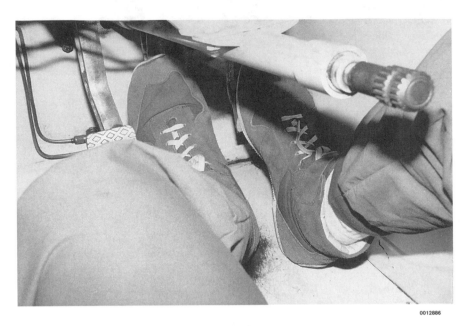

0012886

PEDAL MODULATION. This exercise has the same requirements as the one above, but this time constantly change pedal pressure in the smallest possible increments to reach your reference point. Again, do not brake at the limit on the street for this exercise. For extra practice, try modulating pedal pressure so that no weight transfer is felt in the car when the vehicle comes to rest. For this to occur, you must release pedal pressure at the precise instant the car stops.

LEFT-FOOT BRAKING. Improving left-foot braking skills requires the same practice routine as for any braking skills development. If you drive a vehicle with an automatic, you can practice left-foot braking in daily driving in conjunction with the above exercises. Also practice on the race track if you plan to use left-foot braking. Practice during testing, not during a race. As with all practice exercises, it is best to try this for the first time in a low-risk environment.

Throttle   The key to the fastest possible lap is acceleration. The more time spent on full throttle acceleration, the faster the lap. The goal is to apply full throttle as long as possible approaching a corner and as early as possible at the exit of a corner. The limiting factor is traction. At the entry, traction determines deceleration and cornering speed; at the exit, traction determines acceleration and, therefore, throttle position. Wheelspin indicates too much throttle. Conditions, power, tires, etc., all contribute to how much throttle is too much. Since wheelspin slows acceleration, avoid it. Otherwise, use full throttle as long, and often, as possible.

Fig. 4-25. If you induce corner exit wheelspin, you must either change vehicle paths to allow more power application, or reduce power application. Traction is the overriding factor at the exit, for maximum acceleration as early as possible. Everything you do in a corner is to accomplish that goal. Throttle control is one key factor. Dirt tracks allow more wheelspin. On a dry, slick track like this one, excessive wheelspin is slower. But on a tacky track, wheelspin can help accelerate the car.

0012887

MECHANICAL EMPATHY

Mechanical empathy is vicariously feeling what the car feels. It's being in touch with the various systems of a car, their state of being, and minimizing mechanical abuse to the car. While I believe that 99% of the skills needed to become a winning race driver can be taught, mechanical empathy falls into that elusive 1%. Still, some insights may help you become more empathic with the race car.

To fully appreciate what a tire, engine, shock absorber, or gear box goes through in a race, you must be able to visualize their actions. It can only help to have hands-on experience building a gearbox or engine. When you can get your head into the mechanical processes, you will better feel what goes on, and how outputs to the car affect the mechanical operation and condition of the vehicle.

I have observed numerous students over the years grinding gears with no idea that they are affecting the innards of the gearbox. "If it still runs, it must be OK" seems to be the attitude. Patient explanations have little effect on empathy. If you cannot become a piston or valve, a gear, or a rubber molecule at the tire contact patch for just a few seconds, you probably do not possess much mechanical empathy.

I doubt that a lack of mechanical empathy has a major effect on winning a race, but it probably does when contesting a series championship. Fangio, who possesses tremendous mechanical ability, was the greatest at minimizing wear and tear on the equipment. Jimmy Clark, who was never known for mechanical skills, still possessed incredible empathy for the machine. The common characteristic shared by these drivers was "being one with the car." Neither driver could differentiate between his being and the car. And

THE WINNING DRIVER

You must finish to win.

Drivers often influence mechanical reliability. Abusing the car often leads to mechanical failure. Mechanical empathy improves reliability.

Tools: Discipline, concentration, mechanical empathy, smoothness.

Game Plan: Staying in the race; accepting the reality of vehicle performance; watching gauges and mechanical condition of car. Not over-driving the situation. Dealing in reality now.

Priorities: Keeping the car in good running condition. Drive with mechanical empathy and personal patience.

Practice Exercises: Visualization of mechanical systems (tires, suspension, engine, transmission) and practice of monitoring vehicle systems. Make patience and reality part of your plan.

---

both drivers took very good care of themselves on the race track. The cars and the crew were the biggest benefactors of their ability to feel for the car.

Today, the race driver is much more isolated from the mechanical process. I feel this reduces a driver's ability to show mechanical empathy. Still, developing an understanding of the mechanical workings of a car, and how you can affect the car's well-being, can make you a better race driver.

GETTING IN SHAPE

As with any sport, physical fitness is a key element to success. Being in shape is a tremendous asset for anyone competing in any form of motorsport. Three factors determine the minimum level of fitness needed: event duration, acceleration (both lateral and longitudinal) potential of the car, and level of the sport.

The extreme ends of the spectrum would be the autocrosser running a low-power stock-class car casually in club events vs. the Grand Prix driver. The GP driver must be in top shape, but the autocrosser will also benefit on the track from good physical conditioning.

My area of expertise is driving and car set-up. Conditioning and nutrition are highly developed specialties. I will offer some insights concerning priorities and needs, but not actual methods. I rely upon a trainer to help me in these areas. Dr. Jeff Spencer is one of the best in the country. He works with several elite athletes, including Tom Kendall and Paul Tracy. The benefits I have derived from my relationship with Jeff are considerable. I believe that fitness is so important in motorsports that any driver who is serious about being competitive at any level must address the issues of conditioning and nutrition. Several books offer good information, but the input of a trainer/coach I find invaluable, and highly desirable.

Physical Fitness The winning race driver is most often in top physical condition. To reach a high level of concentration and performance requires practice, discipline, and conditioning. Being in shape addresses these issues. Fitness requires several elements: cardiovascular conditioning , high levels of concentration for long periods, stress management and relaxation, and strength and endurance in several muscle groups

Ignoring any of these areas reduces the potential for long-term success and increases the risk of injury. Let's look at each of these in more detail in an effort to establish priorities.

In my own training program, I prefer to use exercises that will combine activities and meet several needs. This saves some time, but mostly makes the workouts more enjoyable and challenging.

Cardiovascular Conditioning Aerobic conditioning requires consistent aerobic exercise for a minimum of 30 minutes four times a week. Aerobic conditioning begins when the heart rate is elevated within a range at about 70% of the maximum training heart rate. If the heart rate exceeds the maximum training heart rate, the anaerobic threshold is reached, and the lungs cannot supply oxygen to the blood quickly enough to maintain high levels of exertion for very long. Highly conditioned athletes can function in the anaerobic state for only four to five minutes before extreme fatigue and stress begin to set in.

It is important to know your anaerobic threshold for both training purposes and for driving. Some drivers in some cars can experience very high heart rates. For example, during the 1993 Brazilian Grand Prix, Ayrton Senna's heart rate in normal racing conditions was 160 to 170 beats per minute. In tense traffic situations, it elevated to nearly 200.

If the anaerobic threshold is reached or exceeded, endurance and physical well-being are in jeopardy. Consult with a doctor, preferably a sports medicine specialist. A cardiovascular stress test is the best and safest way to learn about anaerobic thresholds and to develop a concrete, effective, and safe training program. This is not an area to leave to chance.

Concentration and Breathing How long can you hold your breath? Not very long compared to the time we can survive without food or water. The Hindu word for breathe literally translates to "life force." The importance of breathing should be obvious. Often, it is not. I have heard several race drivers say that they can control a car more effectively in a corner by holding their breath, the logic being that breathing causes muscular movement. That may be true if you are cutting a diamond, which takes incredible precision for less than one second. But in a car, the logic is false.

In reality, holding ones's breath creates tension in the muscles. This reduces data input sensitivity, or feel, increases anxiety and stress, and reduces the driver's ability to make accurate, smooth control outputs. If there is a single factor in the process of being a skilled race driver, it is breathing effectively.

Pay attention to your breathing. Take full, deep breaths and hold them in for a second or two. Then breath out smoothly and completely. In the race car, you must practice this breathing technique if you are to master it. In addition to improved intake of life-giving oxygen, effective breathing reduces stress, improves overall health, and increases concentration.

I have found Hatha Yoga to be the best means of learning and practicing breathing for me. Yoga also improves muscle tone and flexibility, concentration skills, and is quite invigorating. I do not propose that everyone use yoga as a means to practice breathing, but some form of breathing practice is important. I have often caught myself not breathing properly in the middle of a race. When this occurs, stress, muscle tension, and fatigue all increase. Re-establishing controlled breathing reduces these factors.

Stress Management

Simply defined, stress management is finding effective ways to cope with the stress of life, especially the stress in the life of a race driver. No matter how you live, if you are involved in racing as a driver, stress will be present. The only question is how much. Coping with the stress is the key to progress and success. Managing stress also improves the quality of life.

Several factors can work to help manage stress.

- Recognize the stress
- Determine the cause of the stress
- Understand what you have control over in the process
- Create a plan to take action over what you have control over
- Initiate the action
- Evaluate the effectiveness of the plan and make modifications as needed

Ironically, the least likely cause of stress in the racing environment is driving. Finances, time, sponsor relations, etc., are often much bigger stress sources. Using sponsor negotiations as an example will clarify the process of stress management.

Two days ago, Mark sent a sponsorship proposal by Federal Express to a major corporation. Today, he feels considerable tension in his neck and shoulders. He is also irritable. Mark is stressed.

The first step for Mark to cope with the stress is to recognize the feelings. The irritability and tension are important signs. Next, Mark needs to determine the cause of the stress. In this case, the pending proposal is a likely source. But the real cause of the stress is internal. It is not the proposal that is an issue. It is how Mark feels about the proposal, what it represents to him. In this case, Mark is responding to fear, fear that the proposal will be rejected, that he will look foolish, that he will not have the funds to race, or maybe that he *will* have the funds to race.

Once he acknowledges the fear, Mark can take control of the situation. But what does he really have control over here? Mark has no control over the decision by the corporation, but he does have control over his presentation. If he put the time and effort into the proposal to create a desirable program that meets the marketing needs of the company, he has a much better chance for success and can deal with the reality of a business decision made by the corporate executives, positive or negative.

But that may not be enough. Is it reasonable to expect success from one proposal? Probably not. Mark does not have control over any decision by a corporation, but he does have control over how many corporations he contacts. If Mark sent 50 proposals instead of one, his fear that any one company will reject his proposal is reduced substantially. Creating a plan to contact many companies with a high-quality package will be part of the means to cope with the stress.

Physical tension can be reduced through the continued undertaking of a balanced exercise program. Finally, acknowledging the fear as part of the stress will diffuse the stress even more.

The bottom line concerning stress: Stress is a sign that some issue needs to be addressed. Following these simple steps addresses the issues and creates action to cope with the situation.

Muscle Strength and Endurance Training

In most forms of motorsport, the major concerns for muscle strength are the arms, neck, and shoulders. This is more true in cars with high rates of acceleration, especially lateral acceleration exceeding 1.0 g cornering force. All other strength conditioning will likely occur with aerobic exercise programs.

There are two rules of thumb for endurance training. The first addresses the duration of training. If you will compete in events lasting one hour, then, as part of a training program, aerobic exercise at the 70% training heart rate should regularly occur for one hour in your program. Second, a professional trainer, coach, or doctor should design the program best suited to your needs and current physical condition.

Exercise Programs

There are hundreds of exercise programs that you can use to accomplish any personal goal or fulfill any individual need. Several are more useful for the race driver because they address several needs at once.

I find that two aerobic exercises meet my needs very well. I participate in other physical activities, but mostly for recreation. I find cycling to be the best form of aerobic exercise for me. I enjoy riding and find it challenging. The physical skills of riding a bicycle relate closely to driving a car. Balance, feel, judgement, and visual fields play roles in cycling. Rowing offers aerobic exercise plus upper body development. I supplement aerobic exercise with yoga workouts, which help with flexibility, focus of concentration, and breathing. Alpine skiing is great exercise, and similar to driving. Mostly it is fun.

The most important elements are planning a program that meets needs *and* is manageable. A great program that is not used is not very effective. A

THE WINNING DRIVER

Relaxation leads to speed.
Corollary: Fighting the car creates tension.

To be fast, a race driver must effectively analyze inputs from the car; to analyze inputs, the race driver must be extremely sensitive to feedback; sensitivity requires mental focus; focus requires relaxation; relaxation requires effective breathing, calm emotions, and minimal energy expenditure. Tension reduces sensitivity and increases stress.

Tools: Visualization; attention focus; relaxation techniques; emotional sensitivity.

Game Plan: Learn to relax; then do it in the car. Believe in your abilities and perceptions. Do the work and put in the time to make it happen.

Priorities: Breathing and focus.

Practice Exercises: Meditation, yoga, deep breathing, creating positive, reality-based belief systems.

moderate program that is used will create positive results. Undertake a regimen that you can manage effectively. Any successful training program requires commitment, patience, focus, desire, and effort.

Nutrition

Good nutrition is paramount for good training and effective driving. Nutrition falls into two categories: nutrition for training and diet for specific events.

Nutrition is a very specialized field. Again, several books detail nutritional programs to suit specific needs. And coaches, trainers, and nutritionists can create exact programs for specific circumstances and requirements. Not being such an expert, I can only state that nutrition is a crucial part of the overall plan for the winning race driver.

A HEALTHY DIET. In order to achieve top conditioning for racing, a healthy diet is needed. What is healthy varies from one person to the next. I have found that the best training diet for me includes lots of vegetables and fruit, some fish and poultry, little red meat, and some dairy products. I eat no foods with refined sugar as a primary ingredient. I also limit alcohol intake to two glasses of wine or beer with an occasional meal and do not drink at all three days prior to test driving, longer for race events, especially endurance races. This may be slightly extreme, but the pleasure of consumption is not worth the possible risks of impaired concentration on the track.

PRE-RACE DIET. Before a major event, I will consume more carbohydrates and high-energy foods which are easy to digest. Specific plans must correlate to individual needs for a given event.

FOOD AT EVENTS. On race day, I like to eat a healthy breakfast fairly early relative to the starting time. About an hour before an event, I like to eat some fruit which is high in energy, but easy to digest. I also consume considerable fluids, especially water, before an event. In endurance races, I prefer to have water or an electrolyte replacement drink in the car to fend off possible dehydration. Dehydration can have serious consequences, and can diminish your ability to concentrate. Staying hydrated during an event or race weekend is a very high priority.

Specific dietary needs for pre-race preparations and at events should be planned by an expert who understands your physiological needs and the nature of the competition.

CONCLUSION

A race driver has only three control outputs requiring skills development. Steering, braking, and throttle controls require precise, smooth outputs in order to drive a car to its limits. Many elements come into play to achieve the highest level of skills development. And the conditions existing in the racing environment place considerable demands on the race driver. Physical conditioning and diet are factors requiring in-depth consideration. Ignoring any physical aspect of driving a race car reduces the likelihood of achieving success and increases the level of risk. Creating a plan to develop physical driving skills and mechanical empathy, to reach an appropriate level of conditioning, and to maintain a healthy diet is the first step towards success on the race track. Putting the plan into action, monitoring its effectiveness, and making changes as needed are the next steps on the road to victory lane.

5 MECHANICAL ASPECTS AND CAR SET-UP

The race driver's environment is hostile. Several vehicle parameters can be addressed to improve your comfort in the car, and ease the task of driving. Other tools can be implemented to aid you in gaining knowledge and implementing a plan.

Each area covered in this chapter requires attention to make the driving environment safe, comfortable, and useful for you. While none of these areas will make the car faster, ignoring them can make you slower. Considerable time can be lost due to discomfort, either physical or mental. Paying attention to details in these areas can pay big dividends on the track.

Driver comfort is a relative term in a race car. A more accurate phrase is minimizing your discomfort, for the environment is far from comfortable. However, attention to several areas in the cockpit will assure that you are able to operate the vehicle controls easily.

SEATING

It is crucial that you sit in a position that allows full operation of all controls without struggling against the belts and harness.

There are two important relationships for arm position relative to the steering wheel. First, you should never have to reach forward to fully turn the steering wheel. When your hands are at the top of the wheel, your elbows should have at least a slight bend, with a significant bend desirable in some types of cars. If your arms are fully extended, even if the shoulders are stationary, arm strength will be reduced due to ineffective leverage angles. This is more important in some cars with heavier steering feel. If you must lean forward at all to reach the top of the steering wheel, the seat is too far away. This situation reduces input feel and output control, and induces fatigue.

At the other end of the range, if your elbows strike your body during a full turn of the wheel, you are too close for effective steering outputs.

The pedals should be positioned so you can accommodate full travel without having to stretch forward. The relationship between the brake and throttle pedals should allow comfortable toe-heel downshifting.

The seat itself should offer you considerable lateral and back support and have rigid mountings. Lack of support, or a seat that flexes, will reduce your sensitivity, increase fatigue, and hinder control outputs. Additionally, you should fit snugly in the seat, with minimal padding, to accentuate data inputs from the car.

"Seat of the pants" feel is a crucial source of data. Sliding in the seat, or excessive padding, will filter the data. For safety reasons, the seat mounts

Fig. 5-1. The seating position for a race driver must allow complete and easy access to all output controls and safety equipment.

0012888

Fig. 5-2. You should never need to stretch to reach the steering wheel. Depending upon the type of car and the steering effort needed to turn the car, you are too close to the wheel only if it becomes impossible to turn the steering wheel effectively.

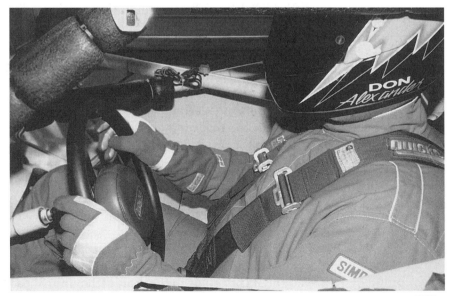

0012890

Fig. 5-3. The brake and throttle pedal position must allow effective heel-toe downshifting on applications where shifting is required.

0012909

Fig. 5-4. Good lateral seat support is very important for good data input sensitivity as well as safety in a crash. A supportive seat can be worth up to a half a second a lap.

0012891

to the chassis should meet NASCAR, SCCA, or IMSA regulation. Minimizing driver movement in a crash will improve the survival chances and reduce potential injuries.

STEERING WHEEL HAND POSITION

The best hand position on the steering wheel allows 180-degree turns of the steering wheel without removing a hand from the wheel.

Fig. 5-5. The hand position on the steering wheel should allow maximum leverage for turns in either direction, and should be comfortable.

Fig. 5-6. When the hands are out of position, leverage is reduced and response time can suffer.

Starting with the hands approximately 180 degrees apart on the wheel allows maximum steering efficiency. With hands separated, maximum leverage is available in either direction. The wide base also improves assimilation of steering feedback to you.

About 95% of all steering can be accomplished from this position without having to move hands or change position on the rim of the wheel. Several techniques work when turns of the steering wheel in excess of 180 degrees must be made. The most effective is the method taught by many police agencies. This method allows both hands to remain on the wheel throughout steering maneuvers. Figs. 5-7 through 5-10 show the way this technique works:

Fig. 5-7. Starting with the left hand at the 9 o'clock position and the right hand at 3 o'clock, a left turn begins with the left hand sliding clockwise around the rim of the wheel to meet the right hand. The wheel remains stationary. When the hands meet on the right side of the rim, the left hand grips the wheel while the right hand loosens its grip.

Fig. 5-8. The turn is initiated by moving the left hand counterclockwise while the rim slides through the right hand.

Fig. 5-9. When the wheel has been turned 180 degrees, the right hand re-grips the rim, both hands being used to continue turning. When it is necessary to begin unwinding the wheel, both hands turn clockwise with the rim until the hands are at the 3 and 9 o'clock positions, then the right hand slides counter-clockwise around the rim to meet the left hand.

Fig. 5-10. At that point, the right hand re-grips the rim, the left hand eases its grip, and the right hand pulls the wheel farther in the clockwise direction.

This method allows both hands to remain on the wheel at all times. There is always adequate wheel travel and leverage and maximum feel is available. Spending a few minutes to learn the technique is beneficial. Most important: use a method which is comfortable *and* allows effective steering output control.

RELATION TO OTHER CONTROLS

You must have access to other controls in the cockpit while firmly strapped in. The gear shift must be easily reached in all positions without causing strain. Ignition and kill switches must be well marked and easy to operate without stretching. A radio switch should be on the steering wheel, operated

Fig. 5-11. The window net release should be able to be easily worked by safety personnel and by the driver from inside the car.

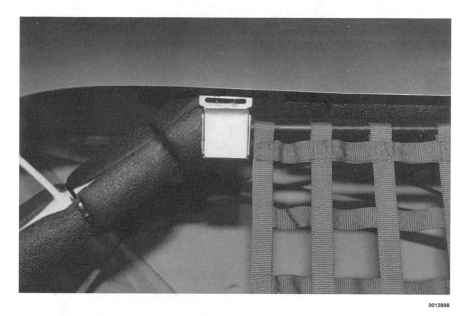

without moving your hands from the normal, straight ahead driving position. A fire bottle handle should be within easy reach, well distinguished from other controls, but not easily triggered by accident. Window net releases should be clearly marked and within easy reach for you as well as by emergency course workers. Radio plugs in the helmet, water bottle hoses, and connections to a cool suit should not interfere with your head movements.

BELTS AND HARNESSES

Lap belts and harnesses serve two purposes. First, they firmly hold you in the car in a crash. Second, the belt system holds you in place in the seat to facilitate data input sensing and to make your outputs easier to accomplish. Both of these purposes are compatible and require the same physical elements. It is important to follow sanctioning body rules concerning belt placement. NASCAR, IMSA, and SCCA have well-defined mounting procedures for effective belt installation. Several of the important criteria follow.

Lap Belt The lap belt is designed to hold you in the car in a crash and to distribute loads over a large area of the body in order to minimize potential injuries. Lap belts must be mounted so that they pass over the pelvic region of the body. This area is the strongest in the body, and best able to deal with the forces in a serious crash.

It is very dangerous to adjust belts in a way that allows the lap belts to ride up over your abdomen. This region of the body is very delicate. Lap belts over this area could cause serious internal injuries in a crash.

To assure that lap belts stay over the pelvic area, anti-submarine belts should be adjusted so that the lap belt cannot move above the pelvis.

Lap belts should always be tightened before shoulder harnesses. Lap belts should be adjusted as tight as possible. After a few minutes of driving they will loosen some. It is very difficult to adjust them on the track, usually impossible. I have never had lap belts that were too tight.

Fig. 5-12. Your belt system should be very snug to maximize protection and your data input from the car.

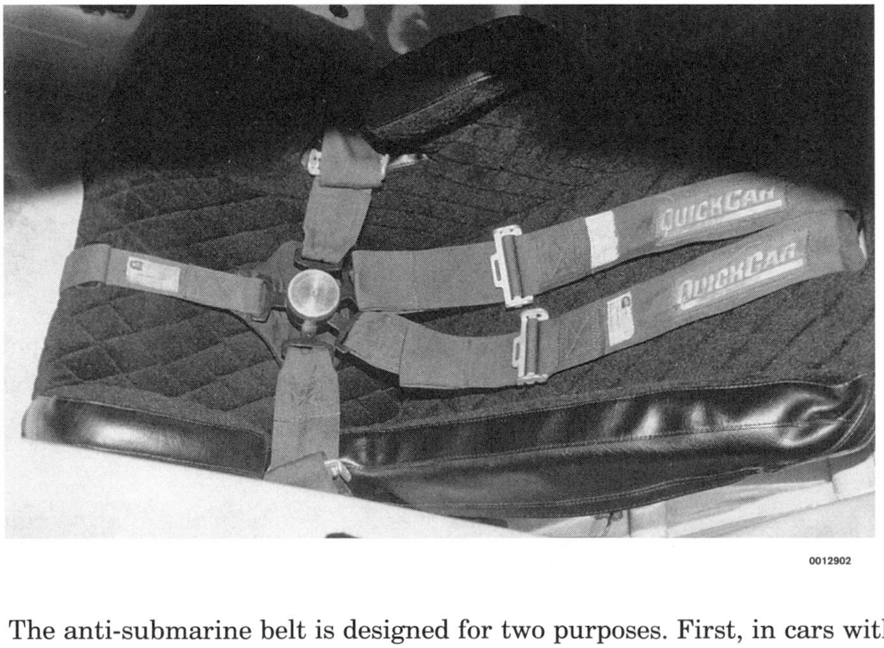

0012899

Fig. 5-13. The 5-point sub belt system is used where the driver sits upright and is intended to hold the lap belt in the best position over the pelvic area. The 3-inch harness spreads loads over a wider area in a crash, minimizing injuries.

0012902

Anti-submarine Belt

The anti-submarine belt is designed for two purposes. First, in cars with semi-reclining driving positions, the belts will keep you from submarining under the dash/steering column.

Second, in all cars the sub belt will hold the lap belt in place, protecting the abdomen from injuries if the lap belt should ride up.

A single, center-mounted sub belt works only to hold the lap belts in place. It will do little to keep you from submarining under the dash. For this reason, a single, center-mount sub belt should never be used in any application where you recline at all.

The best sub belt system has belts that attach to the chassis on both sides of the seat. Often the belts mount at or near the mounts for the lap belts. Sub belts angle forward to the front of the seat, or through an opening in the seat. They wrap around the legs, attaching to the central belt receptacle. It makes little difference whether the belts have a single attachment in the middle, or separate central prongs which attach to the receptacle. This type of sub belt system offers excellent protection by spreading loads over large areas of the lower body, which is very strong.

Shoulder Harness

The shoulder harness is designed to keep your upper body from moving forward in a crash. The upper body is less strong than the lower body. For this reason, it is best to spread loads to the upper body over the largest area possible. The 3" wide shoulder belts do this effectively. The shoulder harnesses should be tightened very snugly. I have found it difficult to ever have these belts too tight.

Sternum Belt

The new design of sternum belt, a short belt placed horizontally between the shoulder harnesses and crossing over the sternum, is designed to keep the shoulder belts from separating in a crash. Drivers have been injured when forces have caused the harness belts to separate, releasing the upper body from the belts. This is much more of a problem in cars where the driver sits upright.

Belt Life

Belt life should be monitored. Belts weaken with age, more so when exposed to ultraviolet sunlight, grease, oil, and water. This weakening allows the belts to stretch more in a crash, which can be very dangerous. Manufacturers recommend replacing the webbing every year or two. The cost, compared to the protection, is minimal. Replace the webbing routinely.

Belt Release

Releasing belts requires some practice, not for normal exit from the car, but for emergency situations. You should practice releasing the belts and exiting the car as fast as possible. Also practice, at least mentally, when to release the belts. Releasing the belts too soon can be more dangerous than staying in the car. If other cars are involved, collisions are possible even if your car comes to rest. Also, in airborne crashes, releasing the belts before you are sure the car is completely at rest is dangerous. Drivers have been killed by releasing belts prematurely.

VISIBILITY

The view out of many race cars is poor in some directions. Seats can sometimes be moved to improve visibility. When the corners or ends of the car are difficult to judge, try a simple exercise to improve the situation. Set up a tall traffic marker or cone, one tall enough to be seen over the bodywork. Drive the car slowly past the marker until you brush it with the side of the car. This will improve your lateral perspective.

Do the same at the front of the car if needed. Roll the car to a stop so that it just touches the marker. This will prove useful to you for drafting and for pit stops.

Fig. 5-14. Gauges should be positioned for easy reading. It is best if all gauge needles point in the same direction when normal conditions exist. Warning lights are much easier to see and can save costly failures. The tach on the dash should be in the driver's normal line of sight.

Gauges

The purpose of gauges is to give you information. If you cannot see the gauges clearly, they are useless. What gauges are needed depends on the vehicle and the team needs. From your perspective, it should be kept simple. You are often too busy to look at gauges for any meaningful data.

Warning lights within your field of vision allow instant response to potential problems with engine systems. A bright light for water temperature and oil pressure is a great tool. Tachometers are important, but after I learn a car, I shift by sound and feel *most of the time*. I still refer to the tach as a back-up to my own judgment, and I use the tach to monitor speed at several locations around a track during practice. A large tach on the dash, within easy eye movement from normal vision directions, is easiest to read. Redline should by vertical, with a high-contrast needle. Other gauges should be mounted so that all needles point in the same direction when indicating normal conditions. I prefer straight up for this purpose.

Mirrors

Mirrors are an important tool for dealing with traffic. They should be mounted so that you can make good use of them without excessive head movements away from the forward visual field. While aerodynamic considerations are important for outside mirrors, visibility to the rear should not be a second thought.

DRIVER SAFETY EQUIPMENT

Personal safety gear for the driver has improved remarkably in the 30-plus years I have been involved in motorsports. The most important criteria is to use good equipment, and maintain it according to the manufacturer's recommendations.

Layers offer better fire protection. I recommend at least a two-layer suit with Nomex underwear. I usually wear a three-layer suit with underwear.

Hands are very susceptible to burns. Driving gloves offer great protection. I do not believe that gloves hurt feel for data-input feedback.

There are many approved helmets on the market. Different brands use different shape headforms for molding liners. One brand may offer a better,

Fig. 5-15. Small mirrors reduce visibility. Really big mirrors can interfere with vision to the front or side. Compromise is important, but it is best to have adequate vision to the rear.

0012905

more comfortable fit for you than another. There is nothing worse than a pressure point from a helmet during a race. If you drive a high lateral G car, consider a carbon fiber helmet to reduce weight and possible neck strain. Open face helmets are more comfortable, but do not offer nearly the protection of a full face helmet.

Driving shoes should first offer fire protection; the feet burn easily. Second, they should offer good pedal feel with a thin sole and reasonable flexibility.

Neck supports, arm restraints, and other items should be considered as aids to improve driving as well as increasing personal safety. Do not ignore the possible use of these items.

DATA ACQUISITION SYSTEMS

The information derived from data acquisition systems is remarkable. Useful information includes lateral and longitudinal forces, engine rpm, or vehicle speed and times, especially segment times. From this data, you can pinpoint specific control outputs and their effects on performance.

Data acquisition systems are very reasonably priced considering the value of the information. Even a very cost-effective product like the g.analyst offers much important data. It is easy to justify investing in some form of data acquisition system if you plan to continue in the sport and improve skill levels.

Video Recording

In-car videos are great fun to watch, especially when you're the driver. Virtually every aspect of driving can be improved by studying videos. Here are some tips:

Use videos in several ways, not just to monitor where you are going. Study steering outputs, hand position, head movements, shifting technique, and pedal use. You can find many errors by studying videos. These videos are best made on test or practice days.

Try to have a video to make comparisons from. Another driver may be willing to trade videos or drive your car to give you a point of reference.

Fig. 5-16. The simple and inexpensive g.analyst is a great tool for driver evaluation purposes, and also helps with car set-up. (See Chapter 4 for a g.analyst readout.)

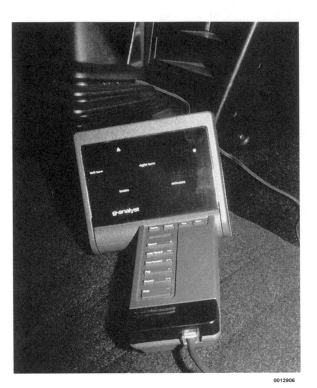

0012906

Fig. 5-17. On-board computers and data acquisition systems provide important data for set-up, tuning, and driver performance.

0012908

In races, videos can be used to study tactics and strategy. Could you have done something differently to make that pass in Turn 2? These videos can also prove useful in protests. But be careful; they may prove you wrong, too!

When using your own videos while learning a new course, try, if feasible, to make voice notes on the video about paths, visual reference points, and any pertinent characteristic you believe relevant to the track. When reviewing the tape, the notes will help you create and modify your plan.

Fig. 5-18. Using videos, you can find out such things as whether or not you tilt your head in a corner. (Some experts feel head tilting is detrimental to performance and perspective. The head angle probably does not matter if you are used to driving that way. The brain can easily compensate.)

When trying to learn a new track, use caution when viewing video tapes made by others. Even if the cars are identical, the perspective will be different, and the driving styles may be worlds apart. About the only real uses of tapes in this situation are for learning turn directions and elevation changes. It is best to avoid creating your plan from someone else's video. Trying to learn a track from an in-car video in Michael Andretti's Indy car when you race a Spec Racer is not very effective.

6 PHYSICS FOR THE RACE DRIVER

While physics is not exactly an exciting topic for many of us, most of what occurs on the race track relates directly to this discipline. To fully understand the skills of a winning race driver, you must also understand at least the very basic concepts of physics that govern a race car.

Vehicle Dynamics

Vehicle dynamics is simply the study of physics as it applies to vehicles in motion. You must understand the basics of vehicle dynamics in order to drive the car to its limits and to have the skills to create the best set-up for given conditions. These are the bare minimum basics for the race driver. Further study is needed to develop a reasonable understanding of this topic, and is greatly encouraged.

Forces

All objects (a car in our case) have mass. To change the state of that mass, i.e., to move it (accelerate), slow it (decelerate or brake), or change its direction (turn), requires force. According to Newton's Law, every action creates an equal and opposite reaction. In other words, forces must always be in balance. While it may seem that a moving vehicle is never in a steady state, it is helpful to remember that all actions such as accelerating, braking, and turning must balance, and the force required for each action must counteract the other forces.

The system is often very complex in a car, but the forces which you can influence or control (braking, accelerating, and turning) all take place at the contact patch of the tire and the road surface. In reality, the tire is creating the force through friction at the tire/road interface. You control when the forces occur by deciding when the controls are used.

If the forces you ask the tires to create exceed their traction capacity, you won't get the results you want. Wheelspin, wheel lock-up, and undesired cornering paths (oversteer and understeer) are all results of asking the tires to do more work than is possible. When this happens, the mass of the car tries to carry it in its original direction (if you tried turning), or the car will not slow or accelerate as quickly as it could.

Insufficient acceleration costs time, but little else. Insufficient cornering or slowing has more serious potential consequences.

Your ability to use 100% of the tire traction in all cases, but not exceed that natural limit, is the essence of a fast lap.

WEIGHT TRANSFER

The forces which cause acceleration take place at ground level. The equal and opposite forces acting to balance the system are focused at the center of

Fig. 6-1. The center of gravity is a point in a car where forces are considered to act equally.

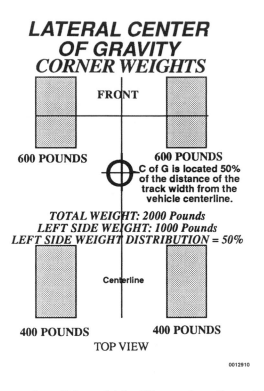

LATERAL CENTER OF GRAVITY
CORNER WEIGHTS

FRONT

600 POUNDS   **600 POUNDS**

C of G is located 50% of the distance of the track width from the vehicle centerline.

TOTAL WEIGHT: 2000 Pounds
LEFT SIDE WEIGHT: 1000 Pounds
LEFT SIDE WEIGHT DISTRIBUTION = 50%

Centerline

400 POUNDS   **400 POUNDS**

TOP VIEW

0012910

gravity of the vehicle. The center of gravity is located at some point above the ground. When equal forces from opposite directions are focused at varying levels, something must occur to maintain equilibrium. That "something" is weight transfer.

Whenever you accelerate, brake, or steer, weight transfer takes place. Weight transfer is always in the opposite direction of the force created by the

Fig. 6-2. Here, due to braking slightly in a corner, weight transfers to the outside as the center of gravity moves.

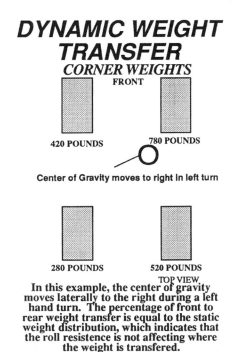

DYNAMIC WEIGHT TRANSFER
CORNER WEIGHTS
FRONT

420 POUNDS   **780 POUNDS**

Center of Gravity moves to right in left turn

280 POUNDS   **520 POUNDS**

TOP VIEW

In this example, the center of gravity moves laterally to the right during a left hand turn. The percentage of front to rear weight transfer is equal to the static weight distribution, which indicates that the roll resistence is not affecting where the weight is transfered.

0012911

tires. In a left turn, weight transfer is to the right. Under braking, weight transfer is to the front; during acceleration weight transfer is to the rear.

Imagine the weight at the center of gravity, which is the entire mass of the car, trying to continue in the original direction when you turn. It attempts to stay still when you pull away from a stop, and attempts to keep going when you want to slow down. You're usually at odds with weight transfer. At least it only happens when you tell it to!

Weight transfer is a major factor in vehicle dynamics, and especially so in racing. We are concerned about weight transfer in four ways:

- How much weight is transferred
- Where it goes
- How quickly it gets there
- When it happens

Tire traction creates weight transfer. The more weight transfer, the more tire traction is used to transfer the weight and the less is available for cornering, etc.

The Amount of Weight Transfer

The amount of weight transfer is primarily a design characteristic. Four factors determine the total amount of weight transfer.

THE FORCE ACTING AT THE CENTER OF GRAVITY. This force is lateral when cornering, longitudinal when braking or accelerating. Both lateral and longitudinal can occur at the same time when braking or accelerating is combined with turning. For racing purposes, we usually assume that the car is being driven to the limits of tire adhesion, so that maximum forces are always being created. You control the amount of this force.

THE HEIGHT OF THE CENTER OF GRAVITY ABOVE GROUND. This is the case where the opposing forces act at different levels. The center of gravity above the ground, where the force reacts, creates a lever arm, like a torque wrench, called a *moment arm*. The length of the moment arm is from the ground to the center of gravity. When a force acts at the center of gravity, it creates an overturning moment. As the name implies, this force tries to overturn the vehicle. The longer the arm length, the greater the overturning moment becomes, for a given vehicle weight and force. Race car designers attempt to design cars with the lowest possible center of gravity to reduce the length of the moment arm, thereby reducing weight transfer. Car design controls this factor.

VEHICLE WEIGHT. The heavier the vehicle, the more weight transfer occurs. Car design also controls this.

TRACK WIDTH/WHEELBASE OF THE VEHICLE. The longer and wider the car, the more it will resist weight transfer. This works like a teeter-totter in reverse. Naturally we want the widest car possible, but not too long, especially since longitudinal weight transfer is less of an issue. Design controls this factor, and design is usually controlled by rules, which limit track width. Otherwise, race cars would be as wide as race tracks. Being on the pole would be all-important, and a major portion of this book would be useless!

Where Weight Is Transferred

Weight goes forward under braking, backward during acceleration, and to the outside in a turn. Simple, right? Wrong! This is where the system gets complex. If the car had no springs, this would be the case if the chassis/body were perfectly rigid. In the springless example, lateral weight transfer due to cornering would be split between the front and rear in a percentage

Fig. 6-3. The cornering force acting at the center of gravity is created by the tires' traction capability. The center of gravity is located some distance above ground. If the height was at ground level, no weight transfer would occur. The track width of a vehicle resists weight transfer.

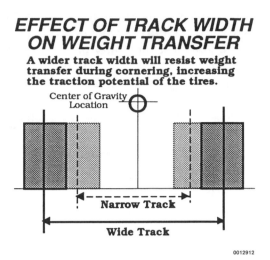

EFFECT OF TRACK WIDTH ON WEIGHT TRANSFER

A wider track width will resist weight transfer during cornering, increasing the traction potential of the tires.

Center of Gravity Location

Narrow Track

Wide Track

0012912

equal to the front/rear weight distribution. Then if the brakes were applied, extra weight would move to the front from the rear, and vice versa during acceleration while cornering.

With springs and antiroll bars, the front-to-rear split changes. The roll resistance provided by the springs and antiroll bars controls the ratio. The ratio of front roll resistance vs. rear roll resistance determines the front-to-rear split of laterally transferred weight while cornering. Maintain the same rear roll resistance while increasing the front roll resistance and more weight transfer will occur at the front, less at the rear.

Where weight is transferred is important because it affects the amount of traction available at the front tires vs. the rear tires. This is crucial for drivers, especially during cornering. This is controlled mostly by the *set-up* of the car and by your control outputs.

The Rate of Weight Transfer

How quickly weight transfer occurs is the third important consideration. The rate of weight transfer affects transitions of the car, in both cornering and longitudinal acceleration. The most important situation occurs when the car takes a set after you turn into a corner. For the car to take a set, weight transfer must be completed, and the tires must reach peak slip angles. If this takes too long, the car's response feels sluggish. If it happens too quickly, you may be unable to sense the car taking a set, which makes it difficult to sample traction and sense the limit of adhesion.

Abrupt use of the controls can cause quick weight transfer, but also cause other problems. The primary controller of the rate of weight transfer is the shock absorber. Stiffer shock rates cause weight transfer to happen more quickly; softer shock absorber settings slow weight transfer and the car's response rate.

Changing the shock rates at only one end of the car will affect the handling balance during transitions. Changing the ratio of bump dampening to rebound dampening will also affect handling characteristics. How each of these changes affects the car goes well beyond the scope of this book, but the information is readily available from several sources.

The shock absorber is a crucial link in the handling characteristics of the car. You should learn the effects of shock absorber tuning. The most effective way to do this is to spend a practice day or two driving with various settings. This is one of the most important skills you can learn. The efforts are well worth the investment.

Note: It is possible for shocks to be set too stiff for some drivers. This most often happens with new drivers in cars equipped with very stiff sidewall tires and stiff shock dampening. The car responds more quickly than the driver can sense. Softer shock rates make it easier for the driver to adapt to the car. With more seat time for the driver, the shock rates can be increased.

When Weight Is Transferred

Weight transfer happens when you tell it to. When you initiate the use of any control, weight transfer is the result. We will see in the section of this chapter concerning tires how weight transfer affects traction, and your responses needed to control this.

TIRES AND TRACTION

The tire contact patch is where the action is! As a driver, it is useful for you to develop an intimate relationship with all of those rubber molecules at the four tire contact patches. They are your link to the planet, and you will be asking considerable work from them. Those little rubber molecules literally have your life gripped firmly in their sticky little paws.

The job of the tire is to make traction. How *much* traction depends on several variables: softness of the rubber compound, size of the contact patch, vertical load (including aerodynamic downforce), dynamic camber angle of the tire contact patch relative to the track surface, track conditions, tire pressure, weather conditions, the phase of the moon, and other, less substantial tricks of those black magic engineers.

You have direct control over only one of these factors: vertical load, which changes with—you guessed it—weight transfer. It is very, very important to understand the effect of weight transfer on tire traction. It will affect how you drive and how fast you go.

Traction and Load

For any tire, in any situation, all else being equal, tire traction will increase as vertical load increases. It's worth restating that: Tire traction will increase as vertical load increases. Simply, this fact is why downforce, which increases vertical load on the tire, increases traction. More weight in the car will also increase traction, but the work which the tires must accomplish will also increase, negating any benefit. But wait! There is a catch here. And it gets worse, not better.

The increase in traction as load increases is not linear. Traction increases at a rate *slower* than the increase in load. In other words, if you increase the weight of a vehicle by a factor of two, the increase in traction is some factor less than two, or about 1.8. Also, adding weight reduces acceleration, so even though there is more traction there is also more work to be done, and the nature of the tire and the laws of physics dictate that more work means less acceleration. The converse of this characteristic is also true. Remove weight or downforce and traction is reduced. Again the relationship is not linear.

The Effect of Weight Transfer on Traction

Any time weight is transferred from one pair of tires to another, the tires gaining weight gain traction; the tires losing weight lose traction. Since the relationship is not linear, the rates of traction gain and loss at the opposing pairs of tires are not the same. The pair of tires losing weight, and therefore traction, are losing traction *more quickly* than the opposite pair of tires is gaining traction.

The potential traction created by tires in a static state is greater than the traction available any time weight transfer occurs. As weight transfer increases, total traction *decreases*. In the design of a race car, the main priority is to keep the center of gravity as low as possible, the weight as low as possible, and the track width as wide as the rules allow. This minimizes weight transfer.

From the above discussion, it should be apparent that when you accelerate, there will be weight transfer from one pair of tires to the other pair of tires. Traction is also transferred in the same direction. This can have disastrous effects.

EXAMPLE. You're flat out in a high-speed corner at a buck and a quarter in a car prone to oversteer, say a Porsche 911. The driver directly in front does something unexpected. You react by lifting from the throttle abruptly. Bad move! You will not need mirrors to see where you came from. You will quickly have a moving experience. The outcome would be pretty much the same in any reasonably good-handling car; it would just happen a little slower, giving you more time to think about what's going to happen to you. What went wrong? You caused weight transfer from the rear to the front, which in turn caused traction transfer from the rear to the front. In this situation, a gradual lift from the throttle would eliminate the problem. Patience and discipline are paramount here.

In a similar fashion, weight transfer can cause problems with abrupt acceleration. Example: You're in a medium-speed corner, and tromp on the throttle hard. The car starts to push like crazy. You must slow to maintain the proper path. What happened? When you accelerated abruptly, weight transferred to the rear tires, and so did traction, causing the front tires to lose traction.

Traction and Weight Transfer as Tools

Using weight transfer can save time and overcome handling ills in some instances. In some low- to medium-speed corners, lifting off the throttle can help point the car into a corner, reducing understeer. How much to lift depends on the car and the circumstances. Experiment with light, partial lifts first. This technique also works in lengthy corners in a car with some basic understeer. By alternating lifts with mild acceleration, you can reduce the steering angle with the throttle lifts, reducing understeer, while at the same time reducing traction at the rear to help steer the car. Returning to the power helps maintain vehicle speed. This technique requires practice, and a skid pad is the ideal spot for this training.

Cars with mild, steady-state oversteer can also benefit from manipulation of weight transfer. A car with slight oversteer can make good use of the extra traction available to the rear tires with medium to hard acceleration. However, if wheelspin is induced, power oversteer will result, making the situation more dicey.

While you cannot change the total amount of weight transfer (without slowing down, at least), or where the weight finally rests, you can affect the rate and the transitional weight transfer. Overall, weight transfer is a fact of life, and learning to deal with it is an important part of the race driver's education. The proper use of weight transfer can save time, overcome some handling problems, and make your job easier. Misuse it and disaster can strike.

Fig. 6-4. In these photos, the tire slip angle can be seen clearly. Slip angle is the twist in the side wall. The tire contact patch moves in a direction closer to the direction of the vehicle than the wheel rim.

0012913

0012914

Tire Slip Angles

For a tire to turn a car, it must develop a slip angle. The slip angle is defined as the difference in the travel direction of the tire tread at the contact patch and the vertical plane of the wheel centerline. In simple terms, the tire twists in the sidewall of the carcass between the wheel bead and the contact patch. The degree of twist is the slip angle of the tire. The wheel always turns farther than the tire contact patch.

Lateral acceleration, or cornering force, increases as the slip angle increases, up to a limit of traction. It then decreases as the slip angle continues to increase, until the tire loses traction and starts to slide. This relationship can be plotted on a graph.

The slip angle where maximum cornering force occurs tells us how responsive a tire is. Lower slip angles for maximum cornering force indicate faster response rates to your steering outputs. This is typical of a low-pro-

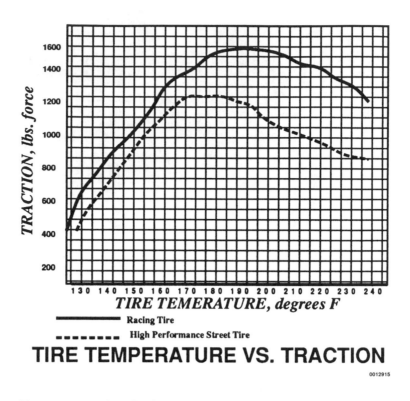

Fig. 6-5. As tire temperature increases, traction also increases up to the point of peak tire operating temperature.

TIRE TEMPERATURE VS. TRACTION

0012915

file racing or ultra-high-performance street tire. The maximum cornering force for a tire indicates the traction created by the tire for a specific application. More cornering force equates to more traction.

Finally, the shape of the curve at the top tells us how quickly cornering force drops off after the peak is reached. This is an indication of how forgiving the tire is. Flatter on the top of the graph shows a more forgiving tire; you have more indication that the tire is beginning to slide. A quick drop-off in cornering force with increasing slip angle after the peak means the tire is not very forgiving; it will lose traction very quickly, without giving much warning. Keeping the car at the limit of adhesion is much easier with a more forgiving tire.

Another useful lesson can be learned from the tire slip angle/cornering force graph. All tires actually have a range of slip angles where near-peak cornering forces are generated. Any driver who corners at speeds creating this lateral force will be driving quite quickly. But *where* you drive within the range does make a difference.

EXAMPLE. Let's assume the range of slip angles for maximum cornering force is from four to seven degrees. Cornering speeds are nearly identical anywhere in that range. So, what is the difference? Tire heat! For a few laps, there will be no noticeable difference. But after a few laps, the tire operating at seven degrees will heat more than the one operating at four degrees, and may eventually overheat, causing a reduction in the coefficient of friction and therefore traction.

Have you ever heard a driver complain about the tire "going off" after 15 laps? It is almost always the driver who drove at the seven-degree slip angle and finished second or third, or went into the fence. The driver running at the four-degree slip angle did a better job of "tire management" than the

Tire Management

How often have you heard, or made, the comment "My tires went off about half way through the race?" What this statement really means is the driver in question is not a skilled tire manager. Managing tires means nothing more than making the best possible use of tires, relative to the situation and circumstances. To be a skilled tire manager, you must know these facts:

1. Tires generate maximum traction at a specific temperature
2. Tires generate maximum traction in a small but specific slip angle range; smaller or larger slip angles create less cornering force
3. Overheated tires wear at a faster rate than tires operating at optimum temperature
4. Higher slip angles generate more heat than lower slip angles
5. Sliding the tires in corners builds heat and accelerates wear
6. Braking and acceleration will heat tires more quickly than cornering
7. Tires operating at improper pressures and improper dynamic camber angles (contact patch not parallel to road surface during cornering) will wear more rapidly on portions of the tread
8. Incorrect handling balance causing one end of the car to lose traction first will increase wear rates at that end of the car

With the exception of selecting the wrong tire compound, you control each of these items exclusively, except #7 and #8, which are controlled by set-up. Set-up is a shared responsibility with the crew. Understanding these parameters allows you to create a plan to manage tires.

The first consideration is the nature of the event, and the type of tire being used. An enduro has much different tire management requirements than a trophy dash or an autocross.

For example, in an endurance race, where tires must be changed at least once, factor wear characteristics with fuel stop requirements. It is usually best to make tire changes at fuel stops, rather than make extra stops to change tires. Since excessive scrubbing overheats the tires and increases wear, you should plan to focus considerable attention on reducing tire scrub.

Second, you will want to sacrifice some speed in areas like corner entry zones, where scrub and abuse are likely to accelerate tire wear. Next, you should be aware that each of the above parameters could affect the outcome of the event near the end. Often the driver with some "tire" left at the end has the advantage. You should make an effort to conserve the tires for the last few laps if the finish may be close.

Finally, before the race even begins, you and the crew must establish the best possible set-up so that all four tires wear at the same rate, and so that no spot on one tire tread wears prematurely because camber or pressure settings were off.

As another example, wear is seldom an issue in a time trial, qualifying or autocross. Here heat build-up is the problem, specifically a lack of adequate heat for maximum grip. Overdriving, sliding the car slightly, excessive steering outputs, and high slip angles—cardinal sins in a race—help in short-duration events.

other driver. His tires lasted longer. (See the sidebar.) The ability to manage tires is one of the differences between the typical club racer and Ayrton Senna or Dale Earnhardt.

Oversteer

Oversteer, which is also called "loose," occurs when the rear tires lose traction before the front tires. They begin to slide first. Technically, oversteer occurs when the slip angle of the rear tires exceeds the slip angle of the front tires. We have seen how you can influence weight transfer to cause oversteer.

Fig. 6-6. Oversteer occurs when the rear tires lose traction before the front tires.

0012916

Understeer

Understeer is the opposite of oversteer and is also referred to as "push." The front tires lose traction before the rears. The technical definition says that the slip angle of the front tires is greater than the slip angle of the rear tires.

Fig. 6-7. Understeer occurs when the front tires lose traction first.

0012917

Neutral Handling

As the name implies, neutral handling lies in the exact middle of the understeer/oversteer continuum. It is the ideal place to be, or at least be near. Excessive understeer or oversteer eliminate your ability to use weight transfer to alter handling characteristics. For you to effectively use weight transfer to drive the car faster, its handling characteristics must be near neutral. Achieving this set-up requires some effort by you and your crew, but the dividends are worth the effort.

**Traction
Sampling**

Tire traction determines cornering force, braking force, and acceleration. Traction can change for many reasons: tire temperature, track temperature, track coefficient of friction, wind, debris, steering, throttle and brake use, tire wear, etc. Since these factors combine to determine the actual amount of traction available, you must monitor grip to drive at or very near the limit of the car's performance envelope. During periods when you are in danger of exceeding the limits of tire adhesion, such as when cornering at the limit, braking, and accelerating out of a corner, you must monitor traction several times a second. This is called *traction sampling*, and it is a complex skill requiring the analysis of many different sensory inputs.

Traction sampling is really part of the *art* of driving a race car. As you become more effective at traction sampling, lap times will become faster, and more consistent.

Everyone who drives samples traction; it is one of the skills needed to drive a car. The average street driver has not developed this skill beyond a rudimentary level, because the average driver rarely approaches traction limits. In order to sense the limit, the limits of adhesion must be experienced and explored.

The process is similar to throwing darts. The first time you throw a dart, you may miss the board completely. It does not matter if you are long or short, left or right. But you now have one acquired data input which will allow you to make judgements and adjustments. If you missed the board low, you know to throw the dart harder. This time, you may hit the board, but still be low. As the number of data points (throws) increases, it is much easier to hit the board, and eventually get closer to the bull's-eye. Highly skilled darts players can place the dart anywhere on the board with incredible consistency.

Driving a car to the limit requires similar skills. Just like darts, practice is the key to hitting the bull's-eye of tire traction. Traction sampling is nothing more than searching for the bull's-eye. The more data points you accumulate in your experience bank, the easier it will be to drive at the limit consistently, and even at the most desirable tire slip angle.

The way you receive sensory inputs which allow traction sampling is varied. The most important is literally through the seat of your pants, which is why "seat time" is so important. But every nerve of your body also senses motions and changes in force. The hands and their contact with the steering wheel offer considerable inputs, especially from the front tire contact patches. The inner ear, with its balance monitors, offers more input. Visual inputs offer you little for traction sampling.

Traction sampling must occur at a subconscious level. If the process is conscious, it will be difficult to hit even the wall; forget the bull's-eye. The conscious mind needs to focus on a positive outcome.

In order to find the traction bull's-eye, you must exceed the limit. Remember that maximum lateral acceleration occurs over a finite range of slip angles, then drops off as slip angles continue to increase. To find the center, you must explore the entire region of slip angles. With experience, the region becomes smaller, and the data inputs needed to find the bull's-eye become fewer. As you develop traction sampling skills, you can more quickly and accurately determine the optimum slip angle at peak cornering force. Errors become smaller and easier to correct.

Most drivers bring at least some level of experience from highway driving, and have already developed traction sampling ability up to a point. The sophistication required to drive fast consistently is rarely developed, however. Several factors will speed the process.

First, you need to spend time at the limit of adhesion. Most of this time, in the early phases of a career, should be spent at the limit but at medium to low speeds. Little time is spent at the limit on high-speed tracks. It is also important to spend part of the practice time making transitions. So how can you learn the fine art of traction sampling?

The first stop is on a skid pad. Driving to the limit of tire traction in a steady-state environment at low speeds is the quickest way to create adequate data points to begin the search for the bull's-eye. By taking lap times on a constant radius skid pad, you can try different techniques to find what is the fastest, and to develop a seat-of-the-pants feel for traction, steering, and speed. The next best place is on a short oval track.

An autocross course is also good traction sampling training, and actually one of the best places to learn transitions at the limit. These scenarios offer the most bang for the traction sampling buck.

To fully integrate traction sampling skills requires seat time. It also requires "feeling" the limit, not conscious thought about the limit. The data flow of sensory inputs is extreme. If you let the data flow, and feel the rubber molecules working at the tire contact patches, you will find the limit. The process is quite natural. Trying to push too hard, or forcing the car to the limit of traction, will assure that you never find the bull's-eye.

The Traction Circle

Many factors affect tire traction, and it is crucial for you to understand the way tires make traction. The rubber molecules at the tire contact patch do not know, or care, in what direction they create traction! Tractive forces can be to the rear under braking, to the side while cornering, or forward while accelerating, or at any point in between.

We can analyze this by comparing the traction forces on a circle, consisting of 360 degrees, with a vertical and a horizontal axis dividing the circle into four 90-degree quadrants.

The circumference of the circle represents the theoretical limit of traction force, with the center of the circle at zero force. Any line emitting from the center of the circle outward is a vector (a graphic representation of a force showing direction as an angle and magnitude as the length of the line).

The vector line will show forward acceleration when its angle is zero, or straight up. It shows braking forces in the opposite direction, or at 180 degrees, straight down. A right turn is at 90 degrees, and a left turn at 270 degrees. The length of the vector line from the center of the circle shows the strength of the force. The limit of tire traction is reached when the force reaches the circle. Any distance short of the circumference of the circle is some force below the absolute limit.

Using only one control output, like braking or steering, will keep the vector on one of the four axes. Combining two outputs, like braking and turning (trail braking), will move the vector line away from the axis.

If half of tire traction is used for turning right, and half for braking, the vector will angle at 135 degrees, or half-way between a right turn only and braking only. If we draw a vertical line from the point on the circumference

Fig. 6-8. The traction circle.

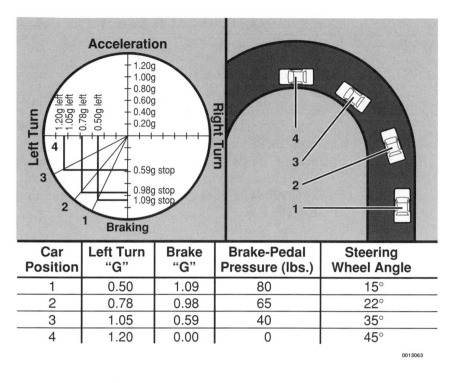

Car Position	Left Turn "G"	Brake "G"	Brake-Pedal Pressure (lbs.)	Steering Wheel Angle
1	0.50	1.09	80	15°
2	0.78	0.98	65	22°
3	1.05	0.59	40	35°
4	1.20	0.00	0	45°

0013063

of the circle to the right turn axis, and a horizontal line from the point on the circumference to the braking axis, we can see how much actual cornering force is created, as well as how much braking force is created.

With the vector at 45 degrees between the axes (135 degrees on the circle), the percentages of braking and cornering are equal, but both are above 50%. The force is proportional to the sine of the angle; in this case both braking force and cornering force are 70.7% of maximum. By using two controls at the same time, there is an apparent gain. It is this reality of traction that allows trail braking and lets you accelerate out of a corner before you complete steering.

Do not, however, be misled by this. You are not getting extra traction; you can only use the available traction to your best advantage. In other words, if you do not make the best use of the traction circle concept, you are giving up speed and performance.

Misconceptions about the traction circle have caused trail braking to be over-emphasized and misused. It is very important for you to use maximum traction available as much of the time as possible. This requires that you keep the traction force vector on the limit as much as possible. Trail braking and accelerating while unwinding the steering wheel at the exit of a corner are the ways to accomplish this.

But it is only necessary to utilize these techniques during transitions. In most cases, braking transitions are very short. Certain circumstances, such as decreasing radius turns or outbraking maneuvers, lengthen the transition period. Because acceleration at the exit of a corner is so important, acceleration transitions are designed to take longer, so that acceleration can begin sooner.

Additionally, this is due to the effectiveness of brakes in deceleration, compared to the ability of the engine to accelerate the car. The more horsepower a car makes, and the lower the gear, the less time is spent in this transition.

In reality the vast majority of time spent at the limits of tire traction, represented by the traction circle, are spent on the vertical and horizontal axes, especially on the left/right and the braking axes. A very small portion of real time is spent in between.

Remember the priorities of your plan. In most situations, the priorities of greatest importance include: a vehicle path allowing early, full-power acceleration; paths using all of the available race track; smooth inputs; driving to the limits of adhesion in all corners; and finding the fastest corner entry speed allowing the best exit. Braking parameters are near the bottom of the priority list.

7 CORNERS, LINES, AND SEGMENTS

The point of motorsports competition is to drive around a track or course at the fastest possible speed, or, conversely, in the least amount of time. Here are the factors relating to achieving that goal.

CORNERING CONCEPTS

Dozens of authors have written about lines and cornering; all of the racing schools teach the basics. While the information is usually correct, it stops short of fully explaining the simple priorities of cornering. What, then, is the reality of cornering?

The Reality of Cornering

Cornering, or more precisely, the fastest path around a race track, must take into account dozens of variables with thousands of possible scenarios. The "perfect line" is a moving target, one which depends upon the interaction of many of these variables. Let's define the "perfect line" in the most concise terms possible.

The "Perfect Line"

The perfect path around a race track is the one allowing you the most time on full throttle power, with the least steering lock. The concept is simple. It is the essence of driving a race car, and should always be uppermost in your mind. The execution is infinitely more complex, and is a major factor in the art of the race driver. Your ability to create a plan to best undertake this concept determines your success. To accomplish this, you must make only two judgements: speed and vehicle path.

Fig. 7-1. There are many factors that affect the "perfect line" around a race track. Your plan must take into account all of them.

0012918

The Correct Speed

The correct speed is always at the limit of adhesion, whether cornering, accelerating, or braking. The most important ability needed to maintain this peak is traction sampling. You must utilize a portion of attention to constantly monitor the traction available. The places where more attention is used for this purpose are:

- Corners where the limits of traction can be exceeded: driving below the limit is slow, since speed is reduced; exceeding the limit will cause tire scrub, at the minimum, and possibly an off-course detour, both of which are slow.
- Corner exits where wheelspin reduces acceleration: excessive power can slow the car, as can too little power. Excessive steering lock can also slow the vehicle.
- Braking zones: excessive braking will reduce deceleration, and possibly overheat or damage the tires and brakes. Inadequate speed reduction can cause excessive tire scrub at the entry of a corner, or a trip off-course.

Table a. Factors Affecting a Vehicle's Path Through a Corner

Factor	Effect
Track Related	
Preceding turns	Dictates speed approaching a given turn, and will determine the entry path into and through the corner
Upcoming turns	Influences the path in the preceding corner
Turn radius/shape	The radius determines vehicle speed. The fastest path in a corner taken flat out will most likely be different from when you must reduce speed at the entry to the same corner. Shape determines the path. 180° corners, such as those on oval tracks, have different requirements at the entry and exit compared to a 90° corner
Track width	Will affect vehicle path if width changes from entry to exit
Banking angle	Banked turns and off-camber corners may require different paths than flat turns
Track inclination	Uphill or downhill corners can alter the perfect vehicle path
Track surface	Areas of rough surface or reduced traction require a change in path
Traction Related	
Tire compound	A stickier tire may allow a different corner path since wheelspin under corner-exit acceleration is less likely
Track coefficient of friction	Changes in friction affect traction and cornering speed, especially under acceleration at corner exit
Track surface	On a bumpy track, the tire of a stiffly sprung car can bounce clear of the track surface, dramatically reducing traction
Debris/fluids	You must alter corner paths to avoid spilled fluids or debris
Tires	As tires wear or heat up, traction changes. You must adjust vehicle paths accordingly
Vehicle Related	
Engine torque	Engine torque can cause wheelspin. To minimize wheelspin, try a later corner apex to make the straightaway as long as possible. The greater the torque, the more important late apexes are to fast lap times
Final drive ratio	The lower the ratio, the greater the torque, creating the same scenario as above
Transmission gear	Lower transmission gears multiply torque, so the best gear for a corner will influence vehicle path as above
Aerodynamics	Aerodynamic downforce increases traction, especially in fast corners. This reduces the likelihood of wheelspin

continued on next page

Making Cornering Choices

Cornering choices, i.e., choosing the fastest path around a corner or race course, is a constant dilemma. This process can use a considerable amount of your attention. It is also a high priority, so the attention is well spent in reasonable, but not excessive, quantities.

One priority dominates all others: corner exit speed. If you always address this priority, your errors relative to other priorities will be less detrimental. The "perfect" path through a corner is the one that allows the fastest corner exit speed. All else is secondary. All of the considerations in the table below will affect this important factor.

Types of Corners

Several types of corners will alter the steps you need to exit the corner at maximum speed and acceleration.

APPROACHED UNDER BRAKING. When braking is required to negotiate a corner, then the corner, by definition, should be taken at the limit.

Table a. Factors Affecting a Vehicle's Path Through a Corner (cont'd)

Factor	Effect
Vehicle Related (cont'd)	
Vehicle condition	A change in the mechanical condition of your vehicle will influence paths. Some corners which previously required braking may now be taken flat out
Handling balance	A well-balanced car, vs. one that has a handling problem or over/understeers, will require a different path
Weather Related	
Temperature	Ambient temperature will change the coefficient of friction between the tire contact patch and the road
Humidity/rain	Dampness or rain also changes the coefficient of friction between the tire contact patch and the road
Wind	Wind can blow sand or dirt onto the track, changing traction. Wind also is a force that affects the vehicle's ability to accelerate, corner, and brake
Driver Related	
Experience, general	If you are a less experienced driver, a later corner apex is often fastest
Experience with the car	Experience with the vehicle usually allows different, more aggressive corner paths
Experience with the track	Knowing a track allows you to drive more aggressively. Later apexes on a new track provide a safety margin while you learn the track
Visibility	In poor visibility, later apexes provide a safety margin. In blind corners, paths should give improved visibility or maintain a level of driver comfort. This is especially true at night
Conditioning	Your physical condition, in general or as an event progresses, may necessitate a change in path to conserve energy or increase the margin of safety (as fatigue sets in)
Strategy Related	
Offensive position	You most often change vehicle path to set up a pass
Defensive position	You change vehicle path to take a defensive position (but not to block)
Traffic	Traffic most often dictates path changes through the corners
Fuel	To conserve fuel in a long race (where pit stops are necessary), you can change vehicle paths to increase cornering speed while reducing corner-exit acceleration
Tires	When you need to conserve tires (which is most of the time in any race), changes in vehicle path will help

Fig. 7-2. Use a late apex in the corner to maximize early acceleration and straightaway speed. However, a late apex is not always the best line for fast laps.

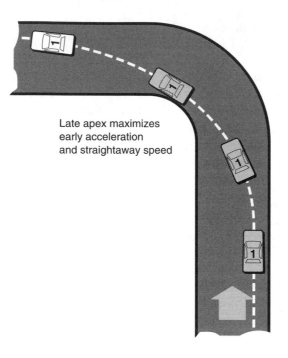

Late apex maximizes early acceleration and straightaway speed

0012919

The first priority in this type of corner is maximum corner exit speed. This requires traction sampling at the exit to control wheelspin, as well as a path through the corner that allows a late apex line.

How late should the apex be? It depends. How fast is the corner? Is wheelspin possible at the exit? How early after the car "takes a set" (all weight transfer has taken place and the tires are at maximum slip angles) can full power be applied?

The second priority is cornering speed, which should be at the limit of traction. This again requires traction sampling.

The last priority is corner entry speed. Overdriving here will cause a speed loss through the corner and later acceleration. This can be more detrimental than being slightly too slow at the entry.

Your goal is to deviate as little as possible from the geometrically perfect line for the corner. If some acceleration is not possible shortly after the point where the car takes a set, the apex should be later in the corner. Additionally, if wheelspin occurs under full throttle acceleration as you reduce steering past the apex, then you need a later apex. However, an apex can only be so "late;" do not overdo a late apex by making the corner much longer than necessary, or reducing speed too much at the entry to accommodate a very late apex.

Certain courses or conditions may make it impossible to achieve a perfect result. You must develop the ability to find the best compromise. Segment times (see Chapter 8) can help here.

Always begin with late apexes when learning a new track or car. Move the apex back in small steps!

AT THE LIMIT—NO BRAKING. When a corner can be taken flat-out, that is, at or very near the limits of adhesion without lifting the throttle or with a small, quick lift, then the priorities change. In this case, the most important factor is reducing tire scrub. Secondary are traveling the shortest distance, and being in position for the next corner.

Fig. 7-3. An apex which is too late is a safe approach since it leaves room to the outside of the corner at the exit. The late apex vs. early apex is shown here.

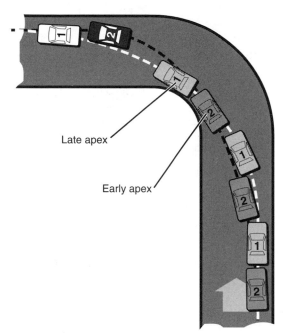

Late apex

Early apex

0012920

Fig. 7-4. The geometric line through a corner is the fast path through a turn, but does not take into account the need to brake and accelerate. Most flat-out corners are taken on the line shown here.

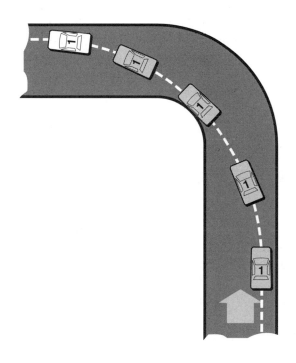

0012921

To achieve this, your primary focus must be minimum steering lock. Excessive steering slows the car *and* heats the tires, which could be a factor in long corners. In this context, the steering wheel works like the brake pedal. Again, compromise is important, and segment timing is a valuable tool.

SLOWER THAN THE LIMIT. In corners where the car is well below the limits of traction, your primary goal is to determine the best compromise between steering angle through the corner, and the path allowing the shortest route to the following corner. The compromise here is between distance traveled and scrubbing-off speed. Segment times again will tell the story.

THE WINNING DRIVER

The fastest race drivers drive the slow corners slow and the fast corners fast.

Slow corners must be driven slowly; overdriving causes tire scrub and speed loss at the exit. This does not imply driving below the limit. Simply do not expect to gain time in slow corners by overdriving, especially at the entry. Fast corners are a much higher priority, requiring focus and attention; speed must be carried to be fast in the fast corners.

Tools: Establishing priorities; patience in slow corners; discipline.

Game Plan: Tackle the fast corners first, where you can gain the most time, then the slow corners.

Priorities: Easy into, and fast out of, slow corners; carry speed and minimize tire scrub in fast corners.

Practice Exercises: Discipline in slow corners; relax in fast corners.

Note: Straightaways fall into this category. If you must cross the straightaway to set up for the following corner, then drive the straightaway like a slower-than-the-limit corner. Minimize tire scrub and steering outputs by using as much of the straightaway as possible to cross over. However, tactical considerations, such as drafting, may overrule this.

SERIES OF CORNERS. In a series of corners, two goals are paramount for speed. First, and most important, is the exit from the last corner of the series onto a straightaway. The priorities like speed vs. distance traveled apply here. Second, keeping the last corner in mind, carry as much speed through the series as possible, without compromising exit speed from the last corner of the series.

Rule of Thumb: In a series of corners, the first corner will have the latest apex. Apexes will become less late as the series progresses. The last corner will be approached for the fastest possible exit.

OVALS. While the basics of cornering apply to any corner, ovals do have several unique characteristics to consider. On many ovals, you will find that the fastest line around the track calls for an early entry into turns 1 & 3, followed by a late apex exit from turns 2 & 4. This is known as a diamond pattern or line. This path allows you to enter the corner deeper, rotate the car at or before the point between the two turns making up the complete corner, and exit the corner with a late apex allowing very early throttle applications and maximum rates of acceleration. This diamond pattern is most effective on a flat or slightly banked oval with tight turns. As banking and turn radius increase, the less useful the diamond pattern becomes.

Sacrificing speed at some point may be necessary to gain speed at a more important point. With the diamond pattern, speed is sacrificed in the midpoint between the two turns to gain more speed at the entry and accelerate early at the exit. Keep in mind that maximum cornering speed is important for the entire turn, not just part of the turn. In some cases, finding maximum traction, or bite, is your highest priority. This is especially true on dirt.

On a banked asphalt track, finding the maximum banking angle is often more important that the best geometric line. Many short tracks have variable banking angles from the low groove to the high groove. Running the low groove, or even using it for a portion of your corner path, with its tighter radius and less banking, will be slower. Running higher will almost always pay off.

Keep these important points in mind:

- Use the diamond pattern where appropriate
- Find traction, either on a part of the track with more grip, or the part of the track that is more steeply banked
- The diamond pattern becomes less important as banking angle and turn radius increase
- Use segment times to see what is really the fastest way around the track

MAKING TRANSITIONS

Transitions occur any time a force changes direction. Going from braking to steady speed is a transition; so is turning from left to right. Acceleration to braking is another. Transitions require smooth steering, braking, and throttle applications in order to maintain balance and rhythm. Ineffective transitions can slow the car, cause a change in path or direction, and could result in an off-course excursion or crash. Transitions require considerable attention and demand specific skills.

From Braking to Cornering

Undertake this important transition with care so that corner entry speed is correct and handling balance is maintained. Braking to cornering takes significant attention, and a delicate touch. At this point, you determine the speed of the vehicle, the path of the vehicle through the corner, and you also influence the handling balance. A lot occurs in a very brief time frame.

VEHICLE SPEED. You establish speed by braking into the corner. Factors include where you apply the brakes, available traction, pedal pressure, and brake release point. The release point of the brake pedal is probably the

Fig. 7-5. One of the most important transitions is from braking to turning. Vehicle path and speed through the corner are determined at this transition. Considerable attention should be devoted to this exercise.

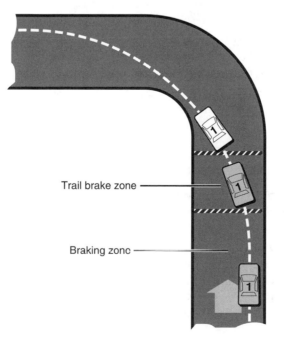

Trail brake zone

Braking zone

0012922

most important action relative to speed into the corner. Get the speed wrong and you lose time, either from slowing too much, or going in too fast. The margin for error is small.

VEHICLE PATH. Vehicle path is determined by the amount of steering lock you apply. Factors include turn-in point and steering angle. If the turn-in is too soon or too late, the path will not be ideal. Too much or too little steering angle will require a correction, causing speed to be scrubbed, or more distance to be traveled. Each costs time.

HANDLING BALANCE. The handling balance of the vehicle is affected by your use of the controls. The major concern is avoiding abrupt movements. If the car tends to oversteer or understeer, excessive movements will exacerbate the condition. For example, on a car with slight understeer, the understeer will become excessive at the turn-in if you brake too hard as the steering is turned. The same situation can occur if the steering wheel is turned too quickly.

At the exit, wheelspin can occur if your throttle applications are too abrupt, causing power oversteer or, in the absence of wheelspin, understeer due to weight transfer. Many other scenarios are possible, and all can be attributed to output errors, not set-up deficiencies.

If you begin to get the idea that the turn-in requires considerable attention, you are right. *The most difficult and important segment of a corner is the turn-in!* You establish both vehicle speed and path at that point. If you are at the limit of adhesion, once the path and speed are established, you are literally along for the ride. You can do little to alter vehicle course until the corner exit.

Always begin by establishing the best vehicle path. Once you establish the path, increase speed in small steps!

From Cornering to Acceleration

This transition is significantly easier than braking to cornering. It becomes easier as cornering speed increases, and is more difficult as horsepower and torque increase. The reason is simple: wheelspin. The goal of this transition is to accelerate as early as possible and as much as possible *without wheelspin*.

In most cases, when the car has taken a set, you apply the throttle to balance the car (no acceleration), then increase pressure until you reach full throttle. You must sample traction to keep the drive tires hooked-up (not spinning). For peak acceleration, low-speed corners and high-horsepower cars require greater sensitivity to traction.

From Acceleration to Braking

This is the easiest of all transitions. Applying the brake pedal requires a smooth squeeze. Making a quick movement from throttle to brake is important, but not at the cost of smoothness.

From Turning to Turning in the Opposite Direction

Often it is necessary to make a quick transition from left to right or the opposite, either for optimum vehicle paths or to take evasive action. Steering must be smooth and precise, else tire scrub will occur. Handling balance can also be upset, causing a spin. Keep in mind that "smooth and precise" does not mean "slow."

This transition can be helped, in some cases, by using the throttle. Lifting off at the proper moment can help turn the car. This is followed by returning to full throttle. This is called *trailing throttle oversteer* and can be

Fig. 7-6. Trailing throttle oversteer occurs when you lift the throttle in mid-corner. You can use this effect to advantage in many instances to help rotate the car into the apex of turn. It is also helpful in countering handling imbalances.

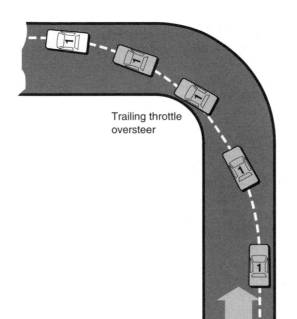

Trailing throttle oversteer

an effective tool for rotating the car into a corner. How much to lift depends on the car and the conditions.

Exercise caution when experimenting with trailing throttle oversteer. Excessive lift with some cars, and any abrupt lift with other cars, can cause a spin. Practice on a skid pad at low speed before trying at higher speeds.

Trail Braking

Trail braking is one of the most misunderstood concepts in motorsports. Let's begin with a simple, concise definition. Trail braking is any time you are turning *and* decelerating (not necessarily braking), at the same time. To be a skilled race driver, you must learn trail braking techniques. You must also learn to use the technique appropriately and correctly.

The use of trail braking, in the vast majority of corner entry situations, is as follows: as the turn-in point approaches, you ease brake pedal pressure, and begin a gentle turn-in at the appropriate time. As you begin steering, release the brake pedal. The exact timing varies based upon the situation, the corner, and the car. When the car takes a set, apply the throttle to balance the car (no acceleration). It is at this point that trail braking ceases.

There are numerous situations where trail braking requires that you carry brake application farther into the corner, or that you leave off the throttle for a period longer than that needed for the car to take a set. The most common of these situations occurs in decreasing-radius corners, passing situations, and on some oval tracks, especially short ovals. In all cases you must reduce braking as the steering angle increases. Brake pedal pressure reduction is a variable, requiring constant traction sampling to keep the car on the edge of the traction circle.

Trail braking is often misused. Instinctively, you may trail brake too far into the corner, reducing vehicle speed more than necessary. This error is often compounded when you realize that entry speed is too slow. Abrupt acceleration usually follows, further upsetting the balance of the car and your rhythm.

Most often, too much attention is focused on braking in an attempt to brake late and deep. Being unsure of the outcome diverts crucial attention away from the turn-in point, speed monitoring, and traction sampling.

The amount of time spent braking around a track is proportionally very small compared to accelerating and cornering. It is a lower priority than cornering and much lower than acceleration. It is better to brake early and smoothly for a turn, giving yourself ample time to shift attention to the turn-in zone well before completing braking.

THE WINNING DRIVER

The PERFECT LINE varies.

The fast line through a turn is the largest radius line; the fastest path around a race course is the path allowing the optimum combination of minimum steering and maximum full- throttle acceleration.

The art of driving a fast lap requires that you have a thorough understanding of cornering concepts, and establish priorities. From this you create a plan, then evaluate and modify it to reflect new data and experience.

Tools: Segment timing; data acquisition; sensitivity to vehicle speed; seat time; patience.

Game Plan: Be open to new approaches for a given car, track, and situation combination. Plan to make changes, and be open to new situations and ideas.

Priorities: Maintain vehicle speed; minimize tire scrub; try different approaches; keep records and charts.

Practice Exercises: "See" the path through a turn; feel the tire scrub and watch steering outputs. Learn the effect of turning the steering wheel.

Fig. 7-7. Each segment of a corner requires specifications.

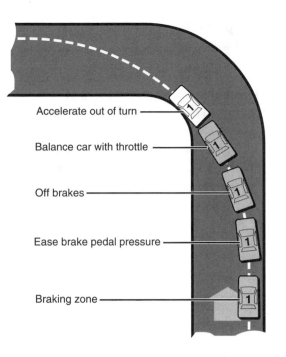

Accelerate out of turn

Balance car with throttle

Off brakes

Ease brake pedal pressure

Braking zone

0012925

CORNER SEGMENTS

In order to fully develop a plan for cornering, and ultimately a plan to lap a course as fast as possible, it is helpful to separate each corner into segments. The segments include the braking zone, the turn-in zone, the point where the car "takes a set," and power application. Each of these segments, or zones, has specific priorities, requiring action and the focus of your attention on specific areas.

Braking Zone

The braking zone is where you reduce speed the exact amount so that the upcoming corner can be taken at the limit of adhesion. If you reduce speed too much, you lose time; too little and the result is tire scrub, or an off-course excursion. The goal is to reduce speed as quickly as possible (braking at the limit of adhesion). The point where you should reduce speed to the lowest point is as the car takes a set, which is at the end of the turn-in zone.

PRIORITIES.

- Correct speed reduction exactly at the turn-in point
- Braking close to the limit of adhesion
- Where braking begins

Note that the turn-in point is very important. Also note that no mention is made of a *fixed* braking point. Where you apply the brakes is important, but only in the context of available traction, car speed approaching the corner, and all the other considerations that play a role in your plan. The braking zone's length and the point where braking begins are variables. Many factors alter the braking parameters. To set a specific braking point is to lose time. Either you begin braking too early, or you carry too much speed into the corner.

PRIMARY FOCUS OF ATTENTION. On the straightaway, as you approach the braking zone, your attention is primarily focused on speed, traction, and the turn-in zone, especially the turn-in point at the end of the zone. The primary plan is to negotiate the corner as fast as possible relative to *existing conditions*. Alter the plan for tactics and strategy, as well as for traffic.

As you approach the turn-in zone, focus more attention on the turn-in point and steering outputs, less on braking and speed reduction. "Banzai" late-braking maneuvers and excessive trail braking often cause you to direct attention to the wrong areas, resulting in a loss of time.

VISUAL REFERENCE POINTS.

- On the straightaway approaching the braking zone: turn-in *zone*
- As the brakes are applied: turn-in *point*
- At the end of the braking zone: corner apex

If your braking point is a visual reference point, you will focus attention in the wrong place. Sensing your current speed and "seeing" where speed must be at its lowest will allow you to compute when and how hard to apply the brakes. Focusing attention on "slowing down" diverts attention from traction sampling and vehicle speed sensing. If you envision the outcome, the brain will compute the details, and inform the body *how* to achieve the goal. You do not need to "think" about the process. Focus on the outcome, which is the "perfect speed" for the corner.

Turn-in Zone   The turn-in *zone* starts where steering begins and ends where you pick up the throttle to balance the car. The car will "take a set" in this zone. If you use trail braking, it will occur in this zone. The turn-in *point* is where you begin steering. No additional steering angle increases should occur after the turn-in zone. Any steering angle increases beyond here indicate a turn-in error or necessary evasive action. The turn-in zone can be very small, especially for a corner where no braking is needed to negotiate the corner at the limit.

The path of the vehicle through the corner is determined in the turn-in zone. Once you plot the path, you are essentially along for the ride. Any time lost due to steering errors is lost forever. Here, the effect of errors can only be minimized, not eliminated. It is obviously best to make very small errors, recognize them quickly, and act effectively to reduce the effect. If speed is too great, or the path wrong, priorities change, with staying on the track, or minimizing the effect of an off-course excursion, becoming most important.

The goal is to establish a path which allows you the earliest acceleration at the exit of the corner, and which deviates the least from the geometrically perfect line through the corner. Your priority is to "see" the path through the corner, and to make early throttle outputs.

VISUAL REFERENCE POINTS.

- At the end of the braking zone: corner apex
- At the beginning of the turn-in zone: through the corner to the exit
- At the turn-in point: the corner exit

"Taking a Set"   A car "takes a set" when steering is complete, when weight transfer has occurred, and when the tires have reached maximum slip angles. This takes a very small, but finite, amount of time. When you drive a car at the limit into a corner, in most cases the car must take a set before you can balance it with the throttle and begin accelerating (in the power application zone). You can distinctly feel the car take a set most of the time. It is possible for the car to set so quickly that you don't feel it; this can be very unsettling, making it difficult, if not impossible, to sense the limit of adhesion.

Fig. 7-8. From the top: The turn-in zone, turn-in point, and apex. What would you use for VRPs to help you in your corner path?

0012926

0012927

0012928

Power Application Zone

This zone is the most important relative to a fast lap, but is the easiest if you have executed the preceding zones properly. Once the car takes a set, throttle outputs can begin. First, the car is balanced with the throttle, but no acceleration occurs. Speed is constant. Next, throttle outputs increase as quickly as possible, without causing wheelspin. This insures peak acceleration at the exit of the corner, and makes the straightaway as long as possible.

Your goal is the earliest possible full power acceleration. Where you can apply full power is dependent upon many factors, such as car torque, turn radius, gear, track conditions, tires, etc. In some cases, such as a low-powered car in a high-speed corner, you can apply full power well before the corner apex.

Important: When learning a car, corner, or new conditions, start by accelerating late at the exit of the corner, and on following laps, begin to accelerate sooner. Make the changes small, since excessive throttle can cause problems.

FOCUS OF ATTENTION.

- Traction sampling; power application; early visual reference points
- At the turn-in point: the exit
- At the apex of the corner: down the following straight and/or into the next corner

Common Errors

In every segment of every corner on every lap, an accomplished driver will make errors. How effectively you manage the errors determines your level of proficiency. The best drivers make the smallest errors, and recover from them more quickly. The more quickly you recognize the error, the smaller your correction will be. Quick error recognition minimizes time loss. Conversely, spending time analyzing the error, especially "beating up" on yourself for making the error, takes time which is better spent making a correction. Most common errors have simple corrections.

EARLY TURN-IN. As the name implies, early turn-in causes a change in vehicle path which results in an early apex or a steering correction. Late braking is often the cause of early turn-in. This is due to the need to feel secure on a larger radius path into the corner, which the early turn-in allows.

USES FOR EARLY TURN-IN. This can be used as a technique for passing under braking, or for avoiding rough or low traction spots on the track. Keep in mind that early turn-in allows more speed to be carried into the corner, but less speed at the exit. It is important to minimize early turn-in when used deliberately.

EARLY TURN-IN ERROR CORRECTIONS. If you find that you have turned-in too early, make a correction quickly. If caught very early, increase steering until you intersect the desired path. Then steer onto the path. Later in the turn-in zone, the best correction is to hold the apex longer until you reach the desired apex, then begin to release the steering at the exit.

OVER-BRAKING. Over-braking occurs when you apply the brakes too hard (not necessarily locked-up) or too late to slow adequately for a corner. Many drivers mistakenly believe that deep braking at the extreme limit of adhesion saves considerable time. In reality, over-braking upsets the balance of the car in the turn-in zone even if speed is reduced adequately to negotiate the desired vehicle path through the corner.

Additionally, over-braking diverts critical attention from the most important priorities: vehicle speed and traction sampling. When you see a wide-eyed driver with a death grip on the steering wheel, praying that the car slows enough to make the corner, you can bet that the focus of attention is in the wrong place. You can also bank on the fact that the driver is over-braking.

It is better to brake a little early, not apply as much pedal pressure, and focus attention on the turn-in zone than to attempt to save time under-braking. Very little time can be saved under-braking anyway. On a typical lap, you spend about 10% of the time braking.

Try this exercise on a practice day with little or no traffic present. Instead of braking for a turn, back off of the throttle very early approaching a corner. The goal is to slow to the correct speed to drive the corner at the limit. Do not exceed this speed! This will allow you to focus all your attention on speed, traction, and vehicle path through the corner long before the corner is reached. You should find that the corner is much easier to drive *at the limit*. After perfecting this, start braking, but brake early and gently at first. Remember to use the beginning of the turn-in zone for a visual reference point. *Brake earlier, with less pedal pressure.*

NOT USING FULL TRACK WIDTH. This should be an obvious error, but it is quite common. In most cases, drivers who do not use the full width of the race track at the entry, apex, and exit, do so as a safety margin. Once you establish this pattern and make it part of your belief system it is difficult to alter. While safety margins are important, especially for new drivers, or when learning a new car or track, this technique is not an effective safety margin.

It is more effective to drive below the limit of adhesion through corners, using all of the track. Learning track dimensions is more difficult, and much harder to "re-program," than it is to increase speed through a corner.

Remember that the fastest path through a corner is on the largest geometric radius. The largest radius requires using all of the track width. Even one inch has an effect. At the limits of adhesion, missing the edges of a 50-foot-wide track by two feet will cost about 5% in speed or about 2% in lost time. It is obviously important to use all of the racing surface.

Start by using all of the track at a lower speed; increase speed in small steps.

EXCESSIVE CONTROL USE. Excessive control outputs (steering, throttle, and brake) all upset car balance. In all cases, traction is lost through wheel-spin (while accelerating), wheel locking (during braking), or extreme tire slip angles (in corners). Gentle, precise, but quick use of the controls will allow the car to remain at peak traction at all times, and improve your feedback from the car. This helps you assess the data accurately and quickly.

IMPROPER LINES. The path of the vehicle is crucial for fast laps as well as tactical maneuvers. The best line in any corner is the one which allows the earliest full-power throttle application.

Causes of improper lines:

- Not understanding the parameters and factors that dictate the best line
- Not creating a plan to drive the optimum path for a car/driver combination under existing conditions
- Inability to mentally "see" the optimum path of the car through a corner

Finding the optimum path takes work and requires considerable attention.

TIRE SCRUB. Scrubbing the tires is like applying the brakes. It slows the car, usually where you don't want to. Scrubbing the tires is caused by turn-

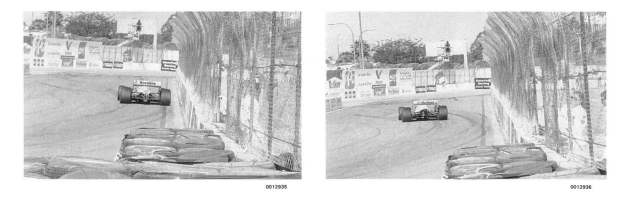

Fig. 7-9. These photos show the difference between using and not using the entire track width at the entry, apex, and exit of a corner. The less road used, the smaller the turn radius and the lower the cornering speeds.

THE WINNING DRIVER

Turning the steering wheel is like applying the brakes.

To be fast requires minimum use of the steering wheel. Turning the steering wheel more than necessary results in tire scrub, which slows the car and overheats the tires. Unwind the steering wheel as much as possible in corners to minimize tire scrub.

Tools: Smooth steering outputs; unwinding the wheel in corners; relaxed style; clear concept of the vehicle path through a turn.

Game Plan: Learn to steer smoothly; "slow hands"; practice unwinding in daily driving.

Priorities: Smoothness; awareness of cornering priorities.

Practice Exercises: Every time you drive, use the steering wheel as little as possible; learn to feel the effect of turning the steering wheel on the tires and on vehicle speed. In long turns or on wet roads, try reducing steering lock, then adding it back to keep the car on its path, but at minimum steering lock and small slip angles.

---

ing the steering wheel too much. Tire scrub occurs any time you turn the steering wheel, but if steering is unnecessary or excessive, you lose time. Excessive steering and scrub occur most often at corner entry. Scrub also occurs in long, sweeping corners and hairpins by operating at too great a slip angle. This slows the car and overheats the tires. Tire traction decreases and wear accelerates.

Correction: Slow steering in the turn-in zone; unwind the steering wheel instead of applying more steering lock when understeer occurs in long corners. By unwinding the wheel, more grip is created, allowing the car to stay on the desired path. As the path widens, increase lock again momentarily, then reduce steering lock. This continues repeatedly until the exit of the corner is reached.

SEGMENT TIMES

Virtually all drivers utilize some tool that allows them to judge how well they are getting around the track. The most obvious of these tools is the stop watch to monitor lap times. Most drivers also check engine rpm at specific points on the track. Often an increase in rpm indicates more speed through a section of track. This may not be the case, however. If time was sacrificed at an earlier point on the track to gain speed at the driver's "check point," then it is clearly possible that the earlier lost time was too much to be made up with the rpm increase. One way to check this is to use segment times.

A segment time is simply measuring the time it takes for a car to cover a specific portion of a track or course. There are numerous ways to accomplish this. But before you begin the process of segment timing, it is important to establish a few priorities.

Priorities for Segment Timing

Your first priority should be fast laps. What is a lap time? It is data which offers you some useful information. If you went faster on a given lap, the lap time is the information that tells you by how much. But the data doesn't provide much other information.

For example, what occurred on lap 5 that caused you to go faster? Was it that you tried a different line, drove harder, had less traffic, made a productive change to the car prior to the session, or encountered improved track conditions? If you know why, you can make real progress; if not, the next fast lap you achieve will be as random as the first one. Additional input must come from another source: you or your crew. Segment times can be a very useful tool in your quest for fast laps.

Your second priority is to have a plan so that results are quantifiable. If you change tire pressures, you make a note of the change *and* the effect. The same applies to making changes in lines, etc. Knowing the change that allowed the fast lap will allow more fast laps.

The final priority is the time through a segment of the track, relative to overall lap times. For fast laps, going faster through a segment of race track is only beneficial if it improves the overall lap time. In a race, however, being faster in a given segment may be more important than lap times if it allows you to implement successfully a given race strategy.

Segment Time Game Plan

Establish your plan before a segment times session. Try only one evaluation per session: either changes to the car or changes to your outputs, but not both. If you want to try a new line or other change in technique, limit it to one turn, so that you can determine the overall effect of the change.

The types of car changes which can be evaluated from segment times are: gearing, overall aerodynamic downforce, aerodynamic downforce balance, and bodywork modifications to reduce aerodynamic drag. Other car changes such as suspension, spring, and antiroll bar adjustments will have an effect everywhere on the track, and segment times are not needed to determine their effect.

The types of changes to driver techniques which can be evaluated are: lines, braking points, and alternate lines for passing and traffic. Possibly the most important use of segment times allows you to try alternate lines through a fast series of turns where you have not reached the limit of adhesion.

Selecting Segments

There are two criteria to use when selecting segments. First, choose a spot on the track where the car has a problem, or where you believe you could gain time. Second, segments should incorporate significant portions of the race track. Break the entire track into segments, but use care in the selection process. The number of segments should correlate to the track configuration, the goals of the test day or session, the time available, the equipment used, and number of personnel available. Attempting to evaluate segment times from ten areas of the track, without the time or people to collect and analyze the data, leads to information overload. A small amount of useful data is much more beneficial than reams of paper which no one has time to review.

When selecting segments and establishing the pre-test plan, prioritize each segment relative to its value and the purpose of the session. For example, the most important segment may be the series of turns leading onto a long straight. This segment should include the entry area of the series as well as a portion of the straight. Or, you may have a problem in a given

Fig. 7-10. When segment timing, divide the track into meaningful sections. Shown as examples are the Street of Willow Springs (top) and Las Vegas Motor Speedway (bottom).

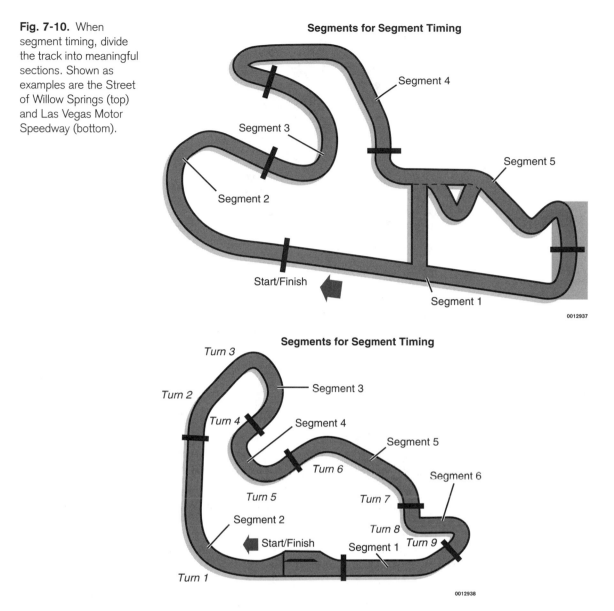

turn; that may be the most important segment. On cars with adjustable aerodynamics, more downforce may be the fastest way around the track, but may cause enough drag so that passing is difficult on long straights. Segment times on fast sections can help determine what works best.

Segments can be straightaways, entire turns, series of turns, portions of turns, or even half of the track. The key is to use segments as a tool to go faster. The segments are created as part of a plan; the plan is not created because you happen to have segment times.

Taking Segment Times

Taking segment times requires a timing device, track reference points, visibility of both ends of the segment, and a method to keep notes. More sophisticated methods are available, utilizing data acquisition systems, video cameras, or products like the g.Analyst and a computer. Radios can make segment timing more useful, allowing you to try more than one segment per lap, since the crew can remind you of the changes to make before arriving at the segment.

Fig. 7-11. Each corner can be further broken down into segments.

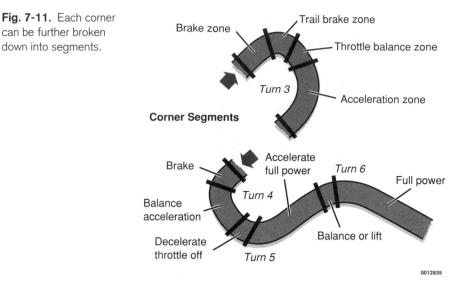

Accuracy of time measurement is crucial. An error of even .05 seconds can negate the usefulness of the times. Keep in mind that if the track is broken into 10 segments, an error of .05 seconds on a segment is like a half-second mistake on the full circuit. That is a very important amount of time to gain or lose.

It is also helpful if the observer, in addition to noting segment times, also records observations about lines, braking points, apexes, mistakes, the set of the chassis, even the squeal of the tires, on each lap. This can be correlated with the data provided by the driver. If you use a radio, someone should take notes covering what you did on a given lap, and your remarks about what occurred. Even more useful is data from an acquisition system like the g.Analyst, Commander, or the video data acquisition system called the DATACAM. This system has on-screen timing so segments are easy to evaluate.

Evaluating Segment Times

On the surface it appears that the only important evaluation is what was fastest, and how did it occur. While in many cases this is true, there are occasions when a faster segment may be detrimental to fast lap times.

Often, a segment speed is not important to overall lap times, but the following segment is crucial. You may need to sacrifice speed in the first segment so that the car is set up to gain exit speed into a faster, more important portion of the race track.

Here is an example. If you create a corner segment, from turn-in point to exit, and time a car on a variety of lines, you will soon learn that the geometrically perfect line, allowing the largest radius through the turn, is the fastest. If you discount the following straightaway, and subsequently the entire lap except the corner in question, overall lap times are affected negatively, even though speed is found on a segment of the race track. If you were to create a smaller segment within this turn, say the turn-in point to the apex, you would again find a great increase in speed if you take an early turn-in, early apex approach. But you would drive off the track at the exit—not the way to make the fastest lap times.

Another misuse of segment times can be the preparation of race strategy and tactics. The goal of the race, to win or place as high as possible, often requires different car settings and a different driving style, or at least different priorities. In close races, where you are pressured by competitors for the duration, and the last lap often decides the outcome, it is important to plan for that last lap, especially the last turn before the checkered flag. An advantage here can win the race, even if speed is sacrificed in other segments of the track.

Here, segment times for alternate lines will help to win races. This important use of segment times is rarely used by most competitors. By finding the fastest way around, then trying alternate lines where passing or defending are likely to occur, you can evaluate what line, or lines, will result in the least amount of lost time. This exercise also allows you to build confidence in your own ability to maintain control and pass competitors and lapped traffic.

Segment times are a great tool, but no one has won a pole with the fastest time in a single segment. Use segment times to try new techniques, to learn new lines, and to test new car settings. Establish a plan and stick to it, so that the most is gained from the effort, either an improvement or a set back. Both will provide valuable information. Collecting too much data can cause more problems than it can solve. Work within the available time frame and logistics. Analyze the data carefully, and make decisions based on the goal, either qualifying or the race. The final judge is lap times, or crossing the finish line ahead of the field.

CREATING PLANS FOR FAST, CONSISTENT LAPS

Fast laps are the primary goal for qualifying, time trials, and other solo events. Your first job is to drive the car at the limit in order to establish the fastest possible lap.

This goal shifts in a race, where winning or placing as high as possible is the primary goal. Absolute lap times are meaningless; consistently fast laps are crucial. Tactics and strategy also play an important role in the race.

Each of these goals requires a plan: to go fast for a single lap in qualifying; to maintain a consistently fast pace for the duration of a race; and to develop a strategy that allows for change as the race progresses. In this section we will address the issues of speed and consistency. Race strategy and tactics are covered in later chapters.

Basic Goal #1: Fast Lap Times

Assuming that the car is properly prepared and tuned for peak performance, creating a fast lap is your first important goal.

Establishing Priorities

A plan requires priorities so that you know where to focus attention and energy. Each race driver and team must establish their own list of priorities for a given event, season, session, etc. Certain issues should always be considered; their relative importance, i.e., their place on your list of priorities, will change based upon circumstances and overall goals.

An important overall consideration is car preparation and set-up. If the car is not reliable, it won't finish. If it is not safely prepared, it will harm your confidence, among other things. If the engine is not tuned for peak overall performance, little chance exists for a competitive lap time. If the handling is not balanced, you will fight the car. And if the chassis is not tuned to create maximum traction from the tires, lap times will suffer. Today, it is a rare circumstance when a driver can make up for inferior equipment and set-up. The optimum set-up for fast laps, as opposed to a race set-up, is important to gain the last few tenths from the car.

The rest is solely up to you. You must be able to focus nearly complete attention on driving the car to the limit for a few laps. Often, as in oval track racing, you have only one lap to warm up, then you're on the clock. In an autocross, there is no warm-up. But even when you have an hour qualifying session in which to find that one fast lap, it is important to learn to "get up to speed" quickly, since modern tires are "fast" for only a few *hot* laps. This is not the time for practice or set-up. If time is needed for that purpose, expect the qualifying results to reflect the situation.

Driver priorities for a fast lap should include:

- Relaxation and mental rehearsal prior to going onto the track. Be comfortable in the car, and make sure everything is adjusted properly, including all safety equipment, especially your helmet and belts
- Considerable attention focused on traction sampling in the braking zone and corners
- Considerable attention focused on speed approaching braking zones and turn-in zones
- Considerable attention focused on vehicle paths in the braking zone while approaching the turn-in zone
- Considerable attention focused on throttle outputs as the end of the braking zone approaches
- Using every inch of the race track, allowing more speed; often this includes using the edges of the track and beyond, such as FIA curbs, etc.
- Making all control outputs smooth, precise, and quick
- Focus attention on steering; unwind the steering as much as possible to keep tire scrub to the absolute minimum
- Leave some of your attention available to monitor the environment, such as traffic, corner workers, gauges, and crew. Never eliminate these vital information sources from the flow of inputs
- Don't overdrive the slow corners. Focus on driving the fast corners fast, and the slow corners slow. This does not mean to drive the slow corners below the limit; don't expect to save time in slow corners. Little can be gained in a slow section; but considerable time can be lost
- Remember to breathe deeply and relax muscles
- Be prepared to break out of your "comfort zone." Driving a truly fast lap is not comfortable, and it is rare to achieve fast laps without stretching your personal "performance envelope"
- Ignore lap times; focus on driving

Important Considerations

For any given race track, especially a road course, some sections of the track are more important than others. You must decide your own priorities, but here are some guidelines:

The Most Important Sections

On any race track, the most important sections are the straightaways, with the longest straight being the most important. While the straights are relatively easy to drive, the speed carried on the straights dictates lap times. Making the straights as long as possible using full throttle acceleration is the key. Longer periods of full throttle acceleration allow more speed on the straights, which minimizes time spent on the straights.

The Most Important Segments

Naturally, carrying maximum speed onto the straights reduces the time spent on the straights. Corner exit speed is, therefore, crucial. The power application zone of a corner is the most important segment. The zone leading onto the longest straight is the most critical. Early throttle outputs and full power application are the keys.

ALSO IMPORTANT.

- Maintaining maximum cornering speed on your optimum vehicle path
- Optimizing vehicle path through all series of corners
- Minimizing speed-robbing tire scrub in high-speed corners and sections
- Braking

Putting the Pieces Together

An integral part of your plan is the analysis of a race track. Understanding the nature and layout of a track will allow cornering and segment priorities to crystallize, and your plan to develop. Your plan must consider the circumstances, including the car, the weather, and your experience. The initial plan should utilize your best estimate of priorities, paths, and visual reference points. Use a course diagram, take notes, and write your plan.

Part of your plan should allow for alterations based on new data. After driving the course, evaluate the plan, and make changes based on new experience and insight. Update your diagram and notes. This makes the plan fluid, and will allow for further changes even while driving. With time, changes to the basic plan will become smaller, but always leave room for alterations and improvements.

Basic Goal # 2: Consistently Fast

The driver who wins the race is the one who runs the most consistently fast laps. One fast lap in a race is meaningless, unless points are awarded for the fastest race lap. It is better to be .5% to 1% per lap slower than your qualifying time for every lap, than to turn two or three fast laps, with the others being 1 to 2% slower as you regain composure or breath. Possibly the most important factor in a race is to be consistently fast while managing your tires. Five blazing laps at the start of a race will not make up for 15 slow laps at the end of a race or session caused by the tires "going off."

Turning consistently fast laps takes intense concentration and practice. The sign of a good *race* driver is the variance in lap times. A variation from the fastest lap of no more than one-half of a percent over a 10-lap period indicates good consistency. Even in heavy traffic, the variation should be no more than one percent. Drivers who maintain this level of consistency will win races. And this is one factor over which you have nearly total control.

How do you become consistent? First, you must be able to drive fast laps. Your plan and your car must be developed and refined to the point where you have complete confidence in both. Next you must practice repeating the same control outputs in the same places lap after lap. Focus on driving, not on lap times. Finally, the secret is hard work and discipline.

Some Keys to Pace and Consistency

If you study the lap times of the best drivers, they are able to turn laps consistently within 0.5 seconds on a 1:30 average lap circuit. The variation is about one-half percent in lap times. On a track with an average speed of 100 M.P.H., that half second translates into nearly 5 car lengths. That is the range to shoot for if becoming a winning race driver is your goal.

- In 10 or 20 lap blocks, look for variance in times, not just the best lap. Doing this will alter the focus of attention
- What is the cause of the variance? If your lap times vary by 2%, is it because one lap was great, but you have no clear idea why? Or did you make a major mistake on one lap which extended the envelope in the opposite direction?
- If the variance was due to a really quick lap, you need to understand what you did on that lap so that you can make it part of your plan
- If the average lap variation was caused by a slow lap, was a major mistake the cause? Were you trying to drive a really fast lap, but ended up over-driving and losing time?
- Within those laps which were within 0.5% of each other, you will find a method to become consistent. Try repeating the session within the range of the average lap times. Forget the fast laps; create a plan which focuses on consistency
- Once you complete a session within the 0.5 to 1% consistency range, try another session where you experiment with going faster, but now focus on whether specific ideas work, and why. If you find better techniques, implement them into you overall plan
- With a revised plan to go faster, now try doing the faster laps consistently. When you find something that works, and integrate that into your plan, you can repeat it over and over. This technique creates consistency
- Remember! In a race, conditions and circumstances change. Lap times may not be a true indicator of consistency. If lap times consistently get slower, tires and track conditions may be the cause. It is important to have a fluid plan to allow for adjustments to maintain peak performance

One of the most important factors relating to consistency, and to driving performance overall, is your physical conditioning.

Basic Goal #3: Planning for Changes

Part of your overall plan must accommodate change. In racing situations, the environment changes, the car changes, and the traffic situation changes. In your plans for lapping as fast as possible and lapping consistently fast, you should include a plan for adapting to changing situations and conditions. If you plan ahead for these changes, it will be easy to shift gears when the need arises. Lacking advanced planning makes changes very difficult, for the human organism resists unexpected changes.

In the course of fine-tuning your plan for fast laps, and again in your plan to lap consistently, you probably accumulated a variety of pertinent data concerning vehicle speed, paths, and traction in areas of the track which you have decided to avoid if possible. This data is likely incomplete, and further experimentation may be needed to fully develop a plan for alternate lines.

GETTING A HANDLE ON HANDLING PROBLEMS

Many handling problems can be attributed to driver error. This is especially true for new, inexperienced drivers. It can be quite difficult to determine if a handling problem is set-up related or driver-induced. The following is a list of clues to help determine where to look first to correct handling problems.

- If the problem is inconsistent, it is most likely driver-induced
- If a problem occurs at every similar type of turn, it is likely set-up related
- If a problem occurs on either left or right turns only, it is likely set-up related
- If the problem occurs at one turn only, it is likely driver-induced

Handling Problems and Driver Causes

Look for these situations to determine if driver outputs are causing handling problems:

- Excessive braking (especially wheel lock-up)
- Excessive throttle application (wheel spin)
- Excessive trail braking
- Jerky or tentative steering outputs
- Steering corrections after corner entry turn-in
  - More steering lock applied to reach apex
  - Reduction of steering lock to reach apex
  - Increased steering lock after apex to remain on racing surface
  - Track space left at corner exit (proper exit requires steady output until car is in straight line)
- Improper line through turn
  - Too early turn-in causing early apex
  - Too late turn-in causing too late apex
  - Not using all of road width at turn-in, apex, and exit
  - In a series of turns, line through first or early turns causes improper line at exit of last turn onto straight
- Too much and too abrupt steering at corner turn-in
- Cornering speed too slow

CORNER-ENTRY AND STEADY-STATE UNDERSTEER. Corner-entry understeer is often driver-induced. The most common causes are braking too late and too hard, excessive corner entry speed, too much trail braking, turn-in too late, and abrupt, excessive steering output.

All of these driver outputs create the same situation. The front tires are highly loaded, causing them to operate at higher slip angles than desired. This causes understeer. Once understeer begins, it is likely to continue through the turn or until speed is reduced. With time, heat builds up, overheating the tires and causing the understeer to become progressively worse.

CURES. Assuming that set-up problems have been eliminated as causes, the best way to cure driver-related corner entry and steady-state understeer problems is to alter driving style. Try the following:

- Reduce entry speed; drive on precise line
- Use minimum steering with a very smooth turn-in
- Reduce or eliminate trail braking; this is even more important for front-heavy cars, especially front-drivers

CORNER-EXIT UNDERSTEER. If a driver is causing corner-exit understeer, it is most likely a continuation of the corner-entry and steady-state understeer problem. If, however, the car is working properly in the entry portion of the turn, and begins to understeer at the exit of the turn, you may be applying too much throttle too soon and too abruptly. The cure is a smooth, well-timed throttle application.

CORNER-ENTRY AND STEADY-STATE OVERSTEER. Corner-entry and steady-state oversteer are not usually driver-induced. However, corner-entry oversteer can be driver-caused under specific conditions. The first situation is when you try to "pitch" the car into a turn. This occurs when you turn in too abruptly, combined with a sudden release of the throttle. A second and more obvious situation occurs when excessive trail braking is used in conjunction with an abrupt turn-in. If rear wheel lock-up occurs, the oversteer will be instantaneous and difficult to control.

The cures are smooth turn-in and reduced trail braking. *Note*: Pitching a car into a very slow turn, such as a hairpin or on a solo II (autocross) course, can be a very effective technique to reduce times. Segment times comparing both methods will determine the best technique to use. This method does not work on faster turns as too much speed is scrubbed off and the chance of a spin increases tremendously.

Mid-corner oversteer can occur due to throttle steer. This is caused by a reduction in throttle pressure, usually an abrupt release of the throttle, in mid-corner. Weight is transferred forward, reducing rear tire contact patch area. The resulting loss of traction will induce oversteer. Oversteer is reduced as speed decreases OR as power is again applied, re-balancing weight distribution.

Throttle steer, used very judiciously, can be a helpful tool in certain types of low- to medium-speed corners where turn-in is troublesome. *Note*: Throttle steer can cause excessive oversteer resulting in a spin, especially in high-speed turns. When driving near the limit of adhesion, under full power, a sudden release of the throttle can induce sudden oversteer, sometimes so much that applying opposite steering lock and throttle application is not enough to correct the situation. If you encounter a situation in a high speed turn where speed must be reduced, a gradual reduction in throttle pressure combined with reduced steering lock is the most effective solution to the problem.

CORNER-EXIT OVERSTEER. The most common driver-induced cause of corner-exit oversteer is early throttle application or excessive throttle application. This is especially true for high-horsepower cars. The cure is more gradual and better-timed throttle application at the exit portion of a turn.

Another possible driver-related cause of corner-exit oversteer is an improper entry line into a turn. If you turn into a corner too early, a steering correction requiring more steering lock at the exit of the turn will be necessary to keep the car on the racing surface. If this is combined with a sudden release of the throttle, oversteer is likely. The most effective cure for this is the correct line into and through the turn. The dynamics of this situation are exactly like pitching a car described in the previous section.

Alternate Lines   Alternate lines, or vehicle paths, are variations to your plan which allow passing, defending position, avoiding areas of reduced traction due to debris or fluids on the track, and dealing with emergency situations. Planning alternate lines allows you to adapt to traffic and changing conditions quickly, without unnecessary diversion of attention, and in a manner which minimizes time lost on the track.

WHICH LINE? The best line is the one which deviates the least from the line you have found best for your plan.

ALTERING SPEED. Be fully prepared to alter speed as needed. Slow as little as necessary, and do everything possible to maintain speed and throttle at corner exits. Minimizing speed reductions will minimize time lost.

OFF-LINE PROBLEMS AND SOLUTIONS. The biggest problem you encounter off-line is usually reduced traction due to dust and debris beyond the area of the racing line.

Though not always possible, it is best to avoid these areas. These spots are easy enough to see, but think about the most likely areas where traction may be reduced, or areas where driving off-line will cause the fewest problems.

Slippery conditions are less likely to be found on the inside of a corner, more likely on the outside. Corner entry areas are usually cleaner than exits off-line. More drivers go off-line in slow turns than in fast turns, so the slow turn offers more off-line opportunities.

If you choose to drive off-line for tactical reasons, it is wise to try off-line excursions in selected areas under circumstances which allow you to sample traction, steering outputs, and vehicle paths without duress. Leave a comfortable safety margin so that you can sample traction without losing it completely.

If you are forced off-line, focus attention on traction sampling, gentle throttle transitions, and minimal steering lock. Alter the vehicle path gently, and as little as possible. Your visual reference points should include where you want to go, not what you are trying to avoid.

In extreme situations, your priority is to avoid the situation; speed and lap times are no longer important. As soon as the situation is rectified, refocus your attention on driving as quickly as possible. Continuing to focus attention on the incident will a) cost valuable time on the track, and b) cause another incident, which you will likely start.

CONCLUSION

While the laws of physics do not waiver, conditions, circumstances, and goals do. The dynamic aspects of racing are ever-changing, requiring you to have a fluid approach, ready to change and adapt to the environment. The goals addressed in this chapter relate to speed around the race track and driver consistency with that speed. In order to achieve these goals, you must create a plan, implement it, evaluate it, modify it, and improve it as necessary. This requires understanding of the issues, prioritizing many variable factors, discipline to implement, judgement to evaluate, and courage and confidence to improve. These are the areas where you have considerable control over the outcome.

8

COMMUNICATION SKILLS

At virtually every level of the sport, racing is a team activity requiring communication. From your perspective as a driver, you must develop communication skills with mechanics, crew chiefs, engineers, sponsors, media representative, race officials, and other competitors. Several principles will help you establish dialog with others.

COMMUNICATION WITH THE CREW

The most important group for you to communicate with is your team. Lack of communication in this area assures problems and makes winning nearly impossible. Good internal communication will help in the efforts to achieve success on the race track. There is one crucial factor when you communicate information to the crew. It is the *golden rule*: all communications from a driver to the crew must be honest and based in reality.

If you do not take responsibility for communicating truthfully, problems will remain unsolved. And worse, reasons for problems become clouded, even hidden. You must accept responsibility to understand the situation and communicate information honestly even if you feel that it will cause personal embarrassment.

Fig. 8-1. It is your responsibility to communicate to your crew, honestly and free from judgement, your concerns about car set-up and team performance.

0012940

Fig. 8-2. The team meeting is an excellent method for debriefing and problem-solving. Michael and Mario Andretti, Laguna Seca, 1992.

0012941

To accomplish this level of communication requires mutual trust and respect by all team members. When the cause of a problem is not easily determined, open-minded discussion will often lead to the solution. But if you feel that the team will let you down if you are truthful and accurate, it will be difficult to communicate. And if the team feels that you will blame the car or the team for on-track problems, little progress will be made and communication will break down quickly.

Terminology

Consistency of terminology is very important in any activity. Considering the highly technical nature of motorsport, you must communicate with a team in a manner that is fully understood. Everyone on the team must use words the same way. The technical elements of language do not matter, but the information does. If you tell the crew chief that the car has high-speed understeer, but you really mean high-speed oversteer, you will likely face a rather surprising situation the next time out. Since you have the most at stake, it is probably prudent that you take responsibility for consistency of terminology.

Areas of Communication

There are five areas of communication within a racing team.
1. Technical communication between you and crew
2. Tactical communication between you and crew chief or team manager
3. Strategy planning
4. Communication between you and outside parties (suppliers, sponsors, etc.)
5. Communication between you and team owner.

You are involved at all levels, but decisions must be made relative to a chain of command. Each person in a team should answer to only one individual in specific areas. For example, a mechanic should answer to a chief mechanic, the team manager to a team owner, etc. The driver should report to and be given directives by the following:

- Technical issues: a race engineer, team manager or crew chief
- Tactics: team manager or crew chief (who is on the radio while you are on the track)
- Strategy: a meeting led by the team manager
- Outside communication: direct, but based upon internal policies
- Communications with a team owner or other official should only be in a meeting with your direct superior

The principle is simple: clear communication requires a chain of command which should not be broken. Responsibilities, duties, and problem solving are much more clear when the chain of command is followed

Areas of Responsibility

You, as the driver on the team, have specific areas of responsibility.

- Car set-up: you should have the final say on the set-up of the car relative to handling balance and gearing. Most often, the engineer or crew chief will decide *how* to achieve that set-up
- Race tactics: on-track decisions are your responsibility. Most decisions must be made too quickly for any type of consultation
- Communication of the reality of the situation to the crew: attempting to alter the reality of a situation by placing blame on the wrong thing makes it difficult to correct problems and move ahead
- Communications with the press and public: the ground rules for such communications should be created beforehand so that a policy is always in effect
- Personal responsibility: in a team you need to express feelings and concerns about perceived internal problems. Issues concerning your safety and team performance should be addressed directly to the person designated within the chain of command. To ignore feelings and concerns undermines confidence and causes additional problems. Facing situations directly and honestly is the first step to solving problems early-on

Judging Reality

One of the problems faced by virtually every race driver is judging reality. Not only is the problem one of adequate knowledge on which to base judgements, but also one of emotions. It can be very difficult to admit a mistake; it can also be hard to determine if a handling problem is caused by car set-up or by your errors.

Individual honesty requires insight and confidence in one's own abilities and in one's humanity. Each person decides a course of action, or lack of action, in this area of life.

Race Communications

One of the keys to success in motorsports is team communication during an event. You need specific information from the crew, and vice versa.

USING RADIOS. The most effective means of race communication is via radio. But like any tool, the radio can be misused. You should understand specific information required by the crew, and tell the crew what information you need during an event.

WHAT INFORMATION IS NEEDED. The following is a selection menu to help you decide:

- Lap and/or segment times
- Time gaps to nearest competitors in front and behind
- Developing traffic situations

Fig. 8-3. For a driver, the radio is an excellent tool as long as you use it intelligently.

0012942

- On-track hazards
- Laps or time remaining
- Laps to a pit stop
- Status of competition
- Changes to track or weather conditions
- Green light or flag at start or restart

The crew will want specific information concerning the car:

- Tire condition
- Temperatures, pressures, and other instrument readings
- Track conditions
- Handling balance
- Where handling problems are occurring
- Any problem so that the crew can prepare for a pit stop

WHEN TO COMMUNICATE. The radio can be disruptive to your concentration. You should tell the crew exactly when and where to communicate. Unless the crew sees an emergency situation requiring immediate contact with you, they should follow your rules of communication by radio. You should also tell the crew when to expect information concerning the car. Specifics may be communicated every lap, or only when something is amiss. In all cases, you or the crew should always acknowledge the reception of data.

DANGER SIGNALS. Any time the crew spots a dangerous situation, you need specific information immediately. Concise language keeps the process simple. Statements like "a spin in 3," "red flag," "blown engine in 1," or "a yellow! Prepare to pit" are direct and simple communications.

PIT SIGNALS. Not all race teams have radio systems. And those teams having radios can expect failures at some point. It is crucial to establish a system for pit-to-driver communications with a pit board and hand signals.

Most of the information is communicated on a pit board. Standard letters and symbols usually refer to specific data:

Fig. 8-4. The crew chief can give you important information instantly, and get feedback over the radio.

0012943

- T = lap time, usually given as the last second plus tenths of the lap time. Example: 23 would mean 1:42.3. Fewer numbers are easier to read; the plan must be pre-determined for clear communication. This is effective unless the driver is very inconsistent in lap times
- + = lead over nearest competitor behind, either overall or in class as pre-determined, usually given in full seconds only
- − = gap to nearest competitor ahead
- L = laps, usually remaining in the event
- IN plus a number = laps to a pit stop
- P = position, either overall or in class
- Other words, like Fuel?, Tires?, etc., are information requests from the crew, asking the driver to check and acknowledge. A thumbs up is OK, a thumbs down is a problem.
- EZ = driver should maintain a comfortable pace
- Hand signals from the crew can be used to communicate specific problems. A thumbs down and pointing ahead could mean trouble is ahead. Other signals can be used also

You often need to communicate information to the crew. Pointing to the ear usually means loss of radio reception, so a switch to pit signals is needed. Thumbs up = all OK; thumbs down − a problem. Raised fingers mean a pit stop in X laps; one finger for the next time around. Pointing to the front of the car and down could mean a front tire problem; to the rear and down, a rear tire problem. Similar signals can be used for overheating or low fuel, etc. The exact signals are immaterial, as long as everyone understands the meaning and the team has practiced using the signals.

READING SIGNALS. Signals are useful only if they are seen by the driver or crew. The location of signaling must be specified in advance, and practiced before a race. Large signs are easier to see, and high contrast is important. The easiest place to see signals is in the middle of a long straight. Glare can sometimes be a problem, so check the light conditions at the time an event will take place. It is also important that the crew see your signals. If they cannot, try something different.

ACKNOWLEDGMENT. It is important that the crew know that you received pit signals. You should always acknowledge reception of signals. In a closed car, a nod of the head is adequate in most instances. In an open car, a slight wave of the hand without removal from the steering wheel gets the point across. Any consistent acknowledgment lets the crew know that you are informed. Lack of acknowledgment always casts doubts.

WORKERS AND OFFICIALS

Course Workers

The corner workers and safety crews are there for you. They offer valuable information and assistance. To ignore their input is dangerous and foolhardy, and can cause serious problems.

When a corner worker or flagger gives a flag signal, you should acknowledge it with a nod or slight wave. This lets the worker know that you received the communication, and it makes the worker feel more useful. They will give you even more information if they feel it is useful to you. At the end of an event or practice session, it is a nice gesture to acknowledge the workers with a wave. They endure terrible conditions to make racing safer for drivers. Additionally, some form of thank you to the workers is appropriate. Who knows? Someday one of them could save your neck.

Fig. 8-5. Pay attention to corner workers and their signals. They often give important information.

0012944

Race Officials   Like any other worker, the race officials are there for you. They deserve to be treated with respect. In most cases, they are volunteers, and very dedicated to the sport. Dealing with officials directly, reasonably, and honestly makes everyone's experience more enjoyable, and can go a long way to solving problems in the future.

COMMUNICATION WITH COMPETITORS

Every individual must determine for himself how to relate with other competitors off the track. On-track situations require certain guidelines.

Passing Lapped Cars   The tactics of passing will be covered later. Passing safely is the responsibility of the overtaking driver. It is best if the driver being passed signals first. At least look for the driver ahead to spot you in the mirrors before the pass. If the driver being passed made your job easier with good communications and lots of room, acknowledge the effort with a wave.

Being Passed   When being passed by a faster car, it is courteous and much safer to point the following driver by. The driver ahead always points to the side where the overtaking driver should pass. Make sure the signal is clear. In a closed car with a roll cage, the arm signal should be moving so that it is very obvious. Make the pass as easy as possible for the other driver without costing yourself too much time.

Working Together   In some instances, drivers can work together to gain an advantage on the field, or catch another car or group. This occurs most often in drafting situations. The most common signal is for the leading driver to signal to a following driver to draft by holding up the right hand. The following driver can acknowledge by nodding or waving back. If the lead driver wants the following driver to pass, a standard passing signal is used.

Signalling Trouble or Reduced Speed   The standard signal for reducing speed or indicating car trouble is a raised hand and wave. Use this signal if you have car trouble and must reduce speed. Also use it when entering the pits. In all cases, the purpose is to warn following drivers that you are going to be slowing, or already have slowed due to a car problem. When coming into the pits, drive off line as early as possible and then reduce speed. Do not reduce speed, then move across the race track. The results can be deadly. If the car is going to come to a stop on the circuit, move to a safe location off the course if possible, and look for course workers. Follow their instructions. Do not exit the car until instructed unless fire is *likely*.

When Another Driver Balks or Causes a Problem   While many will disagree, I believe that it is important to tell another driver if they have balked you or otherwise caused a problem or compromised your safety. A shake of the fist is the common signal for this on the track. If significant, I will seek out the other driver after the event and discuss the situation clearly. Ignoring the situation is asking for a repeat performance. If the situation is extreme, call over the radio so that a crew member can inform the officials, or make a note of the car number, and inform the officials of the situation after the event. You are doing no one a favor by ignoring dangerous or erratic driving by others.

CONCLUSION

Effective communication in all aspects of racing is crucial. Honesty is the first key to problem solving. Creating a plan for each phase of communication will establish chains of command and specific methodology for creating useful and effective dialog. Some means of communication should be established as part of your overall plan.

9 OTHER SKILLS

In today's racing environment, you need to develop many skills to become competitive. Some of those not related directly to the other areas of driving are covered in this chapter.

PRACTICE

Like any activity, racing requires practice to assure proficiency. We have covered several specific ways to practice, and exercises that allow specific skills development. Here we will look at specific ways to practice anything needing more development.

Practice Plans
Track time is hard to come by in motorsport. Making the best use of time is crucial. The principles of time management are not really any different for a race driver on the track than for a businessman creating a marketing strategy. The key is having a plan. A plan allows maximization of results, plus a means to monitor those results. A plan to improve and progress must include practice.

Priorities
One of the keys to create an effective practice plan is to establish practice priorities. While everything needs practice, put the emphasis on the areas of weakness. If you know that braking or shifting is an area ripe for improvement, allot more practice time in those areas. Be very specific about what needs work.

What is it that you do not want to practice? High-speed turns? Or maybe calling a prospective sponsor? Why don't you want do those things? There is a reason! Probably a very strong one. Could it be the "f" word?

Fear can be crippling, and facing it can be difficult. Acknowledging that high-speed corners, or sponsor calls, scare you makes facing it much easier. Those items which you know to be difficult for you to do are the ones you need to practice the most. Of course it's not easy! But it is important if you want to improve and reach your goals. Make the tough stuff a high priority.

Focus
As with driving, practice in any area requires attention. Focus should be complete. The results will be better for what you are currently doing, and it will help on the track as well.

Off-track Driving Practice to Build Skills
There are three ways to practice driving away from the race track. One is to drive, and practice specific exercises, like anticipation or braking orientation. Several exercises are outlined throughout this book. If you are driving anyway, it is a complete waste of time to ignore practicing. Plan to focus on a practice exercise every time you drive.

A second way to practice driving is video games, especially driving videos, which help with concentration. Really focus on anticipation and visual fields when playing video games.

Finally, visualization is an excellent form of practice for many areas of driving, including maintaining mental focus and concentration. This was covered in more detail in Chapter 4.

The most important aspects of practice are to: 1) practice, and 2) practice the most important items. Create a practice plan to improve your weak points and develop your strong ones.

LEARNING NEW TRACKS

One of the most dangerous and difficult aspects of racing is learning new tracks. Like everything else, the task is made easier if you develop a plan. One of the tricks is to prioritize track segments, then focus attention on the most important first. Once learned, you can then progress to lesser levels of importance systematically.

Using Videos, Maps

Any information about a new track is helpful. Maps give a general idea of the direction of turns and the overall circuit layout. Videos offer even more information. An in-car video will show terrain and elevation changes. But do not rely on videos for giving you a complete picture, unless the video is your own. Somehow, everything looks different when you get on the track. Part of the problem is the perspective of a video, especially if taken from a different type of car. Only your on-track experience will tell the whole story.

Fig. 9-1. While track maps are helpful guides, until you drive the track, you cannot expect to fully know its nature.

0012945

Walking or Low Speed Driving

Low-speed driving and walking a circuit are very helpful to learn terrain, elevation changes, surface conditions, and for determining Visual Reference Points. Take detailed notes for future reference. Update them after each on-track driving session at speed.

Picking Visual Reference Points

One of the arts of racing is selecting good Visual Reference Points. Here are some tips:

- VRPs should be close to the race track surface if possible

- VRPs should be within the necessary line of sight at the time you need to visually pick up the VRP
- VRPs should be stationary. Moving VRPs are dangerous, obviously
- VRPs can often be on the horizon, like a building or tree in the background, but within the normal line of sight
- Marks on the track surface work very well as VRPs
- Keep in mind that VRPs are references, not markers where something should happen; they tell how you are doing, not what to do
- Mark your course plan or map with VRPs

Fig. 9-2. The telephone pole at the edge of the track is a good visual reference point (VRP), as is the billboard in the distance. Some tracks also have paint marks on the pavement, or seams, that make good VRPs.

0012946

0012947

0012948

Fig. 9-3. VRPs that are likely to move, such as this motorhome, are useless and dangerous.

0012949

Fig. 9-4. After selecting your VRPs, you should mark up a course map.

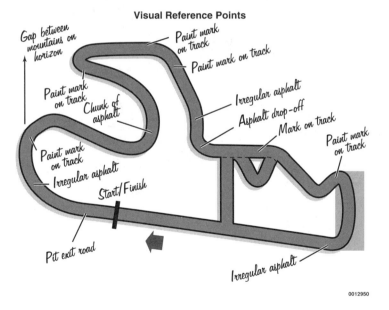

0012950

Make a list or mark a course map with your priorities. After each track session, make notes and observations concerning areas where you might make improvements. Pay special attention to areas where you may be over-driving the entry, especially the slow corners. And remember, take the fast corners fast and the slow corners slow.

Finding the Line

There are several basic points to remember when seeking the optimum line at a new track.

- The line overall will vary, so being close initially is all that matters
- Start with late apexes. This leaves a larger safety margin and also allows you to reduce lap time more quickly since early acceleration is easier with a late apex

- Do not focus on braking while learning a new track. Brake early for corners so that attention can be focused on turn-in points and paths. The braking will come naturally. Remember that when at the limit, on most tracks and in most cars, less than 10% of a lap is spent braking. A well-known driver in the (old) IMSA GTO class encountered a complete hydraulic failure of the brake system at Lime Rock. Within a few laps of adaptation, his lap times were within three seconds of his pole position lap time. *Without brakes!* Early acceleration and cornering at the limit are much more important for fast laps

- Use *all* of the race track. Start off by driving to the edges of the track. If you start at the very edge on entry, turn all the way down to the apex, and exit all the way back to the opposite edge of the track, you are 85% of the way to getting the path through the corner optimized. If you leave room at the edges or the apex, you will have to re-learn the path completely, not make small adjustments to it. In the early stages, while speed is off, drive to the edges of the track so you can see where they are

- Once the path through a turn is in the ball park, work on increasing speed

- With time try alternate lines by making small changes to the path. See if it is a better line

- It can be helpful and save some time in the trial and error learning process to watch other cars on the track, or follow a driver who knows the track *and* is a proven good racer. While helpful, remember that you must learn your own way to drive a track. Watching others can only get you about 75% of the way there

Like VRPs and segments, take notes about paths, especially the ones that were not quite right. Those may work as off-line passing lines or ways to avoid slippery conditions later.

Finding the Limits

One of the keys to fast laps is, naturally, driving at the limits of tire adhesion. To do this on an unfamiliar race track requires a concise plan and patience. Sometimes it is easier to find the limit than the best path around a corner. But in fact, they go hand in hand. The first step is to find what you believe to be the best path, even if you have not yet reached the limits of tire traction.

Once you've found a good path, the second priority is to focus on early acceleration out of the corners. Keep in mind that where and how hard you can accelerate out of turn will change based upon the speed carried into the corner. So if you are very slow into the turn, you will be able to accelerate out of the turn sooner. The path into the corner and through the corner should allow the earliest acceleration. As speed picks up into and through the middle of the corner, the path may need revision for early acceleration. Still, the place to start finding the limit is in the exit under acceleration. Why? This is the part of the corner that will help reduce lap times the greatest amount in the least time.

The third priority is getting up to speed at the turn-in point. To do this requires attention focused on the turn-in zone and vehicle speed. Braking gently and a little early allows more attention on speed judgement and finding the best turn-in point. It is very important to get up to speed here, and will offer the second largest gain in time reductions.

Fig. 9-5. Additionally, you should mark your course map with your corner priorities.

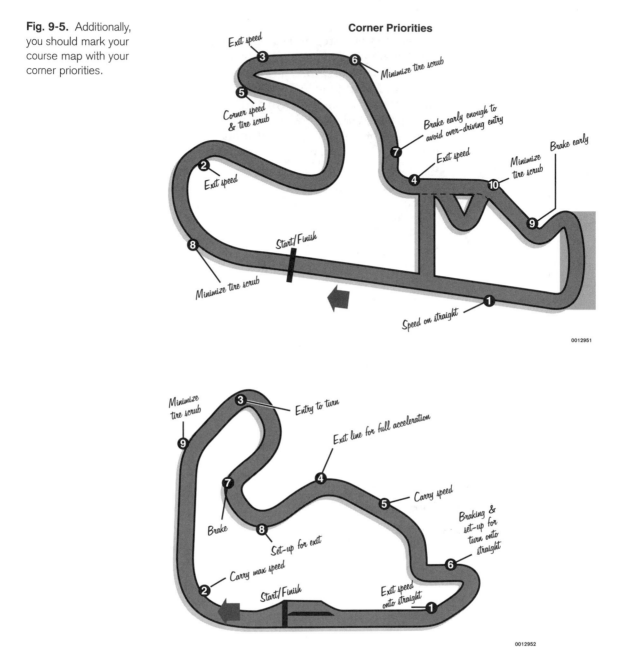

The last priority is the braking zone. As we have seen previously, the braking zone is the area where the least amount of time can be saved, so it is the last priority for driving at the limit of traction.

As an overall criteria to find the limits, take small bites out of the problem. To attempt to find the limit in two or three laps is foolhardy. And the closer you come to the limit, the smaller the bites should be. While learning a new course, much attention is spent on traction sampling. Give yourself the opportunity to gain the necessary experience to accumulate sufficient data points so that the limit is a clear, precise place, not some wild guess that is not repeatable.

Fig. 9-6. Also mark your course map with passing zones.

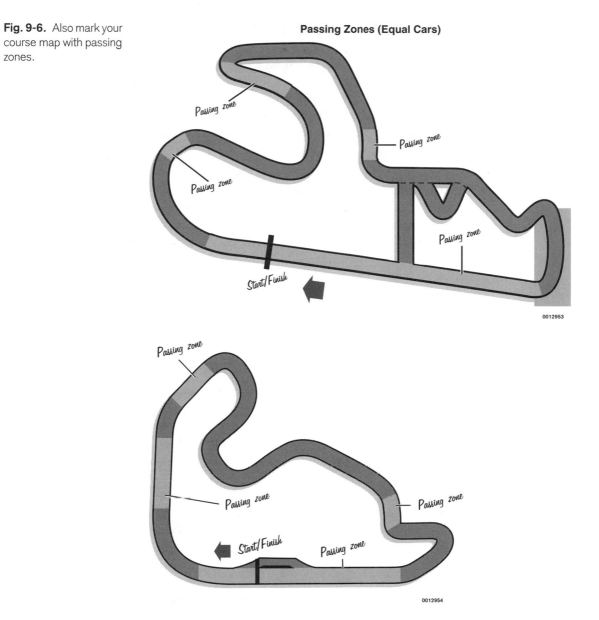

Passing Zones (Equal Cars)

Learning Alternate Lines

Alternate paths through corners are needed for three reasons.

- Passing or defending position
- To find higher traction areas, especially in wet weather or when fluids are spilled on line
- To avoid hazards or bumpy surface conditions

To find the most effective alternate paths requires trying alternate paths. Chances are you have already done so while searching for the optimum line. If you have taken notes, most likely you have considerable data about some good path alternatives. In the areas where the information is weak, or needed, spend some track time trying alternatives.

Keep this rule in mind: alternate paths through corners should vary from the ideal path as little as possible. For example, if you must vary your line under braking and corner entry for a pass and the other car is six feet wide, move over only 6.3 feet. To move a greater distance gives the other driver an advantage.

DEVELOPING TESTING SKILLS

A major factor in auto racing today is vehicle testing. So important is this activity to development and performance, most top teams conduct testing throughout the year. They hire drivers and crews whose primary job is testing for research and development. For the modern race driver at any level of the sport, developing testing skills is pre-requisite to success in motorsports.

You must possess specific driving skills for testing:

- Consistent lap times very near the limits of the vehicle
- The ability to adapt to a new car quickly
- The ability to find the limits of adhesion quickly
- Sensitivity to traction, power, and response changes in the vehicle
- Communication skills concerning the effect of changes to a vehicle
- An open mind willing to explore new ways to approach car set-up

Changing Focus   Unlike learning a new track, or developing driving skills, testing requires you to focus nearly all attention on the car and its behavior. To accomplish this, you must have developed driving skills at least to a predictable level of proficiency. Spending excessive time learning a new track or practicing skills detracts from the primary goal.

When testing, a team should have specific plans to test vehicle parameters. A test could include aerodynamics, new components, tires, shock absorbers, or suspension setting optimization. Whatever the plan is, you must focus attention on the specific goals, what changes are made and how they affect the feel the car, and communicate those impressions to the team crew chief or engineer.

It is excellent training to establish practice sessions where vehicle parameters are altered so you can learn their effects. This systematic approach for you to "feel" changes allows you to learn the effects of the changes both quantitatively and by the seat of the pants. Like any other aspect of driving, testing requires hands-on experience.

The best way to learn the effects of changes to settings is on a skid pad and low-speed course. Aerodynamic changes really need to by tried at higher speeds, but low-speed practice should come first. Depending upon the

Fig. 9-7. Skid pad test sessions are a must for car set-up and for learning testing skills.

0012955

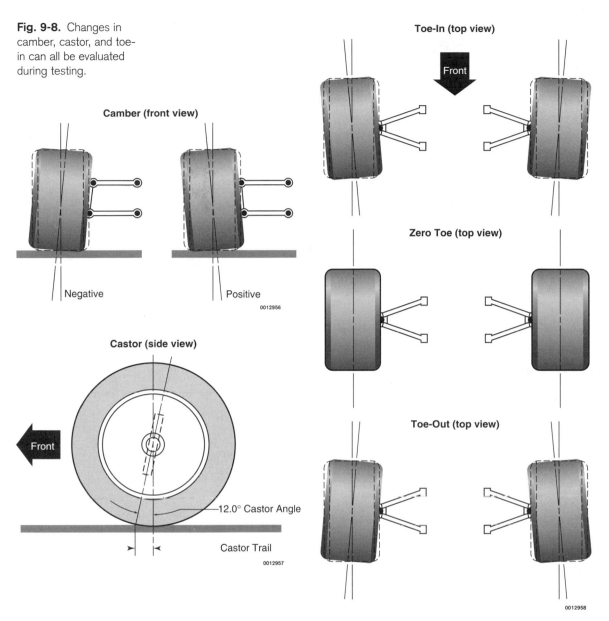

Fig. 9-8. Changes in camber, castor, and toe-in can all be evaluated during testing.

type of car being used, and the ease of changes to suspension settings, several parameters can be altered quickly for evaluation. These include:

- Wheel camber
- Wheel castor
- Front (and rear, if adjustable) toe settings
- Tire pressures
- Antiroll bar adjustments
- Spring rates
- Shock absorber settings
- New vs. worn tires
- Tire compounds
- Wing adjustments/spoiler adjustments
- Tire stagger
- Corner weights, specifically cross weight percentage (wedge)

Fig. 9-9. Tire pressures affect the compliance of the tire contact patch with the track surface.

0012959

Fig. 9-10. Wing adjustments affect aerodynamic handling balance; also consider drag vs. downforce.

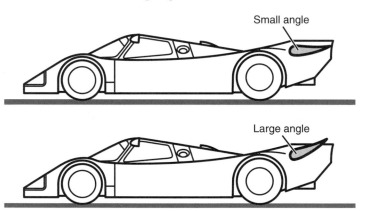

Wing Angle of Attack

Small angle

Large angle

0012960

Fig. 9-11. Tire stagger is the difference in rolling radius (or circumference) of all four tires.

0012961

Fig. 9-12. The cross weights are used to balance handling characteristics from left to right, or to bias them for oval racing.

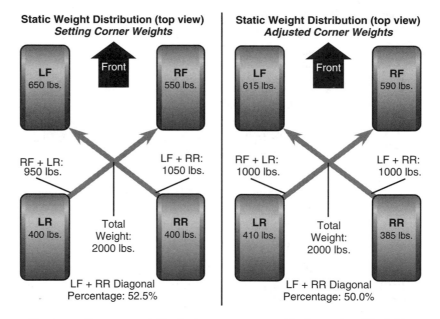

To change the corner weights, the heavy corners must be lowered and the light corners raised. The biggest changes come from the heaviest corners, and at the end of the vehicle with the largest discrepancy.

0012962

Fig. 9-13. Chassis rake affects downforce and weight distribution, and hence handling balance.

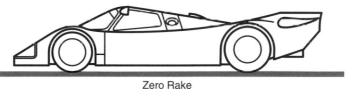

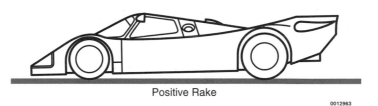

0012963

- Ride height
- Chassis rake (front to back)
- Chassis tilt (side to side) to adjust cross weights
- Ballast location and amount

It is important for you to know how changes to these parameters affect the feel of the car. Changes should be of a large magnitude during skid pad and low-speed practice where the risks are lower. For aerodynamic testing, changes should be smaller at high speeds. Every time a change is made, you should make a note of the effect of the change and how it felt.

Finding a Fast Comfort Level

Once you have the experience needed for meaningful testing, you must be able to drive close to the limits of the car consistently while focusing attention on *what the car* is doing. If you push the car right up to the limits, most attention is focused on driving, not on the car and the effects of changes. Finding a level of driving just below the banzai charge mode should give you a comfort level that allows focus on the important parameters. Try this on a familiar track.

Over the last several years, I have been quite fortunate to undertake numerous test driving assignments. I am able to drive consistent lap times in a new (to me) car within three or four laps. And the time variance for a five to ten lap run is less than .5%. This is considered good consistency, and makes the best use of track time. If I test a car which exceeds the envelope of my experience, it takes longer to reach the limits and consistency is reduced. And my feedback is less concise due to needing more attention to drive the car.

Staying Open-minded about Feedback

What I find the most difficult aspect of testing, and more difficult as time marches on, is maintaining an open mind about inputs from the car and what they are really telling me. Instrumentation makes this easier in some respects, but it can be difficult to look for the real cause of a problem. Every so often, it is important to look at your driving as a source of problems, regardless of experience or skill. Personally, in the past I have often failed to do this, which wastes valuable time. It is important to at least consider all alternatives when looking for a solution to problems with the car.

Part of the problem with car development for a test driver is that the given problem can have several causes, can be masked by other factors, and may have several solutions. While you may have ideas concerning the causes and solutions, your primary job is to communicate what is happening, not how to fix it. Pinpointing the exact problem is much more important for you than attempting to find a cure for it.

Defining Testing Parameters

It should be obvious, but often is not, that a test plan should be created and adhered to for a given session. You must know exactly what to look for, and what communication is expected. It is also crucial that only one change be made per test, and that several laps be run. Times should only be averages for an entire session, not the best lap. Some teams will discard the fastest and slowest laps from the average. This information is much more reliable and meaningful when evaluating the effect of a change.

For the driver, most of the attention should be focused on the area being tested. For example, for shock testing, focus attention on transitions and response rates to steering. If testing tire compounds, you should focus on overall traction at various crucial points on the track. Even though primary focus is on a specific area, some attention must remain on the overall picture. Losing sight of the entire system can have negative consequences.

DEALING WITH ON-TRACK SITUATIONS AND PROBLEMS

Oversteer

When oversteer occurs, it is necessary to regain traction to the rear tires in one of three ways, depending upon the cause.

- Reduce speed by *gently* easing off the throttle. This works when oversteer is caused by wheelspin, or when steady-state oversteer occurs in a cornering situation
- Apply opposite steering lock to keep the car pointed in the desired direction of travel
- Accelerate. This will transfer weight to the rear tires and improve traction. This works well if the oversteer was induced by an abrupt lift from the throttle, or when steady-state oversteer is small

Understeer

When understeer occurs the front tires lose traction. Common causes include abrupt steering, wheel lock-up, abrupt acceleration, and basic car set-up. To correct for understeer, reduce speed, reduce steering lock, slow steering and throttle, and lift off the accelerator to induce trailing throttle oversteer.

Front Wheel Lock-up

Wheel lock-up can occur due to track conditions, the driver, incorrect brake bias, etc. To correct for front wheel lock-up, reduce pedal pressure until the tires are again rolling. This is followed by pedal modulation. You do not usually need to release the brake pedal completely to regain traction. If the front wheels remain locked, the car will not change direction when you try to steer.

Rear Wheel Lock-up

The same technique as above applies. If you steer when the rear wheels are locked, the car will spin quickly.

Spins

If you encounter a spin, attempt to maintain orientation by looking where you *want* to go. Second, control can be regained *if* you do not make excessive outputs. If the steering is centered (wheel in normal ahead driving position), as the car nears the end of 360 degree rotation, it will likely continue ahead.

As soon as you know that a spin will occur, get the clutch pedal in quickly. If a spin could result in possible damage from walls, etc., brake hard to scrub speed. The old adage applies: "When you spin, both feet in."

Cars Spinning, Crashing Ahead

When a spin or crash occurs in front of you, evasive action may be necessary. It is always prudent to reduce speed, but that in itself can cause you to be rear-ended. Attempt to signal cars behind. Most often, if you drive directly toward a spinning car, it will be somewhere else when you reach that point. If walls are in close proximity, be aware that a car can bounce off the wall back into your path.

In crashes ahead, every situation is a little different. Always look for the opening that is easiest to drive into, and reduce speed as much as possible to minimize impact if you get caught in the melee.

Gravel Pits

Gravel safety pits are a wonderful invention. They require little action by the driver, since they decelerate a car very quickly. In most cases, taking a trip into a gravel pit will end the race for you, since it is virtually impossible to drive out of the pit if momentum is lost. A little foresight may help.

My singular experience in a gravel pit occurred while driving a Camaro in a Firestone Firehawk race at Laguna Seca Raceway in California. For several laps, I was dealing with boiling brake fluid by easy braking and pumping the brake pedal on the straights prior to the braking zones. This worked well until three minutes from the conclusion of the race. I pumped the pedal on the main straight prior to Turn 2, a 35-mph, 180-degree turn at the end of the straight where speeds in the Camaro reached about 120 mph. The pedal pumped up fine prior to the braking zone, but when I applied the brakes, no one was home. A single downshift and an attempt to pitch the car into a slide slowed the car very little before I was off course into the gravel pit.

As the car slowed, I actually had some steering control, so I attempted to drive through the gravel to the left, the same direction as Turn 2. But my momentum was inadequate, and I watched the last three minutes of the race from the outside of Turn 2.

Had I driven ahead instead of turning, I would have exited the gravel onto a dirt road, and could have continued on. I could not see the road, and did not know it was there until after I parked. Had I looked over the runoff areas more carefully prior to the race, I would have known about the road, and could have finished the race. The moral: learn not only the race track, but the surroundings as well. It could keep you in a race, or save your life.

Crashing

There comes a moment when the horrible realization surfaces that you are going to crash. Nothing you can do will prevent it. You are merely along for the ride. When you are about to collide with another car or obstruction, several things may help minimize the risk or severity of injuries.

I've always been a strong supporter of good safety equipment, but until I was involved in a big crash a few years ago, I really could not appreciate just how important safety equipment, and creating a safety plan, is to a driver's well-being. But new information keeps surfacing. On the leading edge of that information is the Indy Car Medical Team headed by Dr. Terry Trammell and Dr. Steve Olvey.

WHEN A CRASH IS IMPENDING. When you lose it, and know that you are headed for a crash, what can you do to reduce the risk of injury? According to Dr. Trammell, one of the most common injuries in stock car racing is a broken wrist. "Stock car drivers tend to hold on to the steering wheel in a crash. I know of three NASCAR drivers who broke wrists this year in crashes because they hung onto the steering wheel. Like that would make a difference; if a guy realizes that he isn't doing anything with the steering wheel, he might as well let loose of it, 'cause he isn't driving the car anymore anyway."

The impact transferred to the steering wheel can easily cause a broken wrist or other injury. When you know you're about to impact the wall, another car, or if you get upside down, let go of the wheel and grab your shoulder harnesses. Arms flying around the cockpit can cause injury also.

Dr. Olvey also has some advice when a crash is ready to occur. "You know, it sounds almost silly to say this, but it is better for drivers to relax and breathe prior to making contact. If they're aware they're going to make contact with concrete or a barrier of some type, if you stiffen up and hold your breath you are going to very possibly suffer more injury than if you continue to breathe and try to relax, as odd as that sounds."

Olvey adds that "What we've found with General Motors' studies with the use of the dummies on the sled, where before we thought it would be better to pull your feet up in the event of a crash, it's probably better to leave them on the pedals. It is best if you can relax your legs."

In general, relaxing is good strategy. "Going into a wall at 200 mph and trying to relax is very hard, but we have had two instances of punctured lungs through the years with drivers who held their breath, then on impact the pressure changes blew a hole in their lung. But if a driver can continue to breathe and relax to some extent the chance of that is very slim with the cars the way they are now."

IN THE COCKPIT. According to Trammell, many short track injuries are caused by the driver hitting objects within the cockpit. "Everything should be padded; nothing sharp, no edges—that's the biggest thing we preach in Indy Car racing; file it down, make it smooth. There are a lot of sharp things sticking out in the cockpit of a stock car. The best advice for the weekend warrior is to buy a whole lot of that roll bar padding foam. You can't put too much of it in the cockpit. The driver will still feel the shock, but the closer they get to it, the less the impact will be.

"It's like the Richard Petty theory of hitting the wall. The only way you're going to get hurt is if you take a run at it, and that's true of the driver and the car. The closer he is to the padding, the less likely he is to get banged around by it.

"Additionally, the average nylon-type belt will stretch 20% of its length. It's important to have the belts tight. Getting a running start at the belts can cause injuries. On the other hand, anything that pins you against the seat probably needs to stretch because you want to decelerate slower than the car. If you're going to hit something, the longer the duration of the load, the better. If the force is smaller over a longer time, the injuries will be less. In any case, the driver doesn't want to stop as fast as the car."

DRIVER GEAR. Good driver safety equipment can make a big difference. Arm restraints can save serious injuries in open wheel cars. Terry Trammell has seen the effects of the biggest problem. "Open wheel cars can get upside down easily. The driver's arms can easily get outside the cage. I remember a guy whose hands got scrambled at Indianapolis Raceway Park. He did about six rollovers, got his arms outside the car and his hands just got smashed."

On horse collars, Dr. Trammell feels they can only help. "They probably all ought to wear neck collars, the horseshoe collars, but fasten them so that they will stay on when they crash. We pick up a lot of those collars, even here (at Indy Car events). They fall off, so they can't be worth much. They need to be attached to the harness for stability."

Trammell also feels that the current aluminum stock car seats offer good crash protection. "Drivers need to avoid any kind of steep drop-off in their seat behind their neck; a head rest keeps the back of the seat from acting like a fulcrum for the neck to bend over in a crash." Terry also likes the idea of head side support on seats. "The lateral head supports are a real good idea. Most of the neck injuries are from lateral forces, not the forward and backward like in a passenger car, caused when you get hit or flip sideways."

MENTAL REHEARSAL. I've been a racer and an instructor for a long time. One of the things I've done is to mentally rehearse what to do if I lose control of the car or know that there's going to be an impact. Then I practice going through a series of things like getting the electricity shut off, the ignition shut off. A lot of guys disagree with that because they feel like they're going to practice crashing. Both Dr. Olvey and Dr. Trammell feel that mental rehearsal is a good tool to minimize injuries in a crash.

Steve Olvey says, "I think that could be very valuable to do. Anytime you can anticipate what things are going to be like rather than ignore them, it's easier to cope with. Maybe thinking about how it feels to be on a stretcher on the racetrack being carried to the ambulance or put into the helicopter and flown to a hospital would reduce the fear and trauma. I think with anything in life, if you anticipate those kinds of things and then they do happen, they're easier to tolerate and easier to handle than if you've never given it any thought at all."

Terry Trammell concurs. "Probably every other form of activity where people crash, like guys that drive airplanes, practice what they do in a crash, what's the crash scenario. And it's stupid to say, well I'm never going to crash and if I don't ever think about it I won't ever crash. I think that ought to be just as much of a mental practice session as anything else you do. They rehearse passes and fast laps, why not a crash checklist."

AFTER A CRASH. While we hope a crash never occurs, being prepared is very important. If you have endured a crash and remain conscious, and injuries allow some action, several items require attention. First, shut off the ignition and fuel pump or the master electrical switch so that fuel will not flow from an electrical fuel pump. In some cases, this can be done before impact. If you think that fire is likely, or has already begun, set off the fire bottle. Do not set off the fire bottle if no fire is likely. One may begin in a few moments and you will need the protection of the fire system then.

Unless the car is burning, do not unfasten your belt system until help arrives or you are absolutely certain that you are at rest *and* no other cars are going to impact with you. Several drivers have been injured, some fatally, because they released the belts prematurely. However, if the car is on fire, your priorities change; get out of the car as fast as possible.

Dealing with Car Problems

Car problems are a fact of racing life. How you cope with and adapt to a car problem determines the effect of that problem. By definition, a car problem is something that causes the car to slow. That definition also gives us a clue about solving the problem.

DETERMINING THE PROBLEM. First, determine the nature of the problem. The cause is less important than the effect. For example, if a car is down on power so that it pulls less rpm on the straights, the effect of the problem is less power. The cause could be mechanical, electrical, or fuel related. Chances are you're not going to fix the problem, nor will it fix itself, so minimizing its effects is the goal.

One important decision is required immediately, however. If the problem causing the car to slow stems from overheating or increased engine or drivetrain friction, it may be prudent to make a pit stop. Check the gauges, and attempt to determine whether the problem is terminal before pressing on. A little mechanical empathy helps.

CHANGING THE PLAN. Whether a handling, tire, or horsepower problem, anything which slows the car requires you to mentally shift gears to a revised plan. The reality of the new situation dictates action. What has happened? The car is slower! Where? If you know the previous performance envelope, then you can fully understand the effect of the problem on vehicle performance.

Usually, something has caused the car to become slower. What does that mean? It means that on the straights, top speed is reduced. Less braking is needed to get into a turn for maximum cornering speed. If the car is down on power, throttle applications can occur earlier and full throttle can be reached sooner. High-speed turns may now be flat out.

If the problem is handling-related, which usually means the tires are over-cooked, cornering speeds will be reduced since traction is reduced. But what about braking performance? Or could the tires be overheated, requiring only a few laps to cool off before the pace can be picked up again? You can adapt to any of these scenarios if your overall plan allows for change. If your plan does not accommodate changes, you will be stuck in the old routine, and performance will suffer even more.

MINIMIZING THE EFFECT. A few years ago, I was leading in class at a club endurance race when the engine began to misfire slightly. The power loss was about 15%, enough to cost considerable time on the track. The race was only about half-way completed at the time. The first lap after this occurred was three seconds off the previous lap's pace.

It took about one lap to analyze the problem, determine that it was not terminal, and create a revised plan to minimize the effect. During the next lap, I revised braking zones and corner paths since the straight line speed of the car was reduced. That lap was two seconds off the pre-problem pace. The next lap was one second off the pre-problem pace, and that is where the time lost stayed for the duration of the race. We ultimately finished second with the problem costing about a half a lap on the track.

What would have happened if I had not changed my plan to minimize the effect of the power loss? I would have continued to lose three seconds per lap. By focusing on vehicle speed sensing, traction sampling, and optimum vehicle paths *for the new situation*, I minimized time losses.

PRACTICING PATIENCE AND DISCIPLINE

Both patience and discipline are important virtues. Often you must exercise extreme discipline to reach an objective, whether on the track, finding a sponsor, or in physical training. In the same way, patience allows you to make choices based on the reality of the situation and the relationship to the objective. The need for these virtues transcends the spectrum of racing itself into many aspects of life. Rushing headlong into a situation without regard to the consequences rarely turns out for the best. One example on the track will illustrate the importance of these characteristics.

The one problem characteristic of most race drivers, and virtually all newcomers, is over-driving the entry to a corner. Most drivers believe, for whatever reason, that hard braking and a fast entry into the corners is the essence of speed on the race track. Maybe this comes from watching too many chase scenes on TV cop shows, but it is common beyond comprehension.

It is also very slow around the race track. There is nothing inherently wrong with driving this way; in fact it's really great fun to charge into a corner, toss the car around, and exit in a big power slide. It looks great, which is why it is used in TV and the movies. But if your objective is to get around a race track as quickly as possible, this method is counter-productive. It's not good or bad, right or wrong, but this is reality.

When I have a student who has difficulty understanding this, I will ask them what their goal is. If it is to slide around like a TV stuntman, then they are on the right track. If it is to learn to race, it's time to re-evaluate the situation and face reality. It is at this point that many students start to figure out that this gig is not as easy as they thought. It is also now that they begin to learn how to drive fast. Many students reach the limit quickly, but have priorities mixed-up. Given the desire to learn and make progress, it is at this time where a driver, whether a neophyte or seasoned veteran, must begin to show self-discipline and patience. Without those qualities, learning and progress will come to a screeching halt.

The Fine Line: Aggression vs. Passiveness

In racing, the line between over-aggression and passiveness is very thin. Drivers who are passive rarely win, because they do not take the risks needed to make a crucial pass. On the other hand, the driver who is too aggressive rarely wins, because that driver makes the foolish attempt to pass and often falls off the track in the effort. Few drivers, if any, have found a permanent home in the niche between the two. Patience and discipline go a long way to finding that niche. So does learning from past mistakes.

One of the best drivers ever in a Grand Prix car was Ayrton Senna. He was a joy to watch. Early in his career he showed signs of over-aggressive driving, and has lost races because of that. But maturity seemed to give him a heightened sense of patience. This quality made Senna even greater. The bottom line is, Senna was so skilled that no risks in traffic were needed for him to win in the vast majority of circumstances. By being patient, he usually came out ahead. When that patience faltered, he usually made an uncharacteristic mistake.

When to Act, When to Wait

This question is the key. The answer is difficult to find. It is usually only in retrospect that you really know if you made the right choice. If you think about the action and consider the consequences compared to the possible benefits, you will make the best choice for yourself. If you ignore the consequence/benefit ratio, you will often make poor choices. It's a game of percentages. If you have made your own rules, you are the house. If you haven't, you're playing against the house, and guess who's gonna win!

RELAXATION

Intense concentration and focus require you to be in a relaxed state. Not an easy task in the hostile environment of a race car at speed. Regardless, to reach the necessary mental state requires relaxation. We have looked at stress management skills in Chapter 2; here we will look at the goal and methods to reach a relaxed state in the car.

Releasing Tension

Everyone uses a different approach when they get into a race car in order to gain focus and concentration. I have found that for me, deep breathing exercises have the most soothing, relaxing effect. In most situations, I prefer to get into the car early in order to get comfortable and to focus attention on the upcoming event. Before a race or qualifying, I often feel tension in the form of butterflies. Getting situated in the car and focusing attention on mental rehearsal help to release this tension build-up.

How one does this is not of significance; but doing it is very important. Jackie Stewart, the former World Driving Champion, once described the release of tension, or in his words emotions, as similar to a balloon deflating. By the time the process was completed, just before the start of the event, all emotions were gone and his focus was totally on the job at hand. This process of releasing tension by visualizing a process like a deflating balloon is quite effective.

Many drivers carry on conversations with the crew or others on pre-grid. I find this to be ineffective for me. I tend to ignore the tension in this case, not deal with it directly. The tension is only hidden from view, not dissipated by design.

Practice

Many events in life create tension. Developing a technique to relax in the face of tension is very beneficial, not only when driving a race car, but for improved overall health. The process of visualization, outlined in Chapter 3, can work for pre-grid routines as well. Just see yourself preparing for a race. I know that this process will elevate my heart rate and blood pressure. I also know that deep breathing and focusing on mental practice laps will lower my heart and breathing rates. It helps to practice this routine before using it at a race. This type of dry run can let you determine if the technique is effective.

The goal of any pre-event process should include a means to relax and focus on the job. It is not the time to focus on the result that you hope for. That will take care of itself if you do the work effectively.

MENTAL INTEGRATION

Have you ever had a day where everything you did flowed effortlessly and the outcome was beyond expectation? Have you ever tried to duplicate the experience, but found it impossible? Those good days, most presume, just happen randomly. You just happen to be "on" that day. It's simply chance.

Well, it's not!

The brain is made of two hemispheres, the left brain and the right brain. The left brain controls the right side of the body and vice versa. When peak performance occurs, the left and right hemisphere of the brain are working in unison to collect data inputs, process the data, and create outputs. When we are "in the flow," it is because both halves of the brain are integrated. The opposite of integration is disintegration. And how often have you felt disintegrated?

This is obviously a large, complex topic. What is important is that you can have control of full brain integration. Many of the exercises and ideas presented in this book help to integrate the brain. Relaxation, focus and visualization are among those. The key is to focus on the performance needed to reach an objective, not the objective itself.

Many books and seminars are devoted to these topics. One class that is taught specifically for race drivers covers the mental aspects of driving. The instructor is Ronn Langford, a race driver who also works with teen drivers and in rehabilitation programs for those with severe head injuries. This class offers insights and teaches skills that I have found very helpful. (See the appendix for details.)

CONDUCT AND SPORTSMANSHIP

A sportsman is defined as one who is fair, generous, a good loser, and a gracious winner. Every individual must define for themselves what this means. I feel that sportsmanship should be an integral part of the sport of auto racing. To me, sportsmanship means helping competitors in any way that is not jeopardizing my own goals. I also feel that it is important to play the game by the rules as they are enforced by the sanctioning body. The written rules are rarely enforced to the satisfaction of all competitors. What is fair is not an issue. What is real is the issue, and reality is defined by the way in which rules are enforced. That is why officials are there, and why protest procedures exist.

On the track, the risks are generally high, and to breech rules is foolhardy. To take out another car on purpose in order to win or improve position is not only unsportsmanlike, but dangerous and totally unnecessary. It is a positive step that sanctioning bodies are enforcing existing rules concerning such conduct.

A dilemma always exists for the race driver. Here's an example. In the first ASA race of 1993, Mike Eddy, a several-time ASA champion, ran into the race leader, taking him out. Eddy went on to win the race, but took a lot of heat for the incident. The incident itself was questionable. The lead car appeared to slow in front of Eddy at the exit of Turn 4. Had Eddy lifted, he would have lost several car lengths. By hitting the car in front, Eddy took the lead. He was not black flagged.

It was a tough call for the officials, but in this case I believe they made a good call, because the incident appeared to be initiated by the lead car slowing slightly. Eddy took heat due to his reputation as a very aggressive driver. Had Eddy hit the lead car deliberately, what should have happened? Eddy should have been black flagged. If he had not, the driver he hit had several courses of action. He could have talked to Eddy about the incident. He could have talked to the officials. Both would seem appropriate.

I would have asked the officials if they planned to continue overlooking such incidents. Their answer would define the reality of their rules enforcement. If they planned to penalize such infractions in the future, I would wait to see if that in fact occurred. If they said they were not, then I would remind them that the frequency of such occurrences would increase. Then I would have told the guy who took me out to be careful, since it would likely happen to him.

This is a difficult case. The officials have a responsibility to enforce the rules. If they do not, you must decide what course of action to take. To stand by and do nothing will gain you nothing.

The bottom line is that human nature pushes rules to the limits. The more clearly the limits are set, the easier it is for everyone to conduct themselves like a sportsman. On an individual level, you can be taken advantage of, and feel like a victim by ignoring the situation, or you can take assertive action by dealing with the situation effectively and setting clear limits.

SPONSORS

Finding sponsors and rides is part of the game of motorsports. It is also an area in which I am not an expert. I have made several observations concerning sponsorship and rides over the years that may prove helpful.

If you don't ask for it, you will never get it.

It takes about the same effort to find a $5000 sponsor as it does to get a $500,000 sponsor.

If you approach the sponsor with a viable business proposal, your chances improve.

If your focus is on filling a need for the potential sponsor, your chances also improve.

If you keep your promises, you stand a better chance of keeping a sponsor or a ride.

Playing the percentages works. If you contact one car owner or potential sponsor, your chances for success are small; if you contact 500, your chances are 500 times better.

Sales, and these are certainly sales, are based on emotional needs of the purchaser. Any logical and/or factual presentation will only support the emotional decision. Sales will not be made from the presentation of facts, no matter how compelling they may be.

If you want to progress in motorsports, learn and develop sales skills; they are as important as driving skills.

PUBLIC RELATIONS

Again, I am not an expert in the PR field. It is important to get your name in front of the public. It takes effort, but is actually very easy. Local papers and other forms of media are always looking for stories. Give them yours. It will help you, your sponsors, and the sport in general. As you move up the ranks of the sport, the experience will be beneficial for you.

CONCLUSION

The many skills outlined in this and previous chapters each play a role in the development of a winning race driver. Some are more important than others, and should be higher priorities. But each has importance, and ignoring any will make the road to the winner's circle more difficult. Creating a plan that addresses all of the issues pertinent to becoming a winning race driver is the first step. Now is a good time to start your plan.

10 Qualifying, Time Trialing, and Autocrossing

At first glance, it may seem odd that these topics are combined in the same chapter. The reason is simple. The object of each of these driving disciplines is to turn the fastest possible lap time, so that you earn the best qualifying position in a racing situation, or win the competition in other forms of motorsport. These variations on a theme, while similar, also have dissimilarities, which we will explore.

QUALIFYING

The goal in qualifying is to set the fastest time. In normal qualifying situations, you'll use two methods. In the first, one car (usually) is on the track for a one- or two-lap effort, with only one warm-up lap. Time trials are also usually run in this fashion. The second method sees all of the cars in a group (sometimes split to minimize traffic) on the track at once, and every lap is timed. The fastest lap recorded by each individual driver is that driver's qualifying time. Each of these situations requires a different approach.

Mental Preparation

Since qualifying well brings big advantages, the pressure before a qualifying session can be very high. As with most elements of racing, it is crucial to stay focused on the important priorities before leaving the pits for a run. Mental rehearsal makes focusing easier.

While many factors are important, your mental approach to qualifying can make or break your effort. Trying too hard can cause problems because you focus attention on the wrong areas. As a driver, you must focus all of your attention on driving. If even 10% of your concentration is being used to "push the car harder" or "get the pole," attention is being diverted from doing the job. Additionally, the conscious mind is sending the wrong message. Pushing harder is *not* carrying speed, watching tire scrub, or driving smoothly. It is slowing the car, causing mistakes, and creating erratic driver inputs.

I have had many top drivers tell me that they will go out and focus on a smooth, clean first lap, then tell themselves to really stand on it for the second lap. I've done it myself. The result is almost always a slower second lap. The reason is almost always misplaced attention.

For example, when you say "go harder," you usually will apply the brakes harder going into the turns, and jump on the throttle harder at the exits. A little wheel lock-up going in will upset the car; a little tire spin at the exit slows acceleration. Instead of focusing on a smooth brake application and eye movement through the turn, you tend to focus on a real late brake application and look just ahead of the car, hoping to get slowed down in time.

Then you must suddenly shift attention to the exit, so you mash on the gas too hard while rotating the car, causing wheelspin and a reduction in acceleration. Instead of anticipating, you are reacting and that is slower. It does not take much to cause a loss of a two-tenths in each turn. That can take you from the front row to the back of the grid at most tracks.

In reality, your qualifying laps are nothing more than a couple of normal laps. Sure, your approach is a bit different due to the circumstances, but it's still a couple of laps around the track. If you drive them as nothing more, and have a sound plan, you maximize your chances for a good qualifying run. If you charge onto the track trying to set a lap record, you will probably over drive and end up feeling frustrated with a slow time. Drive the lap or laps like you would practice laps, but implementing your qualifying plan based on the important factors you have considered. Then enjoy watching the competition sweat.

In this situation, I like to get into the car early, get comfortable and relaxed, and visualize a few laps the way I want to run them. I also visualize any changes that I want to make to the vehicle path on the last turn of the first lap, or at the exit onto the timing straight on the last lap. Finally I visualize how I want to drive the warm-up lap or laps, to build heat in the tires.

I then concentrate on breathing and clearing my mind of all thought and emotion, so that when I get onto the track, my ability to anticipate is at its highest level. The relaxation and rehearsal allow me to leave the pit lane at full tilt, as if I had already driven a dozen laps at full speed. No warm-up is needed, other than for the tires.

Many other systems work for reaching peak performance instantly. The key in all of the successful systems is to have a plan for performance, and to internalize the plan before going onto the race track. How this is accomplished, as long as it works for you, is not important.

Single Car Qualifying

With a single timed lap, you must get into the groove quickly. Working up to speed is not a luxury. You must be able to get to the limit immediately, and build heat in the tires as quickly as possible on asphalt tracks. A lack of heat in the tires can reduce traction and cornering speed. Heat is built most quickly with hard braking and acceleration, as opposed to cornering. Since traction will increase as the tires get hotter, the second lap could be faster. Be ready to take advantage of the traction increase.

Fig. 10-1. Short track qualifying requires immediately getting in the groove.

0012964

In the special case of qualifying on a dirt track, you must quickly find the limit in order to "read" track surface conditions. Slight overdriving also helps even though heating the tires is not a major concern.

On long ovals and road courses, the same criteria apply, but with one important distinction. As heat builds up, traction will increase, and cornering speeds will also increase. The further you go into the first lap, the better your traction is likely to become. For you to be fast in this circumstance, you must be able to "feel" the grip of the tires, and respond accordingly. You could have serious problems if you try to brake at the same point used in practice before the tires have heated.

The following methods are used by many fast qualifiers in many forms of the sport. Immediately get up to speed, and sample the traction at the first opportunity. Slight overdriving allows this and builds heat in the tires more quickly. Continue this during the warm-up lap. As you enter the last turn before the timing station, slow slightly more than normal (about 50 rpm), and take a later apex line to allow earlier acceleration and higher speeds on the following straight.

Drive the rest of that lap as close to the limit as possible, being careful not to scrub too much speed, but keeping maximum heat in the tires. Use lines that are the quickest, and on a road course with runoffs, try to use as much "extra" track as possible. Hang wheels off the inside of the track at the apexes, and use the FIA curbs to widen the entries and exits without unduly upsetting car balance. Take great care to stay out of the loose dirt and marbles off the fast line, and to avoid bumps or broken asphalt that may cause traction losses or upset car balance.

On a road course where the last turn is in the opposite direction of the first turn, where you would normally cross over the straightaway to set up for the next turn (assuming that is where the timing lights are located), stay to the exit side of the track leaving the last turn on the final qualifying lap. This will reduce the distance traveled, and consequently the lap time. At a track width of 60 feet, you will travel 55 feet less. At the 120 mph speed, you will save .312 seconds. Try to find that much time around the track! Naturally, you should practice all of these tricks prior to qualifying, if the time is adequate. These are ways to shave precious hundredths from your lap times.

Short track racing adds another dimension to two-lap qualifying efforts. When exiting Turn 4 on the first of two timed laps, be conservative. An error here will cost time at the end of lap one as well as the beginning of lap two.

Creating a Game Plan for Qualifying

Without a doubt, every driver wants to run as fast as possible in qualifying. The goal for most is very clear: the pole, or as close to the front as possible. Reaching that goal is more difficult. Several factors must be taken into account when you create a plan for a fast qualifying lap.

CAR SET-UP. What changes can be made to the car to improve qualifying times? More ignition advance, different tire pressures, more or less wedge. Keep in mind that the car only has to work for a lap or two with no traffic to deal with.

QUALIFYING POSITION. This can make a big difference in strategy and in car set-up. How does the track change as qualifications continue? How will you set the car up for the expected conditions? And how will you drive the track for those conditions? If the track conditions vary from what you expect, how will you alter your driving to compensate?

TRACK CONFIGURATION. The obvious differences are dirt, asphalt, or road course, but other factors must be considered. Where is the starter? Where are the lights for the clocks? Sometimes, a location other than the middle of the front stretch can alter your plan. For example, if the clocks are located beyond the middle of the straight, into your normal braking zone, a different line on your last timed lap of a run could allow you to brake beyond the timing lights, gaining a tenth or two. Be careful! That wall can come up fast. This situation is rare, but does occur. I've seen timing lights positioned on the back straight, also.

QUALIFYING PROCEDURE. Does your track have one lap or two lap runs? Do you get a warm-up lap? Where do you enter the race track? Knowing the answers to these questions helps you to create a sound plan, especially at an unfamiliar track.

One-Lap Runs vs. Two-Lap Runs

Some tracks use a two-lap qualifying procedure while others give you only a single lap. The difficulty with either, but especially the one-lap shot, is a lack of time to get up to speed. This can be further complicated when you enter the track at Turn 4 and go on the clocks at the start/finish line the first time by. Obviously, getting up to speed quickly is important. I have found two tools useful to assist you in accomplishing this.

First, practice getting up to speed quickly. During hot laps, once you know the car is working OK, come in and reenter the track getting up to speed as quickly as possible. If you do this every time you enter the track (except for the first time out for a given event), you will get practice and gain confidence.

The second tool is mental imagery. Run practice laps mentally before you go out to qualify. Close your eyes and visualize running laps exactly the way you want to on the track. You can do this at home before getting to the track, and try it as you are sitting in line for your qualifying attempt. Doing this just before going onto the track gives you a mental warm-up and allows you to get into the groove more easily when the green flag drops.

Qualifying Risk Management

There are two important points about qualifying runs. The first is the exit of Turn 4 just before taking the green flag. Getting a good run off of this turn gives you the best chance for a fast lap. You may be able to alter your line to get on the power earlier than normal by taking it easy into Turn 3. On the second lap, you will not have this option, so plan it carefully. Part of your plan should include a way to deal with the extra speed at the end of the front straight. Practice this plan before you use it in a qualifying run.

On a two-lap run, the important point is exiting Turn 4 on the first green flag lap. If there is a spot to be conservative, this is it. If you blow the exit on this lap, you will affect lap times on both laps, since your exit is slow on the lap you are driving, and straightaway speed will be low for the next lap. For this reason, I prefer to take a good run off Turn 4 as the green comes out, but make the rest of the first lap slightly conservative, especially exiting Turn 4, just to make the show. Then I'll hang it out a little for the rest of the second lap.

Qualifying Set-up

Since this is not a set-up book, I won't go into details here, but the qualifying set-up is often different than a race set-up. Here is one example. In Grand Prix and Indy Car racing, where ground effects and downforce are so crucial, cars are often set up for qualifying with maximum downforce, since this allows higher cornering speeds, and most often faster laps. For a race, the amount of downforce is often reduced, to gain straight line speed. The downforce is sacrificed since passing in the corners is very difficult, but passing on the straights is easy. With too much downforce, drag increases and slows the cars on the straights. A car with less downforce can carry more speed down the straights, and would be more difficult to pass in the one place where passing is reasonable.

The important point is to understand how the set-up varies for qualifying, and to mentally adapt to the changes before setting out for a fast lap. Ideally, you will have tested the set-up prior to qualifying, so that the changes, and their effects, can be easily anticipated during your flyers.

Tire Management for Qualifying   We have discussed tire management already in this chapter, but the concept is crucial. Tires generate more traction as heat in the tread increases, up to an optimum temperature. Beyond the optimum temperature, the traction will diminish. In qualifying or similar situations discussed in this chapter, heat build-up in the tire is seldom a problem. The ambient temperature at the time of a run will also influence this.

In the majority of cases, building as much heat as possible in the tire, as quickly as possible, is crucial, and you can use tire slip angles to do this. (See also Chapter 6.) Whereas in a race you want to drive at the smallest slip angle within the range of maximum cornering force to save tire wear and heat build-up, in qualifying situations, you want to drive at the highest slip angles within the range of maximum cornering force in order to generate heat.

Sensing the difference in slip angles within the range of maximum traction is very difficult. While seat time is important, the extremely high level of sensitivity needed to do this comes under the natural ability heading, more so than any other quality in race driving. You can improve, especially if you get lots of skid pad time to feel what the car does when the tires are overdriven, but the ability to alter slip angles at will is what makes driving race cars an art more than a science.

Ayrton Senna was a genius at making this distinction at will. His qualifying ability was unsurpassed. No one did a better job than Senna. But he showed nearly the same brilliance in a race, saving his tires by driving at the smallest possible slip angles, but keeping cornering speeds as high as possible. At least knowing the priorities gives you a chance to master this technique.

AUTOCROSSING

While very similar to qualifying, the autocross run is distinctive enough to require a different driving approach. The unique problems of autocrossing include visibility, and having only three timed runs on a course you have never before driven. On the plus side, you have a complete lack of traffic, low speeds, and short-term, but high-intensity concentration levels.

From a standpoint of driving technique, adaptability, and car control, I consider autocrossing the most technically challenging of all motorsports. They are ultra competitive, great fun, and I always learn something new at these events. I certainly do not consider myself an expert in this specialized

Fig. 10-2. Autocrossing requires the same attitude as a one-lap qualifying run.

0012969

area, but I have made some observations and learned a few tricks that seem to help. I follow a very distinct pattern of priorities on my three runs.

Before the first run, while sitting in the car, I visualize (mentally run) the course (based on observations during the course walk). I attempt to picture the turns, shift points, and the optimum gear.

On the first run, I overdrive, letting the car slide, focusing on late braking, good paths through the turns, and early power applications. I do not worry about hitting pylons. This run is to learn the course, find the limits for the existing conditions, and build as much heat as possible in the tires. For the same reason (tire heat) I try to get the second run in ASAP.

Before the second run, replaying the first run mentally helps to correct errors and find speed. On the second run, my goal is to drive smoothly, make the smallest possible errors, and put a good, quick, clean run in the books. If I accomplish that goal, the third run is banzai time. I push as hard as possible, using early power applications and the entire lane. I would rather blow the last run going for a really fast time, than to be slower than the second run from being too conservative. I do this only when the second run is clean and quick.

We use an autocross course as part of school training, and newcomers often get lost in the forest of little orange pylons. And newcomers are more prone to hitting pylons. This is a form of the "Bott's Dots Syndrome." They hit the pylons because they look at them. The key is to look at the road between the pylons.

One of the great challenges of autocrossing requires driving at the limits of traction instantly. There is no pace lap, or warm-up. You come out of the gate flat out and never look back. I believe that this type of experience and mindset can only help any race driver learn more about the art of driving at the limit. The type of car does not matter; I've even seen cars with rental company stickers making runs.

CONCLUSION

Qualifying, and the forms of motorsport that are similar in nature, require a short-term, intense effort by you. A realistic analysis of your skills, and the level of risk you are willing to take, will help you to make decisions about your approach to qualifying. In all cases, it is crucial to follow a game plan developed before you set out for qualifying.

Finally, focusing on the important priorities, getting to the limit quickly, managing the tires, using all (and more) of the track, watching traffic, and, if necessary, shifting to a slower mode of driving, are your most important tasks in qualifying.

11 THE RACE

Now comes the payoff. All of your preparation, training, work, and effort now comes to fruition. The point of your pre-race plan is to be in a position to win the race. The point is not necessarily to be on the pole, though that is often beneficial; it is not to set the fastest lap in the race; the point is to lead on the last lap when the checkered flag drops. Absolute speed is not the primary goal; consistent speed over the duration of the event is much more important. Your goal is simply to cover the distance of the event faster than the competition. That margin need only be .01 seconds to win. The prize money, points, or trophies are not greater if the winning margin is larger.

Fig. 11-1. They don't pay more or give bigger trophies if you win by a big margin. An inch or two is enough.

0012970

Several clichés fit:
- You must finish to win
- The race is won on the last lap, not the first lap
- Patience pays
- Consistency is more important than absolute speed
- It is more important to be fast at the end of the race than at the beginning
- It is easier to attack on the straights and defend in the corners. This often dictates car set-up biased slightly for straight line speed

Clichés arise because they are usually true. Each of the above offers an important insight which you should not take lightly.

Finally, before moving to the specifics of this chapter, you should determine your risk/reward ratio for any maneuver you attempt during a race. By risk/reward ratio, I mean "is the reward (higher finishing position, more money or points, etc.) worth the risk needed to get there." Is the risk of a crash worth the possible outcome if the move is successful?

Here's an example: In the 1990 Indy 500, Al Unser, Jr., crashed on the 198th lap while battling for position with Emerson Fittipaldi. The crash was clearly a "racing incident," with both drivers partially responsible. Unser could have backed off, letting Fittipaldi by. He would have been assured of a second place finish, and conceivably, Fittipaldi would have drifted high (Unser's car probably kept Fittipaldi from going off himself), letting Unser get back around a little later. By the same token, Fittipaldi could have been more patient, since he appeared to have a faster car. Another corner and Fittipaldi probably could have made a clean pass. Considering that the 500 is arguably the world's most important race, a lot was at stake. What would you have done in Unser's shoes? Or Fittipaldi's?

It's easy to be an arm chair quarterback. Considering the importance of the event, I probably would have done exactly what Fittipaldi did if I was in his car. And I would most likely have ended up in the fence if I were in Unser's car. The point here is that only you can decide for yourself the risks you are willing to take, but it is an issue worth addressing. You should know the answer before the time comes to make the choice.

STARTS

The most exciting moment in racing is the start. It is also the most dangerous. Very few races are won at he start, while many are lost there. Since nearly all starts are rolling, the unique situation of standing starts will be covered in Chapter 13. All of the material here assumes a rolling start.

Fig. 11-2. The race start—where the fun begins.

From the Pole
There are serious advantages to starting from the pole position. You control the pace of the start, you have a psychological advantage of being the fastest, and you have some control on lateral (left to right) positioning on the race track. Additionally, starting from the front row, or first three rows actually, minimizes the risk of traffic and major spins/crashes in front of you. Being on the pole is a priority covered in the previous chapter.

Fig. 11-3. The car on pole position has an advantage at the start. But the pole car must control lateral position if the advantage is to be useful. Here the pole car moves slightly right to force #2 to the outside (2), then turns in to prevent #3 from passing on the inside (3, 4).

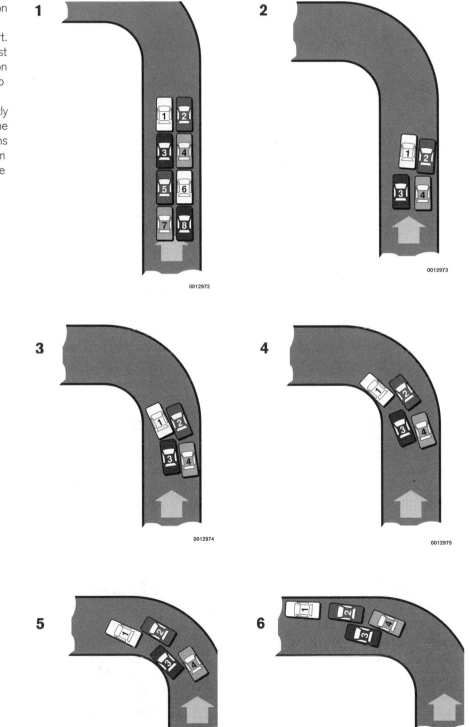

Keep specific criteria in mind as you develop a start strategy. The first issue is pace. How fast should you start the race? To make this decision requires specific knowledge of your car and your competitor's cars. What are your strong points, and what are theirs? If all cars are equal, then the speed is less important from an acceleration perspective. But if cars are not equal, what gear and engine rpm will allow you to accelerate the best compared to the competition? Regardless of the gear selected, always hold rpm at peak torque for the start, as that will give maximum acceleration. The gear selected relates to the speed range determined to be the best. Here are several considerations:

A slow start is best for a car with a horsepower advantage, but a weight disadvantage.

A fast start is best for a car with aerodynamic advantages, either more downforce or less drag.

Analyze the first turn. Since you will likely be off-line when starting from the pole, will a low-speed start allow you to take the first turn flat out off line without braking? This will give you an advantage at the exit, since most drivers will brake out of habit, even if not required. This may merit testing or practice in advance.

Surge starts can be effective. They can also backfire. A surge start is when the pole sitter backs-off, then accelerates again. When the rest of the field responds by lifting, the pole car is back on the gas, giving an advantage if the timing is right. If the pole sitter lifts as the flag goes green, the pole sitter loses big time. This requires that you study the starter so that you can play the odds. Some associations will not allow this type of start, either not starting the race or black flagging the culprit. Overall, this method is a low percentage one. It backfires more often than not.

Practice alternate paths and speed judgement in the first turn from the speed range in which you would like to start.

Fig. 11-4. At the start, cars #2, 3, and 4 pose the greatest threat to the pole car.

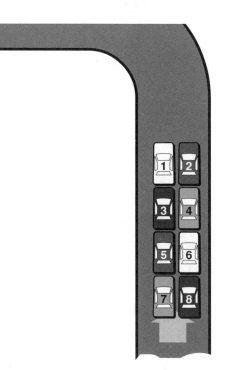

0012978

Keep in mind that the starter can throw the green anytime. If you want the fastest possible start, accelerate early and carry speed.

Be ready to adapt to any situation, even though you control the pace. If the race goes green earlier than you anticipated, you will carry more speed into the first turn than planned. What are you going to do?

The next area of consideration is lateral position on the track. You have two concerns. First you must defend attacks from behind or from the other front row occupant. Second, you must be in position to negotiate the first turn without disadvantage. The two cars presenting the most serious challenge are the other front row starter and the car directly behind. Pay close attention to them after the green falls.

Most associations require all cars to form two relatively straight rows prior to the start. It is crucial to know how well this is regulated. The best case for the pole car is to start as far to the outside as possible, leaving the other front row car as little room as possible. This gives the pole driver an advantage into the first turn relative to the line and control of the other front row starter. It does, however, leave an opening for the car behind. In this case, lower speeds at the start will allow an early turn-in with no major tire scrub as a means to defend from inside attacks. In all cases, the compromise is between optimum path through Turn 1, and defending against attacks. Be prepared for any eventuality. Every start will be different.

Fig. 11-5. The pole car can control lateral starting position.

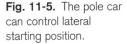

0012979   0012980

Starting from the Outside Front Row

Since you cannot control pace from this position, try to control track location. Attempt to keep the pole car as low on the track as possible while giving yourself the best possible line into, and especially out of, the first turn. On a road course, if Turn 2 is in the opposite direction from Turn 1, holding position next to the pole car through Turn 1 will give you an advantage into Turn 2. The outside front row position is often the best place from which to start.

From the Inside Row

Since most drivers attempt to move to the outside for the optimum line into the first turn, there is often a big hole along the inside at the start. On occasion, one or more positions can be gained by trying the inside at the start. Much of the decision is based on the movements of the cars ahead, and the pace of the start. Slow paces offer the biggest opportunities here.

Fig. 11-6. At the start, a hole almost always opens up for the inside row.

Fast-paced starts dictate moving to the outside for the best path through the first turn. On a slow- to medium-speed start, look for the hole. The farther back in the pack, the better it is to go for the hole with the least traffic.

From the Outside Row

Starting from the outside row gives you the advantage of the best path into the first turn, but requires defense from attacks to the inside. It is best to begin near the center of the track at the start, look for holes opening up in front, and move in the direction of the following car if that car begins to attack. The farther back in the pack you are, or the earlier the race starts, the more helpful this will become.

Fig. 11-7. From the outside row, you must defend to the rear while controlling lateral position; if possible, pinch the inside car down low so that you have the best exit line.

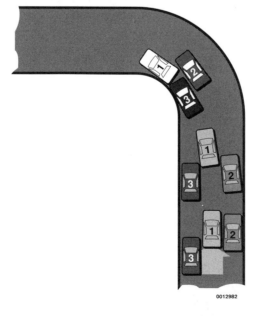

Reading the Starter

The ability to "read" the starter is very important in the attempt to gain an advantage at the start of a race, or minimize any disadvantage. A starter has three basic goals. The first is to attempt to start a race fairly for all competitors, which requires a tidy field line-up. Second, the starter wants a safe start. Finally, the starter sees the racer as an adversary who must be outsmarted.

This final characteristic is far from a negative, for it gives the astute driver a decided advantage. Every starter has his own style; observing and defining that style will allow you to make the best start possible from any position in the field. The only way to achieve this is to watch the starter as much as possible. See where the field is when the flag drops; watch for consistent movements before the flag is waved, like head or body motions that indicate the flag is about to wave. Does the starter raise or drop the flag first? Does the starter always start the race even with a sloppy line-up? Or does the starter have a clear plan for starting the race when the field is slightly out of line? Developing a sense for the procedures of a given starter will allow you to make the best possible start.

Remember that the race starts when the green drops. Most associations allow passing once the green is out, though some do not allow passing until the start/finish line is crossed. First, know the rule. Second, be ready when the flag drops. If you are well back in the pack so that the starter stand is hard to see, and have no radio communication, watch the corner flaggers. They often will signal a green flag somehow, or take away a standing yellow flag. There is almost always some indication that the green flag dropped. This also applies to restarts after a yellow flag.

First Turn Speed

One of the keys to a good start is to focus considerable attention on vehicle speed judgement. The speed of your car as it approaches the first turn is most likely going to be slower than normal, so less or no braking may be needed to negotiate the turn. By judging speed, you can alter speed reduction and vehicle path to accommodate the existing situation. You must judge speed relative to your position on the race track and the position of other cars. It is very beneficial to practice alternate lines and a variety of speeds approaching the first turn so that you have a clear set of "data points" upon which to base speed and path judgements.

First Turn Position

Both your position on the track and your position relative to other cars will determine cornering speed and the path of your car through the first turn. The most important parameter is to create an opening which allows the best exit speed and path from the first turn.

Keep in mind that most drivers will use their "normal" braking point approaching the first turn, even if the speed is slower. This will create opportunities for passes and improved placement on the track. With lower speed, the possibilities for alternate lines increase, allowing many approaches that can gain you advantage. The key: have an open mind, look for openings, and focus attention on speed and paths. Additionally, since starts are often plagued with spins and crashes, be prepared for any possibility, and plan escape routes that give you the best chance to emerge unscathed from the melee.

Patience

Two of the clichés opening this chapter (2nd and 3rd) apply to starts. In some classes, it is difficult to pass, so a good start pays dividends. The question is again the risk vs. reward ratio. Spinning or crashing on the start will

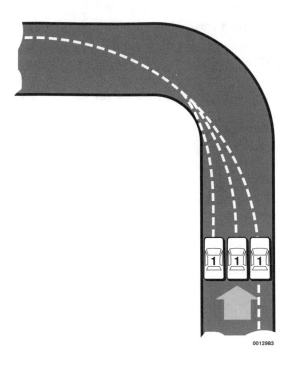

Fig. 11-8. If the first turn speed is low, you have several path options; braking may not even be necessary. But regardless of your entry line, get back quickly to your desired exit path.

0012983

not improve your chances to reach the checkered flag first, so the ability to exercise patience is paramount. By analyzing the situation clearly, a decision about the course of action most suitable is usually very apparent. Take what is there, and do not force the issue.

If no advantage presents itself, accept the reality of the moment, and work on a strategy to improve your position during the course of the race. If you get involved in a situation that costs you time on the track, like spinning cars in front, and you are forced to drop back, accept it, and remain calm. Deal with anger and fear immediately so that you can quickly refocus on driving. This is the most efficient way to gain back the lost ground. Lingering on the situation assures that you will lose more ground.

LEADING RACES

For most drivers, leading a race is the most difficult position to be in. The pressure created in your mind usually causes a shift in focus from driving to watching the following driver. If you start from a position near the front and find yourself in the lead, the best strategy is to attempt to build up a significant lead as early as possible without burning down the tires. A two to three second lead in the first five laps can often demoralize the competition. The key is to focus on driving fast laps, just like a qualifying session, until the lead is comfortable. Then focus on driving your own car; having a comfortable lead reduces pressure and makes it easier to maintain focus on the important priorities.

Keep Calm Of course it is not always possible to establish a lead early on. When the following car is right on your tail, whether fighting for the lead or for 10th place, the pressure is considerable. This is the moment of truth. Can you handle the pressure? It is difficult, if not impossible, to understand the situation effectively without having experienced it.

Let's look at the reality of the situation.

Until the following car attempts a pass, nothing is different about getting the car around the track.

The priorities remain the same: focus attention on the most important ones, like driving fast laps.

If you focus attention on the other car and driver, or worry about losing a position, you have made the other driver's job easier, and yours more difficult.

While it is very easy to sit in front of a computer and say "stay calm," and much more difficult on the race track, that is just what must occur to maintain a lead. Unforced errors are always caused by lack of focus on the important priorities. Stay focused on what you control, not on what you do not control, i.e., the other car/driver.

Driving the Track   While it is important to keep tabs on the following car, the amount of attention to focus there should be small. The overwhelming priority is to focus on driving the track as you would in practice or qualifying. This is true until the following driver attacks for position. An attack is when the following driver actually attempts a pass, not feigns an attempt. A following driver will often move around from side to side to keep you guessing. Until the following driver asserts for position, i.e., overlaps the rear of your car in a real pass attempt, you do not need to respond to the "fakes." The real attack will require a counter-attack.

Blocking   Every association has rules about blocking, and different interpretations of the rules. While there is nothing in any rule book that I am aware of that limits a driver from selecting any path around a corner or, for that matter, down a straightaway, I feel that blocking maneuvers are pointless and actually cost time to the blocking car, and possibly overwork the tires. (By blocking I mean moving to the right on a straight when the following car moves to the right, etc.) The exception is on the last lap. I have found that two tactics are very effective in defending against an attack.

First, force the following car to travel the longest distance to make a pass. For example, when exiting a corner onto a long straightaway where the corner at the end of the straight is in the opposite direction, take as long as possible to cross the straight. Make the driver behind move to the opposite side of the straight first by not leaving room to the inside (relative to the turn at the end of the straight). As the following driver moves, you move. If the follower can draft by into an overlap position, leave a car width at the edge of the track. You have the other car boxed-in. If you take a late turn-in, the car to the outside will never be able to outbrake you into the next turn. And the other car cannot turn-in until you do, without dropping back behind you.

Second, when the following driver attempts to outbrake into a turn, an early turn-in will be the best defense. You can turn-in anytime you want to. If the following car is overlapping you, but not alongside, an early turn-in will force the other car to turn-in when you do. Additionally, the early turn-in will allow later braking and more trailbraking so that you can carry speed deeper into the turn, making the pass to the inside very difficult.

Fig. 11-9. The lead car has the discretion to choose paths. This legal blocking path allows good defense, but does not blatantly move from side to side (which is not legal, though often tolerated).

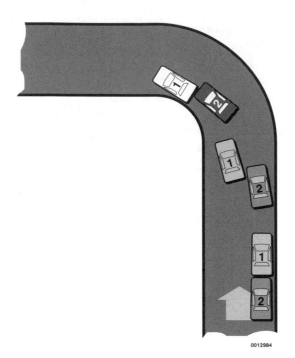

0012984

Fig. 11-10. The early turn-in block is an effective deterrent to outbraking attacks.

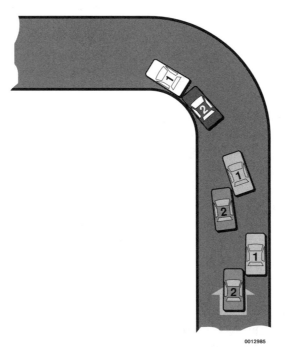

0012985

Note: The rules in virtually every racing association dictate that the passing driver must complete the pass safely. It is the responsibility of the following driver to pass cleanly and safely. I have a personal rule of thumb when dealing with a pass attempt by a following car. If the following driver has asserted position enough so that I can see the front of the other car in my peripheral vision, I will leave room, but just barely enough. In the situation where the other driver is attempting to pass to the inside, I will also tighten my exit line, forcing the other driver to scrub more speed than I do. This

Fig. 11-11. The car being overtaken has the right of way unless you assert position prior to turn-in. I will pass if I have established an overlap (#2, near). Here I know that the other driver sees me. He may still drive into me, but it is then a blatant move. If I have not established an overlap (far), I assume that the other driver will close the door on me, as I would in the reverse situation. Then, you must either back off, drive off the inside of the track, or collide. You can attempt to coerce the other driver, but don't count on success. Some drivers are mean and nasty.

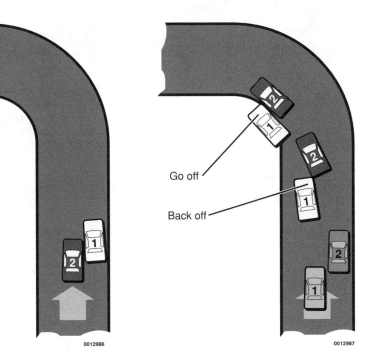

helps to repel the attack. On the other hand, if I cannot see the other car in my peripheral vision, I will close the door and turn all the way to the apex and/or the edge of the track at the exit, should the attack be to the outside.

There is a risk associated with closing the door. If the other driver is a jerk, he can take you out very easily by holding position and letting you drive into the nose of his car. The lead car here is very vulnerable. If your association does not enforce the rules, it may be necessary to leave the other car room when you are uncertain of its position.

I have found this system to be about 80% effective, maybe more. And I am completely comfortable with this method.

Important: If you turn in too early, the other driver can gain an advantage at the exit of the turn, and set up a pass on the next straight, which will be difficult to defend. Additionally, if you use an early turn-in as a means to block the car behind, you are leaving the door open for an outside pass into the corner.

When to Relinquish the Lead

There are many occasions when letting the following car pass without taking defensive action is in your best interest.

When a following car can draft by on a straightaway. In this case, defensive reactions are rarely effective for very long, and defensive moves have two negative consequences. First, tire scrub is increased, and second, cars following farther back can gain time on you. You can always come back with a well-timed counter-attack later. The exception to this is on the last lap of a race.

When your plan requires careful tire management. The passing driver may be over-driving and burning down tires. Pressing a defense may cause you to do the same. This can be a tough call and takes considerable discipline. The exception is near the end of a race, or in a short race, like a trophy dash, etc., where tire management is not an issue.

Fig. 11-12. When passing under braking into a corner, the passing driver is in a vulnerable position until clear ahead, as shown in the overhead view. The sequence of photos shows that you are vulnerable from behind as well. The Mustang is bumped and thrown off line into the wall.

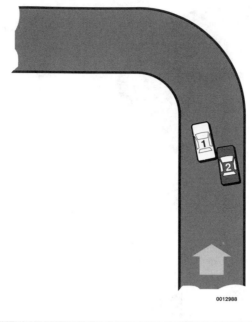

0012988

0012989

0012990

0012991

Fig. 11-13. The outside pass is very effective if the leading driver turns in too early or slows too much at the entrance.

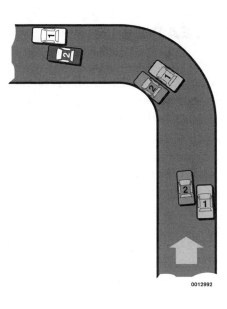

When you know the other driver is inconsistent. If you are consistent, and the other driver is not, you will find it easy to come back with your own attack in a few laps. The exception to this is in the final 3 or 4 laps of a race.

When you think the other driver is in too deep. In this case he may scrub off speed at the exit, spin, or crash. Attempting to stay with a driver who is over-driving will lead you to the same fate. Reality-based judgement and discipline are needed to enforce this. There is never an exception to this.

When you are within a lap of a pit stop. When a pit stop is approaching, fighting for position is really a low priority, and doing so takes away focus on making a clean entry to the pits and stopping on the mark.

When the attacking car has asserted position by drawing even when entering a turn. At this point the attacking driver has pulled off the pass; attempting a defense at this point is locking the corral after the horses have escaped. Short of knocking the attacker off the track, little can be done. It's time to focus on a later attack.

Fig. 11-14. When a driver asserts position while you are braking, it is best for you to relinquish the lead since the attack is effective. You can then counter at the exit.

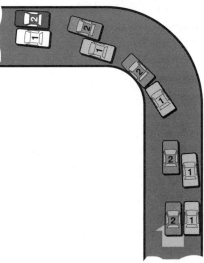

FOLLOWING THE LEADER

While it is always best to lead when possible, being second to the leader of a race is, in many ways, more fun. It is much easier to drive your own race while pressuring the leader, or patiently waiting for him to make a mistake and leave an opening for a pass.

Driving the Track

Even when following the leader, it is important to drive the race track, not the other car. If you are caught up in the flow of the lead car, it is easy to be caught out by the leader's mistakes, or "tricks."

Many years ago I learned a valuable lesson, almost by accident. I was not leading the race, but dicing for position with another driver, who was right on my tail. The pressure was tremendous, since the cars were equal, with no advantage to either car. I was constantly fending off attacks while braking, and the tires on my car were wearing rapidly from the pace. Lap after lap I drove as consistently as I was able, never varying paths, braking points, etc., except to turn in early as a defensive tactic.

Finally I decided to try a tactic I had never seen. With about five laps left in the race, I waited to apply the brakes for about six car lengths beyond the normal braking point. I had to change my line, and do some serious car control antics to stay on the race track. The following car was sucked into my ploy. The driver applied the brakes as late as I had, but without a plan to compensate for the problems late braking would cause. He had been lulled into complacency by my consistency, driving my race, not his own. When he realized he was into the corner too deep, he locked the brakes and spun. I gathered up my car and gained about 40 car lengths by the time he recovered. Needless to say, he was no longer a threat for that race.

The chance of successfully implementing the same ploy twice with the same driver is very slim. I expected the other driver to be really angry about the maneuver, but he was too embarrassed to say anything. My guess is he probably used the ploy himself at some point. The moral of the story is: drive your own race against the track, not against other cars.

Drafting

Before the advent of wings and sophisticated aerodynamics, drafting was both more effective and easier. Cars with little horsepower differential and similar aerodynamics are not easy to draft by. Timing and patience are required to effect passes from a drafting situation.

Every car has different drafting characteristics; until you drive a given car in a draft, it is hard to determine what works, and what doesn't. There are several general rules for drafting:

- Drafting is more effective as speed increases
- At least with some types of cars it seems to be better to draft by with some momentum, without easing off the gas as you pull up behind the leading car. In other words, do not back off and stay in the draft, but pull out of the draft when needed as you approach the lead car
- Cars with wings and ground effects will lose downforce in a draft. How much depends upon speed, the corner, and the aerodynamic characteristics of the cars involved. Be prepared for less traction when drafting

- It is best to attempt a drafting pass only when you know that the pass can be completed successfully. Not being able to complete the pass can place you at a tactical disadvantage to the lead car, and open the door for a following car
- Staying in a draft for too long can cause overheating problems. Watch the temp gauges

Fig. 11-15. Parking behind the car ahead makes the pass more difficult (near). It is best to gain momentum in the draft before passing (far). Without momentum in equal cars, it will be tough to make a pass. Timing is important: pass too soon and the other driver can counter; too late and asserting position under braking will be difficult.

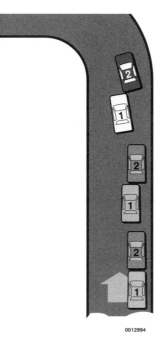

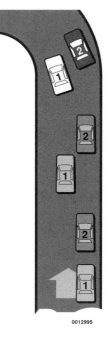

Fig. 11-16. Be careful when attempting a draft pass. Watch and defend to the rear.

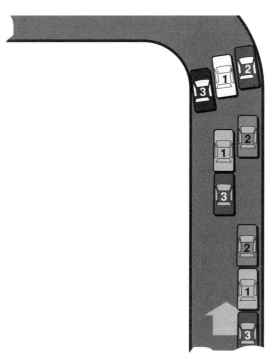

Applying Pressure

The act of following another car applies mental pressure to its driver. Attempting to apply additional pressure by "filling the mirrors" of the lead car is a popular tactic to rattle the leader. When I am in the lead, I find this tactic ineffective for two reasons. I know that when a driver following me is doing this, he is focusing more attention on me, or on passing me, than on driving. Additionally, he is using tires, brakes, etc., more than I am, giving me a slight long-term advantage.

The reality of the situation is this: if the lead driver is going to be rattled by such tactics as moving left and right to fill the mirrors and create an impression of an attack, chances are that driver will be rattled simply by the presence of a following car without the extra effort. And if the lead driver is not rattled by being followed, it's unlikely that the lead driver will be rattled by the extra tactics.

You must choose an approach, be it the patient, relaxed approach, or the more aggressive, mock-attack approach. In any case, it is crucial to maintain focus on the really important priorities.

Watching for Mistakes and Advantages

One of the nice aspects of following the lead car is the opportunity to analyze the techniques of the lead driver. If the driver shows signs of inconsistency, you can use that to advantage. If you find you are slightly faster on a specific section of track, then at some point you can use that to advantage. There are several mistakes to watch for. They include:

LATE THROTTLE APPLICATION AT THE EXIT. You can use this to advantage on the next straight by leaving a small gap and getting on the power earlier, allowing more speed to be carried on the next straight. If you follow too closely, you will be unable to get on the power early enough. Timing is important.

EXCESSIVE SLOWING AT THE ENTRY TO A CORNER. This is the perfect scenario for outbraking attacks.

EARLY TURN-IN. This, on rare occasions, can allow for outbraking to the outside. It can also allow earlier throttle application if the other driver does not adjust the exit line and get back on the power early enough.

ANY INCONSISTENCIES IN LINE OR SPEED. These can open the door for an attack.

OVERDRIVING. If the lead car is overdriving, especially at the entry of the corner, you can often count on tires going away late in the race.

Fig. 11-17. One of the most common tactical mistakes is to follow too closely. If the other car is late getting on the power, leave a gap ahead, get on power earlier at the exit, and use the momentum to drive by.

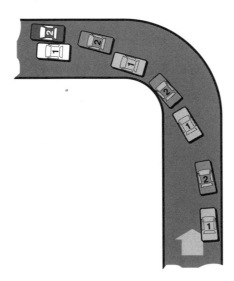

0012997

Fig. 11-18. When attempting an outbraking pass, use the draft and be patient (A). Pull out to pass in the braking zone (B). Assert position as early as possible, before turn-in if you can (C) and the corner is yours (D). Other scenarios can also be used effectively.

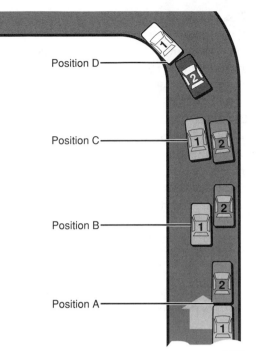

Fig. 11-19. Using the same approach as in the last example, outbraking to the outside can be very effective if the car ahead turns in early to defend position. Alter your path for an apex one car width from the edge of the track, and set up for early power application.

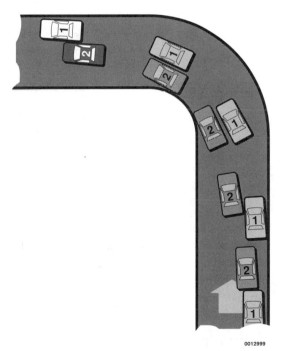

Avoiding Mistakes

Naturally all of the items to look for when following the leader (or any car you may be engaging for position) are important to avoid; this is even more true if you take the lead position. Before you attack, you must be able to drive your car and the race track.

PASSING (ATTACKING)

If you find yourself in a spot to attack for position, some guidelines will be helpful. Some of these have been covered already, but will be repeated here for continuity.

There are four basics types of passes:

DRAFTING. This was covered in detail earlier. It is usually the safest and most effective pass.

OUTBRAKING. This is often effective, but also creates counter-attack opportunities for the other driver.

EARLY ACCELERATION. This pass requires timing and patience. It is very effective, difficult to defend against, and safe.

Fig. 11-20. The Early Acceleration set-up requires patience and timing. When executed effectively, the other driver will claim that you are cheating because you were able to "power by" on the straightaway.

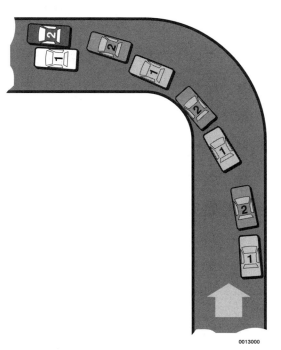

0013000

THE PICK. The pick needs traffic situations to implement. While very effective, it is also the most risky since some of the slower cars creating the traffic situation may be unaware of your presence. This pass requires anticipation, alternate line knowledge, assertive positioning, the ability to take advantage of the situation instantly, and perfect timing. An escape route is a good idea should you misjudge the scenario, or if the plan goes awry.

The Set-up

Each type of pass with the exception of the pick requires a set-up. A set-up requires planning and patience. Some times the set-up can take many laps, other times only a turn or two.

Your set-up plan should include two elements. First is a pre-determined attack, such as "I will initiate an attack at Turn 3 on the next lap." Second is an "If–Then" statement, such as "If the lead driver does X at Y, then I will attack." At least one of these elements needs to be in effect before you initiate the attack. When a driver is very consistent, then the pre-determined attack is usually the operative element. If a driver is inconsistent, then the If–Then statement is the operative element. Here are examples of each.

Fig. 11-21. One of the most effective ways to pass is the pick set-up, using slow traffic as a pick. Anticipation is the key element to this pass.

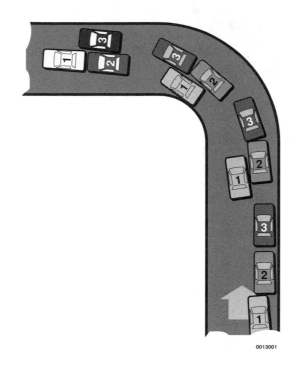

0013001

You are following Joe, who is very consistent. After several laps, you have learned that Joe is consistently feeding in power at the exit of Turn 7 later than you can. You feel that you can make a pass at will by taking advantage of this. This requires an early-acceleration set-up, and a pre-determined attack at the time you decide is most advantageous.

You are following Mark, who is very fast, but inconsistent. You notice that Mark varies his turn-in point and braking technique going into Turn 9. You feel that you can make a pass *if* Mark brakes at the 3 marker entering Turn 9, but that you cannot if Mark brakes beyond the 3 marker. Your plan now includes an If–Then statement. If Mark brakes at or before the 3 marker at Turn 9, then I will attack. This scenario could also include a pre-determined attack element. If Mark is very aggressive, and you expect a

THE WINNING DRIVER

The fastest and most effective path when attacking for position puts the other driver off his perfect line.

You need to force the other driver onto a longer path at the entry of a corner or on a straight while you deviate the least from your perfect line at the exit of a turn or on a straight.

To make a pass of a competitor with equal speed, you must have corner exit speed that at least matches his. Minimum tire scrub and early power applications are crucial.

Tools: Visualization, seat time.

Game Plan: Work on the best line for outbraking going in, but early power application at the exit.

Priorities: Making the pass for more than one turn. A pass is only good if it cannot be counter-attacked quickly. Excessive dicing can cost time relative to other drivers not involved.

quick counter-attack, it may be advantageous to wait for the last few laps before attacking. In this case your statement could be "If Mark brakes at or before the 3 marker *after* lap 25, then I will attack."

Without the operative statements for the set-up, the chance for a successful attack is reduced, and the possibility for a counter-attack increases.

Outbraking

Outbraking attacks are the most obvious. Specific parameters will make the maneuver a high-percentage one.

You must assert position before the lead car turns into the corner. By asserting position you must be within the range of peripheral vision of the other driver. Ideally, you are alongside so that no doubt exists that you are seen. If you are not even, the other driver can legally "slam the door shut" on you, so be ready to back down.

You must plan an alternate path through the turn that deviates as little as possible from your ideal path. This is crucial at the exit or you can expect a counter-attack which is likely to be a successful one.

You must be able to get back on the throttle as early as you would in a non-attack situation. The more you deviate from this, the more likely a successful counter-attack will occur.

Fig. 11-22. By asserting position in an outbraking pass attempt, you leave no question as to the outcome. On the other hand, if another driver gets under you without asserting position, be careful! You are in a very vulnerable spot. If you turn into him, even though you can legally, you are likely to be spun out if contact occurs. Unless the other car gets black flagged, you lose two ways. If you try to outbrake, this is the best position for turn-in, since you (#1) now control the entry line.

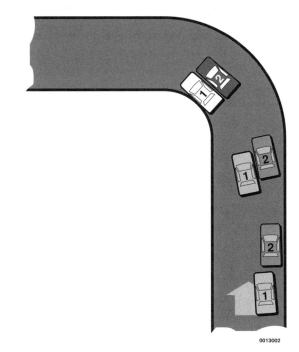

0013002

Several mistakes are common when attempting outbraking attacks:

TURN-IN TOO EARLY. An early turn-in allows the other driver to defend position easily since that driver is on a more ideal path into the corner. The other driver cannot turn in until you do if you have effectively asserted position before turning in. If anything, a later than normal turn-in is beneficial.

MOVING TOO FAR TO THE INSIDE. You must leave room for the car you are attacking. You do not need to leave enough room for two cars. The width of the lead car plus an inch or two is enough. More than that and you are forcing yourself to take a path into the corner that is even less desirable.

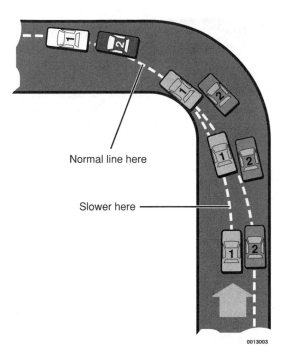

Fig. 11-23. When outbraking, you must plan an alternate line that allows a reasonable entry and a normal early-acceleration exit.

Normal line here

Slower here

0013003

A PATH WHICH DEVIATES EXCESSIVELY FROM YOUR IDEAL PATH. This will allow the other driver to counter attack at the exit, or possibly even defend position at the entry.

EXCESSIVE SPEED REDUCTION. If you slow too much, expect the door to be closed at or near the apex.

FAILURE TO ASSERT POSITION BEFORE TURN-IN. If you fail to draw even by the turn-in point, expect the other driver to close the door on you.

Fig. 11-24. If your alternate line is too early, the other driver can easily defend position due to your early turn-in. Also, if you move too far over to pass under braking, leaving the outside car too much room, that driver can easily counter your attack by following you in early.

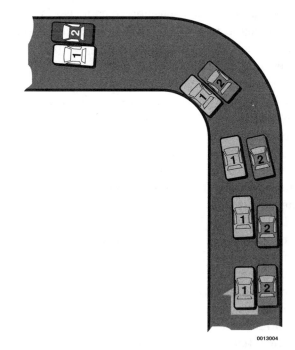

0013004

Fig. 11-25. If you turn in too early and the other car does not counter at the entry, expect an exit counter-attack due to your poor position and line at the exit.

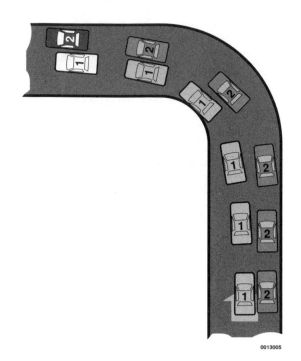

0013005

Alternate Lines

One of the elements of passing and defending is to drive on alternate lines. Without practice, it is difficult to know what you can and cannot manage when deviating from the ideal vehicle path through a turn. The middle of a race is a poor time to find out.

Unless the other driver blows it, he will hold his preferred line into, through, and out of the corners. That means to make a pass, you must drive off the best path through the corner, or at least some portion of the corner. This is precisely why passing an equal car is so difficult.

The key to making a pass is to choose an alternate path that allows you to accomplish your goal. Here is an example. If your goal is to pass under braking, how can you improve braking performance? On most short tracks, you brake and turn (at least a little) at the same time. Part of the tire's traction is used for cornering, the rest for braking. Change the percentage if you want to out-brake your rival. Take a straighter line into the corner so more of the tire traction can be used for braking. There will be a price to pay in mid-corner, however. Since you entered straighter, you must now rotate the car more for the exit. You will have to sacrifice mid-corner speed to pass under braking, but you must be in a position to get on the power early, or the car you pass entering the turn will get back around you at the exit.

In this scenario, when you get underneath the lead car going into the turn, that driver cannot rotate his car until you rotate. The trick is to rotate your car at the best time for you, forcing the other driver to rotate after you. Then you can drive off the corner on the line that allows you the best corner exit acceleration.

The same applies to passing at the exit. Drive a different line into and through the turn that allows you to use more tire traction for acceleration earlier than the other car. This allows you to carry more momentum down the straight, giving you the advantage into the next turn. Many drivers make a crucial mistake when doing this. If you follow the lead car too closely into and through the turn, any momentum advantage you gain will be lost because you will have to slow to keep from hitting the car ahead. A clear mental picture of your desired path through the turn and well-executed timing will allow you to make the pass more easily, and to stay ahead.

Track Position   One of the keys to passing is lateral track position; that is, where you are left-to-right relative to the car you are trying to pass. When alongside another car, it is common courtesy and good etiquette to leave the other car racing room. Two questions arise here. How much room to leave, and when you must leave room. There are many opinions, but the most practical course is to leave the other car just enough room. If you are on the inside, leave just over a car width to the outside wall. How much over a car width? How good is your judgement, or how large is your pit crew? A foot should be considered liberal. The same applies to leaving room for a car trying to pass to the inside.

The second question is more a judgement call. When do you need to leave racing room for the other car? My rule of thumb: leave room when the other car is within your peripheral vision. If you try to pass to the inside going into a corner, expect the other driver to close the door if he cannot see you alongside. I always assume the other driver cannot see me unless the nose of my car is even with his "B" pillar.

On the other hand, if you do not see the car trying to get underneath you, or you attempt to slam the door shut from the outside, who is really at risk? The car lower and slightly behind usually is at less risk. If you are higher and ahead, when you turn down, your rear quarter panel will likely hit the front of the lower car, causing you a problem. Giving way is usually better than a spin or a trip into the fence. Great care must be taken in this situation. You really need to decide in advance how far you are willing to push either situation *before* it arises, and be willing to accept the consequences of your decision regardless of the outcome. If you do not accept the consequences, the time you spend fuming at the situation will render you ineffective as a driver. Most often the lower car comes out OK and the lead car spins. It is really important to know where you want to be on the race track and to know where the other cars are located.

Defensive   When under attack from a following car, defensive measures are your first
Measures   priority. A defensive tactic is intended to stop an attack from a following car before it has a chance to succeed. Certain attacks lend themselves to defensive measure, others do not.

Attacks based on your inconsistency, driver errors, superior corner exit speed of the attacker, or drafting are, by nature, difficult, if not impossible, to defend against once the attack is initiated. In these cases, the good offense is your only defense. In other words, drive your race with consistency, good corner exit speed, and very small errors. A drafting or early acceleration attack are indefensible if you have allowed the situation to occur. If you find yourself in a situation where another driver attempts the pick attack, it is difficult to defend against. Here a strong, assertive offensive position in traffic is the best defense.

Only the outbraking attack consistently lends itself to defensive moves. When attacked under braking, the first line of defense is the early turn-in. A turn-in before the other car draws even allows you to control the path

Fig. 11-26. The failure to assert position under outbraking or an early turn-in leads to counter-attack to the outside.

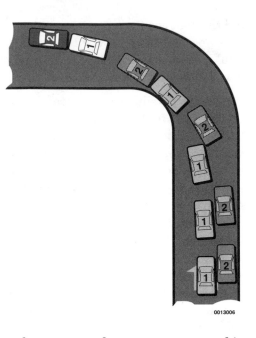

0013006

into the corner and to carry more speed into the turn under trail braking. Nine times out of ten, the attacker must give way to you. Turning in too early can leave the door open for an outside pass attempt, so do not turn in until the other car has overlapped your rear bumper/tail/wing.

The second line of defense occurs when the attacking driver has asserted position, but is either carrying too much entry speed, or has chosen a vehicle path that will scrub off corner exit speed. In either case, let the other car pass, since you will be able to easily repass when the attacker falls off the race track or scrubs off speed.

As always, though, a good, solid offense is the best possible defense. By focusing on your job, i.e., driving your car and the track, you stand the best chance of foiling all attacks before they are started.

Fig. 11-27. If the car attempting to outbrake you at the entry overdrives the entry, you can counter-attack when the other car is forced off line or the race track at the apex or exit. Patience is helpful here.

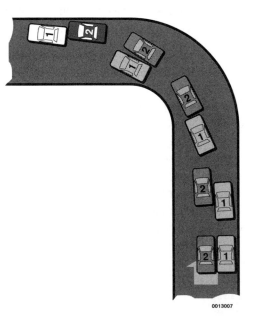

0013007

THE WINNING DRIVER

Always attempt to force the other driver to travel the greatest distance in his attempt to pass.

The fastest and most effective path when defending position allows your exits to follow your perfect line, but allows a defensive entry to the corner.

An effective entry when defending position allows you to exit correctly, at speed, with early power application, and forces the attacker to adjust speed and path, losing any possible advantage.

Tools: Off-line practice; early turn-in; assertive positioning.

Game Plan: Know what effect driving on a defensive line will have on you. Know when to take a defensive posture.

Priorities: Maintain position, but relinquish when needed; do what you can to get back on the power as early as possible at the exit; exercise patience and good judgement.

Practice Exercises: Visualize before an event; drive off line in practice; keep a "book" on the competition.

Counter-attacks

A counter-attack occurs after the attacker has actually completed a pass successfully. All of the attack scenarios, including the pick, lend themselves to counter-attacks. To counter-attack, you quickly attempt to repass the attacker, usually in the same corner or following straight. Beyond that point, the plan is to create an attack of your own.

A drafting counter-attack can occur when the attacker makes the pass too early on a straight, allowing you to catch the draft and attempt a pass before the braking zone. This move is often totally unexpected by the attacker, and therefore effective.

An early acceleration attack can be countered in exactly the same way.

The outbraking attack has two (at least) counter-attacks. The most common is holding an outside position, wheel-to-wheel with the attacker, forcing the attacker onto a less desirable path. This counter is especially effective when the next corner is in the opposite direction from the corner where the attack began.

Fig. 11-28. Sometimes a wheel-to-wheel counter to outbraking attacks is effective, and gives you the advantage if the next corner is in the opposite direction.

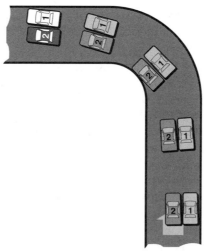

0013008

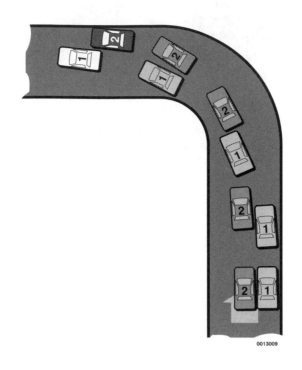

Fig. 11-29. If the attacker asserts position at the turn-in, an early acceleration crossover counter-attack can work at the exit or the following straight.

The second counter-attack is the crossover. If the attacker has taken an early turn-in, he may slide wide at the exit. This counter-attack requires a later than normal apex, allowing early acceleration and a path that leaves one car width to the outside of the track at the exit.

Early power application and the optimum path will allow you to move to the inside with momentum and make an immediate pass at best, or a pass on the following straight. This is a common counter-attack on oval tracks or where the following turn is in the same direction as the turn where the attack was initiated. Like an attack, the counter-attack requires practice and pre-planning if you expect good execution. These counter-attacks are high-percentage moves, but only if well conceived and executed. Poor planning and bad timing make these more dangerous.

Attack Timing

When is the best time to initiate an attack? Several criteria must be considered to make a good choice.

- If the lead driver is fast and consistent, opportunities to attack with a chance for success are few and far between. It is best to act when opportunity knocks
- If you have found a weakness in the lead driver, and if not under pressure from behind, you can choose almost anytime to attack. The best is probably as close to the end of the race as possible, since the chance for a counter-attack is less likely, and the other driver will have little time to mount a new attack on you
- If under pressure from behind, but attempting to pass the lead car, it is often best to attack as soon as possible, especially if the car behind will be unable to follow you through successfully. This may create the opportunity to give yourself a little breathing room
- If the lead driver is erratic, or overdriving, patience will allow for an easy pass when the leader's tires go off, or the car falls off the track. If you're under pressure of attack from behind, it may be best, as above, to attack sooner rather than later

Anticipation Used in Passing Situations

One of the most powerful uses of anticipation comes in passing situations. The following illustrates an actual situation in which I found myself during an endurance race at Willow Springs International Raceway.

The first illustration shows the typical fast line through a series of turns where this incident occurred. What is not shown is that most of this section is uphill. The steepness of the climb increases at the apex of Turn 3, levels off between the two apexes of Turn 4, and quickly descends from the second apex of Turn 4 towards Turn 5A.

The event was for SCCA Improved Touring and Showroom Stock cars. The cars involved were in a variety of classes, with varying levels of performance. I was driving an ITA Mazda RX-4, which is designated as car 1 in the diagrams. Car 2 was an ITC Datsun, car 3, an SSB, car 4, an ITS 240Z, car 5, an ITB VW, and car 6, an ITB.

The following commentary is my thought process as the situation unfolded:

At the mid-point of Turn 2, I saw a group of cars approaching the exit. They were all traveling at different speeds, and I anticipated a possible traffic problem, and a passing opportunity under braking for Turn 3, which is an excellent place to pass. (#1)

As I approached Turn 3, I decided to attempt a pass of car 5, possibly car 4, but when cars 3 and 5 pulled to the left to pass, this became impossible. (#2)

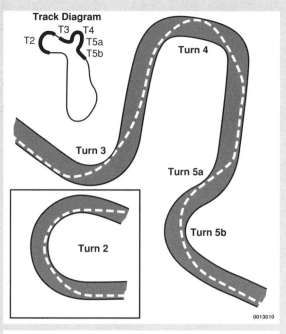

0013010

1 Turn 2

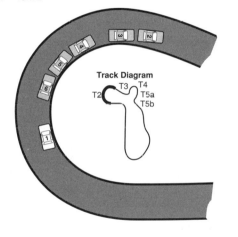

0013011

2 Turn 3 Entrance

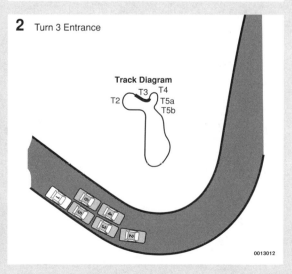

0013012

Since the lead car (car 2) was going slowly, and stayed to the left exiting Turn 3, and the other four cars were two abreast up the hill, traffic slowed considerably, proceeding well below the limit. (#3) Two possible options presented themselves. The first was to stay in line, taking the normal early apex approach to the first apex at Turn 4. Then, at the exit, with a very late apex and early power application, I could pass one or two of the cars. This was virtually a sure bet. Less certain was option two.

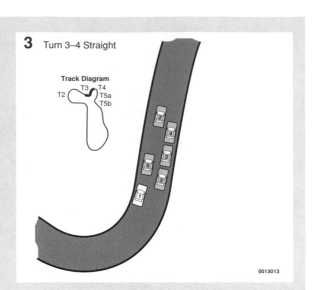

3 Turn 3–4 Straight

Track Diagram

If, as is common, all of the cars held relative position, and tried to stay as close to the fast line as possible, a hole would be open on the inside between the first and second apexes of Turn 4. (#4) Since this is not a normal passing area (passes are rare on this spot), few drivers would recognize the opportunity, even though speeds were less than 70% of normal, allowing a path that could not be held at higher speeds. This option would let me pass at least three cars, maybe four, and minimize the time lost, since the next good passing opportunity was on the back stretch, three turns later. And the speed lost at the exit of Turn 5, which leads onto the back stretch, would cost even more time. At this point, I chose to stay to the left at the exit of Turn 3, well off the normal line. (#4) This gave me additional time to watch the situation unfold, but also give me a choice between the two options.

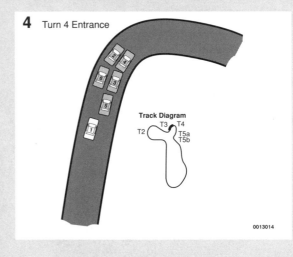

4 Turn 4 Entrance

Track Diagram

Four factors allowed me to anticipate the situation, and to make a decision. First, we were moving so slowly that I could literally drive anywhere on the race track, and even accelerate with no chance of losing traction. Second, my field of vision allowed me to see that the paths of the other five vehicles, even though they were in two rows, would carry them high, to the left just past the first apex of Turn 4, leaving a nice path along the inside. Third, the five cars were tightly grouped at this point, and no one, other than car 3, would attempt to pass. (#5)

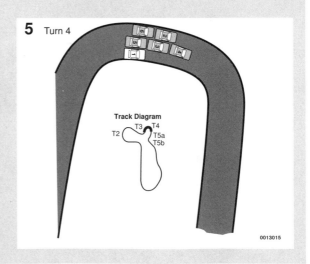

5 Turn 4

Track Diagram

Finally, I was able to anticipate that under full acceleration, I would be able to get next to car 3 *before* the second apex of Turn 4, and that its driver would have sufficient time to see where I was positioned. Additionally, car 4 would be clear ahead, and not impede my attempt. (#6) The worst case scenario would see car 3 turn into the side of my car, but since I was certain that I would be well within his field of vision before the apex, I felt this risk was minor.

Naturally, driving aggressively, I chose the second option. I successfully passed four cars between the first and second apexes of Turn 4, a distance of about 150 feet. (#6) And, since I was under full power, but below the limit of adhesion at the second apex of Turn 4, I held a tight line at the exit and passed car 4 under braking into Turn 5A, another area where passing is unusual. (#7)

At the time this incident occurred, I was racing for the class lead, so every tenth of a second was crucial. On this particular lap, I lost a half a second vs. a traffic-free lap. Had I joined the parade, I would have lost at least 3 seconds, and possibly more.

I was able to make this pass by anticipating the situation. Seeing potential problems unfold and having an open mind allowed me to see an opportunity that few drivers ever see. By anticipating other driver's options, and seeing their moves (more anticipation), the scenario unfolded exactly the way I anticipated. I was in a position, physically and mentally, to take advantage of the situation.

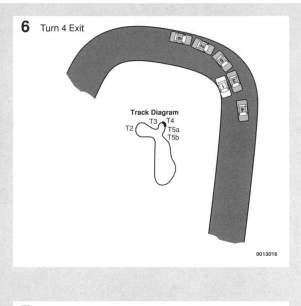

6 Turn 4 Exit

Track Diagram

0013016

7 Turn 4-5 Straight

Track Diagram

0013017

8 Turn 5

Track Diagram

0013018

This shows my line through this section of course. Compare it to the first illustration. At no time did I feel that the maneuver was risky, because I was well below the limit, as was everyone else. I could have easily driven off the inside of the track at the second apex to Turn 4 with no damage, and the driver of car 3, who was startled by my presence inside of him at the apex, easily changed directions to avoid me, with little loss of time for him. Anyway, I was clearly ahead of him at the apex, and left him no choice but to give room, or hit the side of my car. I never doubted the outcome, though I was very surprised that one of the other cars didn't exercise the same option before I had a chance. My thought at the time was "I don't believe they're letting me do this!" They did.

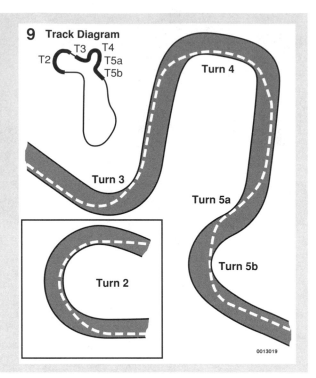

9 Track Diagram

Turn 4

Turn 3

Turn 5a

Turn 5b

Turn 2

0013019

DEALING WITH TRAFFIC

Race traffic is both potentially dangerous and a great challenge. We have studied attacks and defenses. Traffic situations are defined as those situations where you are passing or being passed, but not racing for position. Each scenario has specific parameters which allow for the minimal time loss and reduced risks.

Reading Traffic

On the surface, the ability to read traffic seems to be a sixth sense which some drivers are blessed with. I suppose there is some truth to that, but mostly, reading traffic takes work, like all other aspects of racing. Six skills are necessary to read traffic effectively.

ANTICIPATION. See the sidebar on *Anticipation and Passing Situations* in this chapter.

SPENDING ATTENTION ANALYZING OTHER DRIVERS' MOVES AND ACTIONS. You must be good enough as a fast driver to divert attention to race tactics and analysis. This and anticipation can be practiced every time you drive on the street by watching what other drivers do behind the wheel and "knowing" the outcome before it happens. Just pay attention to other drivers. And it makes highway driving much safer and more fun.

THE ABILITY TO "SEE" ALTERNATE VEHICLE PATHS AROUND TRAFFIC. Seeing alternate lines past traffic requires practice and experience. It is like playing chess and seeing several moves ahead.

AN OPEN MIND THAT CONSIDERS ALL OF THE RACING SURFACE "USABLE." The race track is there to use; use it all.

THE ABILITY TO DIFFERENTIATE BETWEEN A HIGH-RISK, LOW-PERCENTAGE PASS AND A LOW-RISK, HIGH-PERCENTAGE PASS. This does require experience, but mostly a clear concept of reality, patience, and discipline.

DESIRE AND A WILLINGNESS TO ASSERT FOR POSITION. You must want to get ahead and be willing to assert yourself to do it.

**Overtaking
Slower Traffic**

There are two primary goals when overtaking slower traffic: minimizing time loss, and reducing risk. The ideal situation occurs when the driver about to be overtaken points you by. The ideal situation does not always exist. In cases where the driver being overtaken does not signal, you must assume that the other driver has not seen you approaching from behind, nor have the blue flags been observed. You should assume that this driver will take a normal line, and will squeeze you off the race track at the entry or apex if you attempt to outbrake without pulling even. It is very important to assert position in this case. Other passes are less risky, and less likely to cost you time. Overall, passing slower traffic is easier than dicing for position if you anticipate and plan ahead.

There are four places where overtaking slower cars usually occurs:

- *Straights*. By far the easiest and the safest place
- *Braking zones*. A good spot if you assert position prior to turn-in
- *Mid-corner*. Slower cars can be passed in mid-corner, especially on long sweepers, but the danger is high unless the driver in the car being overtaken signals you by. If you are unnoticed by the other driver, an inside pass is safer than an outside pass. If two slower cars are dicing, it may be impossible to get around them. Creative communication is effective in these situations
- *Corner exits*. This is a very high-percentage overtaking location, especially if you have a horsepower advantage

There are four attributes needed by any driver to be proficient at overtaking slower traffic.

- *Anticipation*. The more adept you are at anticipating situations as they develop, the easier you will find this task
- *Judgement*. Closely related to anticipation is judgement. Being able to accurately judge the relationship between time, speed, and distance is crucial. While some drivers are blessed with natural ability to judge these, all drivers can improve with practice and experience
- *Patience*. In many instances, giving a little ground now will save more time later
- *Timing*. Like judgement, timing requires practice and experience

THE WINNING DRIVER

The fastest line in traffic allows minimum deviation from the *perfect* line.

When planning to pass slower traffic, plan in such a way as to minimize your movement from the best line, especially at the exit of slow and medium turns, and throughout fast turns. When being passed, give room where it hurts you least.

Tools: Visualization, good judgement, off-line knowledge.

Game Plan: Force the other driver to give room; hold the best possible line; slow in and fast out is crucial. Focus on early power application at the exit.

Priorities: Maintain exit speed; minimize tire scrub in fast turns.

Practice Exercises: Seat time in traffic.

MINIMIZING TIME LOSS. The other driver can minimize your time loss and make passing easy by signalling, but even that is not always very helpful. The most effective way to save time is to anticipate closing rates between you and the car you are overtaking. Patience and timing are key.

The best places to pass from a time standpoint are straights and under braking. If it is not possible to make the pass there, or in mid-corner, the exit will minimize time loss *if* the move is well-timed. Many drivers make a major mistake when attempting this. They will stay right on the tail of the car being overtaken through the corner, then power by on the straight.

To lose the least time, it is crucial to be on the power at the exit as early as possible, preferably as early as you would with no traffic ahead. You must alter your path for the exit and leave a gap ahead so that you can be on the power early, but not need to lift off the throttle to avoid a collision with the car being overtaken. If this move is well-timed, you will be on the power early, make the pass as you enter the straight, and carry nearly normal speeds down the straightaway.

Even if the driver being overtaken has not signaled to you, by taking a path which allows a pass to the inside, you can still pass to the outside at the exit if the driver ahead leaves room. Planning to pass on the outside eliminates your options, unless the driver ahead has signalled you by to the outside at the exit. Without a signal, you cannot be certain, so leave options open until the situation unfolds.

Fig. 11-30. Patient overtaking is usually more successful. Here the driver behind is either attempting to pass without a good set-up, or is faking a pass to rattle the lead driver.

Being Overtaken

The flip side of overtaking is being overtaken by faster cars. I have found being overtaken, without losing excessive time, to be much more difficult than overtaking. It is very easy to spend too much attention on the mirrors. The most important aspect of being overtaken is to make the job of being passed as easy as possible for the overtaking driver. To do that, you must signal, and don't slow down if you can possibly avoid it. Slowing beyond what is needed to change your line *slightly* will only throw off the overtaking driver's timing, costing both of you excessive time.

WATCHING THE MIRRORS. If you race a car which you know will be overtaken often, make sure that the mirrors are easy to use with good visibility. The best places to check the mirrors are those areas where you have the most "spare" attention. Here is a list to consider, in order of preference:

- Exiting a corner onto a straight
- On a straightaway
- Prior to braking for a corner
- As the throttle is picked up at the exit of a corner
- In the middle of a long sweeper
- While braking, before turn-in

The place that you should never check the mirrors is after you have committed to a corner after turn-in. This is a really stupid place for the overtaking driver to attempt a pass. But a word of caution: there are some really stupid drivers out there.

In an enduro, I was driving a slower car, and being passed by a line of four cars in a difficult portion of the track for overtaking. I was able to easily point the first and second cars by at the exit of a turn without having to reduce my speed, but did not point the third car by, since I needed to move into position for the next turn.

My plan was to give the third and fourth cars the inside of the next turn, allowing them the best possible exit onto the long straight following the corner. If I pointed them by to the outside, even though it was slightly earlier, they would have been off line, and would have lost speed all the way down the long straight.

Well, the third car in line decided to pass to the outside before the turn-in. He had no signal from me to do so, and drove into the passenger door of my car. This driver attempted to pass in a spot where it was difficult, and foolish, for me to check the mirrors. His action showed a complete lack of judgement, patience, anticipation, and timing. Damage was minor, and the incident cost me almost no time, but it cost him a position. After the race we had a brief discussion. Even though this driver has a reputation for such behavior, I doubt that he will exercise such a blatant lack of patience the next time he attempts to overtake me. The unfortunate aspect of this driver is that he is very fast, often leading races, but his lack of patience and discipline cause him to make foolish moves, often at the expense of a win on the track.

SIGNALING. A good passing signal is the first step in being overtaken effectively. There are three rules for effective signaling.

- You point the overtaking driver by to the side you want the overtaking driver to PASS, not to the side where you are going
- Make sure that the overtaking driver sees the signal. It is always a good idea to give a signal with movement so that the driver/drivers behind you can distinguish the signal from a roll cage crossmember or wing element, etc. If you want the following car to overtake to your right, for example, point to the right and move the entire arm vertically a few inches so that the signal is obvious

- Give the signal early enough so that the driver following has adequate time to respond. If the overtaking driver does not respond by the time you anticipated, check the mirrors and drive your line. Signal again when it is feasible for the other driver to overtake effectively *in your judgement*. Often the overtaking driver cannot make the pass when you thought it was possible. When you again think it is possible, signal new directions at the appropriate moment

MINIMIZING TIME LOSS. Even though you are being overtaken by a faster car, you are still likely to be vying for position in your class, so your goal is to lose as little time as possible when being overtaken. This is the same goal as the overtaking driver's. And the criteria are the same. Some places are better than others around the track; patience now can save precious hundredths later.

The Psychology of Passing

The psychological side of passing works like most areas of racing: confidence works wonders. If you believe you can make a pass, you have a much better chance. If you're not sure, the odds work against you.

The other half of the equation is the psyche job. Some drivers watch their mirrors too closely and are affected by pressure; others are not. One of the most common tools that can be used effectively is to apply constant pressure to the lead driver. This can be done with consistent pass attempts, either in the same place or in varying locations. The danger here is that by attacking, you can overheat tires and you become vulnerable to attacks. Applying pressure through consistent driving, always being in the exact same place on the track lap after lap, is possibly the best way to intimidate.

The most effective method of psyching is to make a clean pass quickly and easily while at the same time making it very difficult for others to pass you. By doing that, it becomes easier to make passes on all drivers later. That is how Dale Earnhardt became the "Intimidator." Again, confidence in your ability and commitment to making the move are your greatest assets.

Patience

It has been said often that patience is a virtue. Those words were meant for the race driver in a passing situation. Patience is a critical factor in several ways. A patient driver attempting to make a pass has several advantages:

- Is more open to developing situations
- Is in a better position to take advantage of mistakes by others
- Is more likely to force mistakes by other drivers
- Crashes less
- Is prone to focus attention on the most important priorities
- Manages tires more effectively
- Rarely is repassed
- Is often more effective at holding off pass attempts

The impatient driver most often uses up the tires quickly, misses opportunities, gets repassed easily, suffers from red mist (clouded judgement), hits the lead car while trying to pass, fades as the race progresses, and rarely wins.

Patience, like most virtues, requires commitment and practice. The effort is worthwhile.

Passing and Tires

In the scenario opening this article, one of the factors keeping the second-place driver behind was the state of the tires on that car. When you attempt a mad dog pass under braking, the front tires heat up. That means less traction, so the pass becomes less likely to succeed. Do this three or four corners in a row, and the tires get even hotter. The car starts to push, and as the race progresses, the situation gets worse.

To make a pass successfully requires tires that are optimum for the job. Keep the tires cool while waiting for an opportunity. Here is where it is best to set up for a good run off one corner, which requires cooler rear tires for peak traction, then use the front tires for outbraking into the next turn when they are at their optimum traction. This makes the pass more certain and more likely to stick.

If you abuse your tires, passes become more and more difficult. You soon find yourself in a defensive position, trying to hold off the cars behind. If you abuse your tires early in the race, you will be a sitting duck at the end of the race or long green run. It is also helpful to create a car set-up that allows for easier passing. And if you know you will need to run off line to make passes, get the car working for off-line situations, then practice driving on the most likely passing lines. This will give you a distinct advantage.

Anticipation and Judgement

As with overtaking, anticipation and judgement are paramount for being overtaken easily. But when being overtaken, timing and patience are less crucial.

RESTARTS

Rarely can a restart offer the opportunity to win a race, but restarts provide plenty of opportunities to lose races. Restarts are somewhat unusual in road racing, but happen often in oval racing.

RESTART PRIORITIES. Regardless of your position on the track, the first priority is to not lose ground to the other cars, either in front or behind. A second priority, also very important, is to attempt to gain distance and position on other cars.

RESTARTS AND THE RULES. It is important to know the rules concerning restarts. Can you pass as soon as the green flag waves? Can you move laterally, or must you stay in a single-file line? And more important than the written rules is the manner of enforcement. What will the starter let you actually do on restarts? Will the enforcement be different if you are leading, in the front half of the pack, or at the back? Asking these questions, even if the answer is uncertain, will allow you to create a general strategy concerning restarts. Then you have a better chance to respond to the tactical situations as they present themselves.

RESTARTS AND THE STARTER. Knowing the starter's techniques is paramount for making good restarts, regardless of your position in the field. Will the starter throw the green flag in Turn 3, Turn 4, or on the front straight? Can you accelerate before the flag waves? Will the starter throw the flag if the leader backs off trying to oscillate the field? Will the yellow come on if the leader gains a jump on the rest of the field? Study the starter to learn the technique employed. Then you have more data to create your tactical plan.

RESTARTS AND THE TRACK. The layout, and the condition of the track, can each influence your restart strategies. For example, if you are leading on a restart, do you want to accelerate early, causing a brake application into Turn 3, or do you want to accelerate later, so that no braking is needed into Turn 3? How are the track conditions? If the track is slippery, you may want to try a different approach than if the track has good bite.

RESTARTS AND YOUR CAR. As in the above considerations, your tactics will change based upon the status of your car. Are the brakes functioning at 100%? How's the handling? Does your car have an advantage on a particular piece of race track? If the handling is off, or the brakes are less than optimum, a later acceleration run into Turn 3 would be better for you, so that you do not have to brake into Turn 3, or drive at the limits of traction through Turns 3 and 4.

RESTARTS AND THE COMPETITION. It is always important to know the competition. What is the likely restart procedure for the drivers around you? Some drivers are passive on restarts; other are very aggressive. Some will attempt to pass before the green flag, others will lag behind, costing themselves, and you, time and distance on the race track. Knowing what the other drivers around you may be up to will assist you in developing a tactical plan that has the best chance of working to your advantage.

Restarting from the Lead

The best place for a restart is in the lead. The leader has a psychological advantage as well as a physical one on the track. If you find yourself in the lead on a restart, there are several things to consider in order to gain an advantage, or at least maintain position.

- Plan your restart at the optimum engine RPM as described in the start section of this chapter
- Begin to accelerate at the point on the track that works best for your set-up or car condition. If your car pushes going into a turn, don't accelerate going into a turn; wait for the exit, unless, of course, the green is already flying
- Have a clear idea of when the green will come out. Try to accelerate before the green is shown
- If you see the car behind drop back to make a slingshot pass, either accelerate as the other car drops back, or wait until the other car begins to accelerate. If you wait, the other car must back off to stay behind you. That is the optimum time to stand on it
- Find traction, especially on dirt. If you don't, the guy who does will pass you

CONTROLLING THE PACE. When in the lead, your big advantage is controlling the pace. Avoid being over-anxious. Set the pace to allow peak acceleration, and stand on it when you know the time is best for you, unless, of course, the green comes on before that point on the track.

Restarts Near the Front

It amazes me how often drivers of cars in the top four or five on a restart seem to be sleeping behind the wheel on restarts. Unless you plan to try a slingshot pass, stay close to the car in front, accelerate when that car accelerates, and keep an eye (or ear if you have a radio) out for the green flag or light.

Drive the path that offers you the best traction or tactical position. Remember that all the cars behind you are trying to get by, so defense should not be ignored. While it might be great to gain a spot, it is terrible to lose one on a restart.

Be sure to consider all of the options, listed above, that the leader may try to keep you out of first place on the restart.

GETTING A JUMP. Getting a jump on other cars is an aggressive tactic on restarts. To do so requires that you lag back slightly, time your acceleration just before the green (or just before the car in front begins to accelerate) and carry momentum past the car ahead. As with most aggressive moves, this one has inherent risks. You could jump the start, be forced to back off at an inopportune moment, or end up in a compromised position. Many factors must be considered when choosing this tactical attack.

Restarts from the Back

Restarts from the back of the pack often create great opportunities for passes. Know when the green comes on, or when the leader begins to accelerate. Plan which way to go before the restart, high or low. You must consider several factors, including traction, the probable path of cars in front, and the likely place you will be when the green flag falls.

LOOK FOR THE HOLE. When starting from the rear, keep an open mind, look for openings, and keep alert for other drivers missing the green flag. Other drivers' errors can create passing opportunities for you.

Be Willing to Pay the Piper

If you want to attempt to gain an advantage on restarts, you must understand the possible hazards, and accept them. If all goes wrong, and you cannot make the intended pass, or even if you get passed in the process, stay focused on your job. Wasting time beating up on yourself for getting aced will only make the situation worse. Maintain a positive attitude by accepting responsibility and dealing in reality, not focusing on the negative or wishing things had worked differently.

ASSESSING THE COMPETITION

Knowing the competition is important. It helps in the anticipation process if you have a solid idea concerning the actions, skill level, and awareness of another driver. And it does not matter if the situation is a dice for position, overtaking, or being overtaken.

Creating a "Book"

One way to integrate knowledge about other drivers, and your impressions of their behavior on the race track, is to create a notebook on the competition. How you format your notes is not important; keeping the notes is! The areas of importance include:

- Consistency
- Predictability
- Assertiveness
- Tendency to overdrive
- Tendency to be overly aggressive
- Co-operativeness in overtaking situations
- Ability to manage tires/car
- Patience
- Mental discipline
- Reaction in a racing situation
- Overall attitude
- Response to your actions

Dealing with the Intimidator

Many drivers earn reputations as intimidators on and off the race track. The reality of the intimidator is most often a driver who lacks true confidence in his own ability and compensates by showing aggressive behavior. If you happen to be an intimidator, sorry if you're offended, but if the shoe fits....

Some drivers have this reputation because they are very talented and take risks others are not likely to take. If you fall into that category, you are very fortunate indeed, since you have a built-in advantage. Dale Earnhardt and Ayrton Senna come to mind as members of this small group.

To deal with an intimidating driver requires one of two tactics. First, ignore the aggression and focus on driving your race, assured that the efforts of the intimidator are probably costing him time and giving you the upper hand. This method is by far preferred. Second, try turning the aggression around by giving the intimidator a dose of his own medicine. This usually works in the same way that standing up to the bully in grammar school eliminates the problem. This is clearly a last resort, but occasionally it is the only way to deal with the situation, and most effective off the race track.

Pit Stops

In many forms of racing, the pit stop is an integral part of the race. Chances are that you will never win a race because you made a great pit stop (this is from a driver's perspective, not your crew's), but you can sure lose them by blowing a pit stop. One factor is of utmost importance when making pit stops. Because pit stops are extremely dangerous for your crew as well as every crew on pit lane, it is absolutely crucial as a driver to mentally change focus from racing to making pit stops before you begin to slow down to come into the pits. Like any aspect of racing, making pit stops requires attention, focus, and a plan. Without a conscious shift of attention, it is very difficult to deal with the needs of slowing the car, watching for parked traffic and other cars pulling into and out of the pit spots, and hitting the exact marks required by rules and by the needs of the crew to service the car.

To make effective pit stops, you need a plan which should include the following elements.

Know the rules regarding pit stops. Infractions can cost a race due to time penalties or disqualification. Some possible infractions include fueling procedures, number of crew over the wall, pit lane speed violations, running over tires or air hoses, and many others.

Pit stop communications. Some of this was covered in the Communication Skills chapter. You should have a distinctive crew signal or sign board marking your pit spot, and it should be visible from as great a distance as possible. The minimum distance is double the length needed to decelerate the car from pit entry speed to a stop at the pits. You must be able to see where to stop in order to do so effectively. Over-shooting the pit spot can be disastrous to your chances. Additionally, one crew member only should be responsible to signal the driver out of the pits, and the signal should be very clear and consistent. Even with radio contact, hand signals are still the most clear. Words like "No" and "Go" are easily confused over a radio with all the noise in a pit stop.

The exact position of the car in a pit stop should be pre-determined and practiced every time a driver enters the pits during practice, even if entry speeds are reduced. And the pit marker board should also be used every time the pits are entered.

Like many aspects of racing, a little discipline and patience pay great dividends in the long run. Sacrificing some entry speed to assure a clean stop is almost always worth eliminating the risk of infractions or over-shooting the pit spot.

THE LAST LAP

Most often the last lap is a non-event from a tactical perspective. Other times it is the moment of truth, the last chance to take a shot at victory, or fend off an attack. In these cases, the entire race was, or should have been, planned to gain an advantage for the last lap.

Positioning

When planning for the last lap, position is everything. During the race, if it comes down to a shoot-out on the final lap, you should know your strong points and weak points, as well as those of your chief adversary. The goal is to take advantage of your strong points, and the other driver's weaknesses, while defending or countering your own weaknesses. We have already explored many of the attacks and defenses. The last lap is different only in the fact that it is your last opportunity. Where will you attack, or how will you defend position based on your best estimate of the other driver's likely attack?

Asserting for Position

If you are attacking for position, where is the spot that allows you the greatest advantage? If early in the lap, can you defend during the remainder of the lap?

If you are defending, where will the other driver attempt to overtake? What is your highest percentage defense?

In all cases, make your decision as early as possible, preferably several laps before the end of the race. Create a scenario that is most likely, but have one or more back-up plans should the first attempt fail. And when you attack or defend, assert for position strongly. Now is not the time to pull punches.

Sprint to the Finish Line

Since most start/finish lines are on straights, your last shot to attack, or last need to defend, will likely be on a straight. If you are attacking, exit speed from the last turn is everything. If you can carry momentum, it is crucial to time a pass so that you are ahead at the line. A little subtle practice on the laps leading the finish will give you clues about the best timing.

If you are attacked on the last straight to the finish, you have two important tactics. As with the attacker, exit speed is crucial as a defense. Equal or superior exit speed makes an attack very difficult. Second, force the other car to travel the greatest distance to make the pass. At the same time you should travel the shortest distance to the finish. After all, this is the last lap. Who cares if you get passed into Turn 1 after the checkered flag!

So often I have seen this scene. On a track where the last turn is in the opposite direction from the first turn, a driver must move across the straightaway to set up for Turn 1. Even when leading, most drivers will move over on the last lap as they have on every other lap. If the track is 60 feet wide, you just drove an extra 60 feet that was not necessary. You also allowed the following car the option to travel only 54 feet if he was drafting you, and less if not. At 120 mph, you have spent .3 seconds the other driver did not spend. And even if the other driver was drafting, but stopped lateral movement one car width to the inside of you, he saved .03 seconds. That's nearly half a car length. But if you stay to the exit side of the race track, the other driver must travel the extra distance, costing the other driver the precious time. If the other driver moves out of the draft to pass to the outside, move with the other car after a slight overlap is established. This will cause both cars to scrub speed, but will affect the passing driver more, possibly enough for the following driver to lose momentum from the draft.

When battling for the lead, or for position, and it looks like the fight will continue to the last lap, create a plan with options for the last lap. And do it early enough to test the plan subtly before taking your final shot.

Reading the Race Track

In a previous section, I explored the need to adapt to changing traction conditions during a race. The track, and the people around its perimeter, can give you valuable information. First, you must use it; second, you must understand its meaning.

The Caution Flag   The most important flag is the yellow flag. It says that a dangerous situation is about to confront you. Be prepared. If the yellow is waving, it means that you may need to stop to avoid the situation. In road racing, it also means that no passing is allowed unless you are *clearly* waved past by the other driver. In oval track racing, a yellow means to cease racing, either immediately, or at the start/finish line on this lap. (You should know which applies to you.) The oval situation is more clearly defined, and little interpretation is needed. In road racing, the message is less clear. How much to slow is open for interpretation. The fact that you cannot pass is not.

The first problem facing the driver is the level of danger. A waving yellow can mean anything from a car spinning off the race track, which is a minor hazard, to a major crash where the track is blocked. Clearly one situation requires a different degree of speed reduction than the other.

The second dilemma relates to what other drivers do in response. They cannot pass you, but if they decide to slow less than you in the area of the yellow flags, they will gain time, either pulling ahead more, or catching you from behind. Unfortunately, there is no good resolution to the problem, only common sense advice.

First, if the area ahead of the initial yellow is clearly visible to you, you will have a little time to evaluate the situation for yourself. Second, if the area ahead is blind, you must rely on the judgement of the corner workers and how you interpret their signals. This clearly falls into the area of risk management, and each individual must choose how to deal with this risk. The most important concept here is this: make the choice of action in this situation part of your plan. You will not have time to think about consequences vs. rewards as the situation occurs. Also, leave some flexibility in your plan to accommodate unexpected situations. It is foolish to leave this decision to chance.

Signaling

When you encounter a yellow flag, it is important to signal to following drivers that you are slowing. The same signal is used in this case as would be used anytime you are slowing below normal speeds on the race track. Raising a hand so that it is visible from behind is the standard method of signaling. This should always be done when slowing, but is crucial when encountering a potentially dangerous situation.

Reading Corner Personnel

If any corner workers, or race workers in general, happen to see this, here is my personal Thank You. The job undertaken by race workers is miserable, hard work often in extreme conditions. And the pay sucks. The skill, quality of work, and dedication of these people is just amazing. Without them, racing would be considerably more dangerous, assuming we could race at all.

Corner workers offer you considerable information you do not have access to otherwise. It comes in two forms. The flags are the most obvious and the most common by far. But you can also gain insight from the reactions of the workers, especially in a yellow flag situation. Facial expressions, running to the scene of a crash, animated hand gestures, etc., can all indicate an extreme situation where great caution is needed. Additionally, it is important to understand that the race workers on course are there to assist you by making passing easier and safer, by warning of danger or hazards, and by helping you when you are in serious trouble.

What the Flags Mean

If you do not watch for flags, they do you no good. It also makes you a dangerous driver. You must use some attention to check all of the corner worker flag stations on every lap. You simply cannot afford to miss important information.

There are eight flags, some shown only at start/finish, and some with different meanings for oval racing vs. road racing:

GREEN. Shown only at s/f, indicates that the race has started or is in progress; also indicates the moment when the bull ceases.

YELLOW. Shown anywhere; static indicates danger, waving indicates extreme danger with a possible need to stop on course to avoid a situation. No passing is allowed at anytime until the yellow flag is passed on a road course. A full course yellow indicates no passing at all. On ovals, some associations indicate no passing immediately, others indicate racing back to the s/f line is allowed.

YELLOW WITH RED STRIPES. Slippery conditions exist just past the signal; exercise caution. Slippery conditions can be sand, gravel, spilled fluids, rain, etc. Typically, this flag is used in road racing only, and is shown for only two consecutive laps. Just because the flag is removed does not mean that the slippery condition has been removed. The flag is shown to educate the drivers about the condition, not about the removal of the condition.

BLUE WITH YELLOW DIAGONAL STRIPE. The passing flag is shown anywhere. It's not really a passing flag. It is shown as a courtesy to drivers who are about to be overtaken by a faster car. Just because you are shown the flag does not require any action on your part. It is a good idea to check your mirrors, though.

BLACK. When shown at s/f or at a designated black flag station, this flag means "come into the pits for consultation with race officials; you're in deep trouble." The black flag with an orange ball, also called the meatball flag, is the mechanical black flag. You come into the pits to have your car checked, since something important is hanging off the back, or leaking all over the race track. When a black flag is displayed at other points on the track, it means that the race is being red-flagged for a serious reason. Slow immediately (remember to signal) and proceed slowly to the area of the s/f line. Do not enter the pit lane. You will be directed to stop and park at a designated spot along the edge of the s/f straight. This is a real bad flag to miss. It is dangerous to ignore, and the officials will be really angry, and rightfully so. You can lose your license over this one.

RED. The race is stopped; see above.

WHITE. In road racing, a white flag indicates that slow traffic is ahead on course. Most often this is an emergency vehicle or tow truck, but could also be a slow-moving race car limping back to the pits. In oval racing, shown only at s/f line, it indicates that the last lap has been started as you cross the line.

CHECKERED. The race is concluded.

Exiting the Race Track

When leaving the race track for the pits, you usually must reduce speed. Signal to following drivers your intentions to slow and enter the pits *before* you slow down. The raised hand signal is used for this.

Entering a Hot Track

When leaving the pit area to return to the track, stay to the inside (the same side the pit exit is on) all the way through the first turn, until you are up to speed. It is very dangerous to move across the race track so that you have your favorite line into the first turn. That line will look somewhat less appealing if you are speared by a car closing at 100 mph.

Off-course Excursions

If you take an off-course excursion due to mechanical problems, when you drive off course, move as far as possible from the race track to an area safe for you, the workers, and your car. If your trip to the boonies was unintentional agriculture racing, follow the instructions of the corner workers before attempting to re-enter the race track. Any time you go off course, for any reason, look for a corner worker and follow their instructions before you exit your car, unless of course you are burning. The workers have better visibility and a more complete picture of the situation. And they have been trained to respond to your needs effectively.

Corner Workers, One More Time

At the end of a race or practice session, I have always acknowledged the job done by the corner workers by waving to them on the cool down lap, as do many drivers. This small gesture is a simple sign of appreciation for enduring crummy working conditions and possibly dangerous situations. I truly appreciate what the workers do for our sport. I have a pet peeve concerning those drivers too arrogant and self-centered to participate in the traditional acknowledgment to the workers. It's something all drivers should do!

12 RACE STRATEGIES

A race strategy consists of a plan created in advance based on the best information available. While the situation is going to change as an event develops, having a strategy in advance helps you and the team focus on priorities, strengths, and weaknesses, allowing each to play a part in the overall picture.

A lack of strategic planning assures chaos and reduces the chance for a successful outcome for an event or season. For a given event, it is important to develop a team strategy in order to "stack the deck" in your favor. It is immaterial if the event is the Indy 500 or a local autocross; a strategy will help you to achieve the best possible results.

DEVELOPING RACE STRATEGIES

Before creating a strategy for an event, you should take a hard look at the reality of your situation. The following factors should be considered before creating your strategic objectives:

- Your skill level
- Your experience
- Crew skill level
- Crew experience
- Overall budget (which indicates both the performance potential of the race car, and the ability to provide all of the performance elements for the given event)

Where you may be positioned relative to each of these factors is neither good nor bad; it is simply the reality of your situation. For example, if you are in your first season of racing, with a three-year-old car, tires which are two races old, an engine 50 horsepower less than the fastest cars, an inexperienced crew, and a budget half the size of most teams, your strategy for an event will be very different than that of Penske Racing preparing for the Indy 500 with three drivers, nine cars, and a budget large enough to run a third-world nation. Your situation is not bad, while Penske's is not good, although it may "feel" that way. The situations are simply reality and must be taken into account to create an effective strategy for an event.

Parameters   Several physical parameters must also be considered when creating a race strategy. They include:

- Grid position
- Experience in starts

Fig. 12-1. Different types of racing call for different strategies. Darrell Waltrip leads at Phoenix, 1992.

0013021

- Experience and skill in traffic
- Weather
- Track conditions
- Competitors
- Event length
- Car set-up
- Car performance characteristics relative to event duration
- Driver's physical conditioning

Pit Stops Races requiring pit stops require special strategic consideration based on fuel mileage, tire wear, and caution flags. The goal is to create a strategy based on fuel needs. Included in the strategy is an allowance for caution periods. Refueling "windows" will allow for a strategy which can respond to the dynamic nature of a race as it develops. Included in this part of the overall plan are factors such as current position on the race track, pit space location, rules governing yellow flags, the number of cars on the lead lap, distance to cars ahead or behind in the race, points structure, and the need to score points for a season-long championship as opposed to finishing position in the race. By developing a strategy in advance which allows for each of these variables, you can implement a quick decision with a better chance for success.

Fig. 12-2. Pit stops play a key role in racing strategy. Ernie Irvin's and Geoff Bodine's teams go head-to-head at Atlanta, 1992.

0013022

Tire Wear When an event duration exceeds the wear capacity of the tires, part of the strategic planning must include tire wear considerations. As with pit stops, tire wear requires careful consideration in several areas. Tire wear "windows" can allow for tire changes during caution periods. Other considerations mirror those of pit stops for fuel. But the most important consideration is the "time" value of a tire change. How long does a pit stop take vs. the reduction in lap times by running on fresh rubber? This question requires an answer, or the risk of ineffective stops and lost time is likely.

Last Lap In many cases, creating a strategy based on the last lap of a race can mean the difference between a victory and a lesser result. This is especially true of races in classes where cars are equal in performance, especially in sprint races where no pit stops are needed. Several factors require consideration:

- Race track configuration; specifically, is it more important to defend for position in the last corner with cornering speed or with straight line speed?
- On the final lap is it better to lead, or be in a position to pass by drafting (or any other way)?
- Should the car be set up for maximum downforce, maximum straight line speed, or some compromise? (Remember that it is easier to defend position in a corner than on a straight, so straight line speed is usually more important than cornering speed, even if overall lap times are slower. If you can carry speed on the straights, you can usually pass a car with better cornering speed on the straights, and defend position in the corners.)
- Will building an early lead be more effective than saving the car and tires for the last portion of the event?

Changing Race Strategies Races never run according to plan. Regardless of the brilliance of your strategy, the situations of a race will unfold in a manner different than you anticipated. The reason is simple: you have no control over the track, the

Fig. 12-3. On dirt tracks, where available traction can change often throughout a race, you need to have the ability to modify your plan and race strategy.

0013023

weather, or your competitors. A race requires a strategy which responds to dynamic changes as the event unfolds. The most important element of a strategic plan is the ability to accommodate change. This open-minded approach allows for the widest range of possibilities, and creates opportunities for you that may be missed by others with less flexible strategies, or no strategy at all.

THE WINNING DRIVER

The fastest race driver is the one who turns the steering wheel the least, accelerates at the maximum the greatest percentage of a lap, and the one who spends most time at the limits of adhesion while staying on the race track.

Corollary: The fastest driver is the one expending the least energy inside the cockpit for a given lap.

Explanation: This is the point of driving fast in a race car, and everything applies to this.

13 PLANS FOR DIFFERENT TRACKS

RACING ON ASPHALT SHORT TRACKS

Priorities for Fast Laps

Like any situation, the most important priority for fast laps is corner exit speed. Getting on the power early, smoothly, and with no wheelspin is very important. Smooth throttle applications are the key.

The second priority is maintaining maximum cornering speed. On most tracks, in most types of cars, good cornering speed means fast laps. Lightweight, high-horsepower cars can get momentum back quickly, but cornering speed is still crucial. The bigger the turn radius and the higher the banking, the more important cornering speed becomes.

The third priority is getting into the corner. Hard braking is not nearly as important as getting into the corner at the fastest speed. The exception to this is when trying to make a pass under braking.

Fastest Lines

The fastest line around an oval is the path allowing the earliest throttle application, highest cornering speed, and straightest line into the turns under braking. The tighter the turns and the flatter the track, the more likely the entire width of the track will be used in the corners. As banking angle and turn radius increase, the exact line becomes less important. More than one groove will probably be fast through the turns, but you will still use all of the track width at the exits and entries to the turns.

Finding Traction

Cornering speed on an oval is affected by three factors: 1) the coefficient of friction between the tires and track surface, 2) the smoothness of the racing surface, and 3) the banking angle. Pay attention to the track surface. Rubber, fluids, dust, and heat can all reduce traction on all or part of the track. Keep your eyes open.

Bumps can cause the tire contact patches to bounce off the racing surface, reducing traction for a split second. You might be able to compensate with the setup (softer springs and shocks), but that may slow the car in other areas on the race track. The other alternative is to avoid the bumps as much as possible. Be open to trying alternate lines. Some compromise will be needed. You just have to find the best one for your car, set-up and driving style.

Banking angles play a big factor, and they are not always consistent. The fastest speeds will be found on the steepest angles, assuming that traction is equal, which is not always the case. It is helpful to know what the car will do on flatter areas of the track before you need to drive on them. You're probably going to run there to make passes.

Braking Techniques

On most tracks, you are braking and turning in at the same time, so some of the tire traction is used to turn. Too hard on the brakes can cause wheel lockup followed by a spin, or cause the car to slide (push or loose depending on brake balance).

Early brake applications, with less pedal pressure, will keep the car balanced, let you judge speed more accurately, keep the car from getting upset entering the turn, and allow earlier throttle applications. Be easy on the brakes to go fast. The most important thing you can do while braking is focus a lot of attention on speed and tire traction. Focus on hitting the best cornering speed as early as possible, ease off the brakes, and roll on the throttle. Apply the gas as if an egg were between your foot and the throttle pedal.

Visual Priorities

It is very important to keep your visual field well ahead of the car. Keep your eyes up, and look down the race track. When you exit a turn, look down the straight to the deceleration area. As you approach the turn, move your eyes as far through the turn as possible. Before picking up the throttle, move your eyes and visual field all the way through the turn to the exit

Fig. 13-1. Brake smoothly to enter the corner. As you get into the corner, use more steering and less braking since you need more traction for cornering. The entry rule of thumb is more steering equals less braking. Keep in mind that deceleration occurs even when you release the brakes, so ease off the brakes as you apply more steering lock. In most cases on asphalt, by mid-turn you will be at the lowest point on the track.

Fig. 13-2. After you pick up the throttle to balance the chassis, near or before mid-corner, you must begin to unwind steering as you apply more throttle. The more you unwind steering, the more traction is available for acceleration. Plan your exit path to allow earliest maximum acceleration. Remember, wheelspin is slow.

Fig. 13-3. As you exit a turn onto the straight, use the largest radius so that you can unwind steering as early as possible and accelerate more quickly.

0013026

Fig. 13-4. Mid-turn handling problems can get you into trouble. In the first photo, this driver has applied opposite lock to try to correct an oversteer slide. If he lifted abruptly, the car would whip back and point head-on towards the wall. A little opposite steering lock and rolling off the throttle will correct the problem and cost the least amount of time. In the second photo, the car is pushing. Here, straighten the steering and roll off the throttle slightly. Hard acceleration will carry the car to the wall.

0013027

0013028

and the next straight. Save some visual attention for the lights, the flagmen, and other peripheral factors. The sooner you can pick up a yellow flag/light, the sooner you can avoid a potential hazard.

Alternate Lines   You will need to have an alternate line, or several lines, to make passes. Often, a single groove exists from qualifying or heat races. Worn rubber lays just above the groove. Moving higher than the groove will cause the rubber chunks to collect on hot tires, reducing traction. It is possible to move the groove by moving slightly higher on the race track for a lap or two. After awhile, another groove will be drivable. But if you're leading, it is best for

Fig. 13-5. These photos show a variety of alternate lines. To use alternate lines, you need to practice them. You must also make sure that adequate traction is available in the upper groove. Tire rubber and dust can reduce traction. If you needed to use the higher groove during a race, move up about a tire width each lap to slowly clean the new groove of debris.

you to leave a single groove. Watch for others to move the groove. You need to know if it is there so you can use it too, or so you can defend against pass attempts.

Banking Angle   I have already talked about banking angle relative to cornering speed. Another important factor on banked tracks is car control. If you get loose in a turn, be very careful. An abrupt lift off the throttle will cause the tail of the car to slide down the banking and point the nose right at the wall. Over-correcting the steering can have the same effect.

If you get sideways, it is usually better to not correct the steering, but add left steering lock and let the car spin down the banking. This not always the best reaction, but it usually keeps the car off the wall, or at least reduces speed significantly before you contact the wall. There is no best answer here. Give some thought to what you feel is the best response, then practice that response using mental visualization so that you will react the way you want to when the situation occurs.

Changing Priorities for the Race

During a race, priorities will change. Where speed and lap times are the key in practice and qualifying, getting to the front and leading the last lap are the goals of the race. A car set-up and driving technique that allows for maneuverability and consistency are the most important priorities. Sheer speed for a few laps will not necessarily put you in victory circle.

Reading a Changing Race Track

Changes to the track condition are more subtle on asphalt than dirt. Oil, dust, and rubber on the track all change the traction. It is important to devote some visual attention to monitor the track surface, especially during the race. The best indication of changing conditions is from seat-of-the-pants feel. Overdriving is slow. Be as smooth as possible. It's easier to sense traction when you are smooth with the controls. Abrupt steering, braking, and throttle applications will cost traction and make optimum speed and acceleration more difficult to sense. A considerable amount of your attention should be devoted to sensing traction. Even more attention is needed to monitor traction as conditions change.

Success on an asphalt short track takes smooth driving, precise use of the controls, and an eye for subtle changes to track conditions. In traffic, being patient can pay big dividends. Racing on short tracks is challenging and demanding. It is a great place to learn driving skills and techniques for handling traction. You can learn skills on short tracks in a short period of time that you may never learn on any other type of race track.

Fig. 13-6. If you get too high into the junk out of the groove, all you can do is slow down and watch the world go by underneath.

0013034

Fig. 13-7. Position is everything. If you try to pass up high, you need to squeeze the lower car down at the exit so you gain an advantage. On the other hand, if you are the lower car, you want to push the higher car up as much as possible so you can unwind the steering at the exit. The goal is to gain the advantage at the exit by accelerating sooner and harder than the other car. In the first photo, the lower has a clear position advantage as the cars begin to exit the turn. In the second photo, the high car has enough overlap to force the lower car down at the exit.

Racing on Dirt Tracks

One of the most challenging aspects of racing is dirt tracks. The ever-changing surface conditions make winning on dirt the ultimate challenge for car control skills and traction judgement. Driving styles and priorities change constantly. The speed difference from a damp, tacky track compared to a dry, slick track is simply amazing. The skills you must learn to be successful on dirt apply to any type of racing, and those drivers with solid dirt racing experience have a distinct advantage in other forms of racing. And, racing on dirt ovals is great fun.

Priorities for Fast Laps

As with any other type of racing, the number one priority is getting off the turns with maximum acceleration. There is a major difference, however. When a dirt track is really tacky, sliding the car and inducing wheelspin off the corners helps acceleration. When sliding, the edges of the tires, especially the outside edges of the right side tires, create "side bite," which helps turn and slow the car. It also allows very early power applications.

Fig. 13-8. On a good, tacky track, you can enter hard and slow by sliding the car. When the track is fast, you usually have more than one fast groove. Note that the rear tire is spinning. This is driving the car forward while it slides sideways, keeping cornering momentum up.

0013037

This keeps momentum up and gets the car out of the turns and down the next straight faster.

Side bite works a lot like skis on snow. The edges of the tires dig into the tacky dirt surface the same way a ski's edge digs into the snow. The sideways attitude of the car works like the curved shape of the ski to steer the car. The edge of the tire provides the force to cause the slowing and change in direction.

When you pick up the throttle, the lateral grooves in the tire create a forward thrust by shearing the dirt surface. The more shear, the more forward drive, so wheelspin will drive the car forward, at least up to a point. Too much wheelspin is still not the ideal. How much is right is determined by the driver. This fact makes driving on dirt a serious art form.

Of course, when a dirt surface begins to dry, this all changes. The shear provided by dry dirt is virtually non-existent. On a dry track you must rely on the traction between the tire's rubber molecules and the racing surface. And on dry, slick track surfaces, the traction is small. You must adapt a style more like that used on asphalt with little traction. You must be very careful applying the throttle on a dry, slick track for optimum acceleration. And the drier the track becomes, the truer this is. Focusing attention on traction is a high priority.

Fastest Lines

The fastest way around a dirt oval depends completely on traction. Two factors contribute: surface condition and banking angle. On a good or bad track with uniform traction, two or three grooves may be nearly as fast. Finding the best line is the key. There are no set rules. The seat of your pants is an important element. In most cases, the fastest line will change as a race progresses. The driver who adapts the quickest has the best shot at winning.

Corner Segments

Just like on any other type of track, on dirt the most important corner segment is the exit. When the track is tacky, some wheelspin will accelerate the car faster. On a dry track, exit wheelspin should be slower, though some wheelspin is inevitable since it helps keep the slide angle off the corner.

The entry on dirt varies considerably depending upon the track condition. On a tacky track, sliding the car works to get into the corner; as the track dries, sliding into the turns is less effective. Experience is the most important.

Fig. 13-9. Wheelspin is inevitable on dry dirt. Here the car is in mid-turn, but the drift angle is perfect. The car is sliding through the corner, but already pointed down the front straight and accelerating.

On a tacky track, drift angle in the corner and keeping momentum up are important through the turns. When the track turns dry and slick, a straight line in under braking works well, followed by a mid-corner rotation of the car. The straighter the car is pointed at the exit, the faster the acceleration will be.

On dirt, the throttle is used as much as the steering to steer the car. This is especially true in racing situations where the radius of the turn must be tightened or increased to handle passing and traffic situations.

Fig. 13-10. When a dirt track is dry and slick, most slowing is done in a straight line, with the brakes. When speed is reduced, pick up the throttle and set a drift angle that will give the car a good, straight run off the turn. The top photo shows a near perfect angle while the other photo shows too much drift angle. In this case power was applied too hard.

Fig. 13-11. This car is pushing slightly at the exit. This is a slow way out of the turn. This can be driver-induced, by abrupt steering use, or caused by car set-up.

Fig. 13-12. Loose at the exit is also slow because the rear tires cannot drive the car down the track as hard. Again, the cause can be the driver on the gas too hard, or the car set-up.

Fig. 13-13. These photos show a near perfect corner-exit drift angle on a tacky dirt track. The straighter the front tires, the more the rear tires can drive the car forward instead of using bite to corner the car.

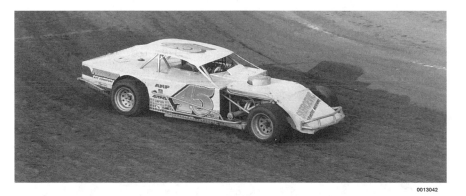

Braking Techniques

On a tacky track, use the brakes only to set the car into the corner. If the track is really sticky, you may not even touch the brakes. Tire side bite from the sideways slide of the car is enough to reduce speed.

On a drying track, use more brake to slow the car into the corner, though keep pedal applications light. Since the line is more straight into the corner, you have to rely on friction between the tire and the track surface to slow the car.

When the track is very dry, straight line braking with light pedal pressure is the fast technique. Locking a brake can cause a spin or a push into the fence. Brake bias adjustments are very important. You must develop a good feel for traction under braking. It is similar to driving in rain or ice. Traction is low. You must use what is there and not try to take more than possible. Overdriving a dry, slick track is easy, but costly.

Visual Priorities

As with any type of racing, keep the eyes the up and looking as far down the track as possible. On the straight, look into the braking zone. As you slow the car, shift visual attention to the mid-point of the turn and on through to the exit. Keep ahead of the car.

An additional visual priority is much more important on dirt. You must watch the track surface for changing conditions. This will help you find the best traction. You must also watch what other cars are doing. They may have found traction sooner than you, or they may lose traction running in a different groove. Let your competition educate you.

Alternate Lines

Unlike asphalt where alternate lines are primarily used in passing and traffic situations, alternate lines on dirt are also used to find more traction. The best way to do this is to try different grooves. Sometimes one groove is so much faster that you must run in that groove or lose ground. Other times, two or more grooves will be about as fast. If grooves are nearly equal, use them all. You will need the experience for passing. Even when two grooves are equally fast, passing can be very difficult. Mistakes by other drivers still give you the best opportunity to get by. Patience pays dividends. Do your job and wait for the other driver to blow it. Be in a position to take advantage of the situation.

Banking Angle

While always a consideration, changing banking angles in the turns of a dirt track are less important. This is more true when the track is dry and slick. If the low groove has less banking, even no banking, but more traction, that groove will be faster. Even if traction is only slightly better on the low side, the shorter distance traveled can make it the fast way around.

Basic Car Set-up

For side bite on a tacky track, more weight transfer to the outside tires is beneficial.

On dry, slick track, the set-up is more like an asphalt set-up, but with softer springs and shocks. Brake balance is crucial. If bias is too much to the rear, the car will be very loose and hard to get hooked up at the exit. If the bias is to the front, the car will push, making it difficult to rotate the car into the corner. A slight rear bias is most advantageous. It is really helpful to have cockpit-adjustable brake bias so that you can fine-tune the balance as conditions change.

Fig. 13-14. Over the cushion is dangerous and slow. This is survival time. The first photo shows a push, the second is loose. Throttle control and easy steering movements help you get back where the traction is.

0013045

0013046

Fig. 13-15. These shots show a good slide right up the cushion going into a turn. At this point, getting the front wheel straight helps drive the car off the corner. The second photo is the best drift angle for a good exit. It's really hard to be consistent on a track this dry.

0013047

0013048

Changing Priorities for the Race

You can count on track conditions changing on dirt. The question is how much. With experience, you can change your driving style to suit the conditions. If a big change occurs during a race, this is your only option. But if you know that the track will change during a race, you can try for a compromise set-up. The compromise that works most often is to set the car for late in the race, especially if the track is certain to go dry and slick. It is a little easier to adapt a dry, slick set-up to a tacky track than the other way around.

RACING ON ROAD COURSES

Nearly everything that applies to going fast on any track applies to road racing also. Getting off the corners fast is the most important criterion. Keep your eyes up, looking far ahead, and move your visual field ahead of the car. Shifting gears and driving in wet conditions are the major differences.

Fig. 13-16. In a series of turns, it is important to use a line that uses the entire track. The last turn in the series is the most important. Position your car for good acceleration at the exit. It helps to look as far down the track as possible. Winston Cup action at Watkins Glen.

0013049

Shifting Gears

While it is unlikely that superior shifting skills will win races, you can bank on losing races due to poor shifting. The basics are simple; the execution crucial for peak performance and transmission reliability.

UPSHIFTING. The upshifting process from first to second, second to third, and so on is the simplest. The important factors include quickness, precision, and smoothness. The most common mistake occurs when you attempt to force the shift too quickly. A light touch on the gear lever, with a smooth, precise, and quick movement, creates the most consistent and fastest shifts. Applying heavy pressure to the shift lever causes missed shifts, which can damage the transmission or over-rev the engine.

Using the clutch should also be straightforward. A quick, well-timed movement of the clutch pedal is all that is necessary.

TOE-HEEL DOWNSHIFTING. The one area most likely to cause problems for newcomers to road racing is downshifting. First, let's define the purpose of

Fig. 13-17. Shifting should be one of the easiest jobs of a race driver, but often is poorly executed. Holding gear lever gently, and making patient but quick shifts will save time both on the track and in the shop for maintenance.

0013050

downshifting: the reason to downshift is to be in the best gear for acceleration at the exit of the corner. Downshifting is not used to slow the car. That is the job of the brakes. Driving a race car quickly requires peak acceleration around as much of a track as possible. Peak acceleration requires that you be in the correct gear to begin acceleration in the exit zone of a corner. If you use the wrong gear, acceleration is slowed, or the engine may be over-revved. The best gear to use is the one that falls within the engine rpm range between peak torque and peak horsepower.

The problem with downshifting is that you often have to change gears and brake at the same time. And in order to make a smooth transition from one gear to the next, you must raise the engine revs to the correct rpm for the next lower gear. If you don't raise the revs, wheel lock-up can result, which is very undesirable when braking at or near the limits of tire traction.

Let's look at the simple process of downshifting without braking. Release the throttle and the car decelerates due to engine compression and drag. Depress the clutch pedal, move the gear lever from fourth to third, and release the clutch.

When the clutch pedal was depressed, the engine revs dropped toward idle speed. When the clutch was again released, the engine revs raised up to the correct speed for the new gear to match the road speed of the car. Either the clutch was slipped to accommodate this, or the transition was very abrupt, possibly even causing the drive wheel tires to chirp when the clutch pedal was released.

This situation can be averted if engine rpm is raised to the correct level to match road speed in the new gear *while the clutch is depressed*. A well-timed "blip" of the throttle while the clutch is in will raise rpm. If the clutch is released at the proper instant, engine rpm will match road speed and a very smooth downshift will result. This is the method you would use in a car with a synchromesh transmission.

If you drive a car without a synchro transmission, an additional step is required. Double clutching, as the name implies, requires the clutch be de-

Fig. 13-18. This photo shows the proper heel-toe position.

0013051

pressed and released twice. The first release occurs when you shift from one gear to neutral; the second release of the clutch occurs in the desired gear. The blip of the throttle takes place when the gear shift is in neutral and the clutch is released. This allows the output shaft of the transmission to accelerate to the same speed as the driveshaft, allowing a smooth transition to the next lower gear.

Many race cars have non-synchro gearboxes. You must use the double clutch method when shifting with the clutch, or learn to shift *without* the clutch. (See the **Clutchless Shifting** section below.) Many racing schools teach double clutching to save wear and tear on the gearbox, but the best way to shift is without the clutch, since it is faster and smoother.

Now let's add braking to the scenario. The problem of downshifting becomes much more complex; you must manipulate three pedals with, usually, two feet. Hence the toe-heel concept. Use the toe (or ball) of the right foot on the brake pedal, while blipping the throttle with the heel (or side) of the right foot.

The toe-heel downshift takes co-ordination, timing, and a soft touch to execute properly. It is an art, and considerable practice is needed to master the technique. Every time I drive a stick shift car, which is most of the time, I practice this technique. After nearly 30 years of experience, I could still improve.

Let's take a step-by-step look at the procedure for toe-heel downshifting in a car with a synchro transmission.

1. Right foot lifts from throttle and moves to the brake pedal. The toe or ball of the foot is used to apply pressure to the brake pedal

2. When the engine revs drop sufficiently to downshift to the next lowest gear without over-revving, the clutch pedal is depressed with the left foot

3. At the same time, the gear lever is moved to the next gear down

4. As the gear lever is moved, the heel, or side, of the right foot rolls onto the throttle pedal to lightly depress it, to raise the revs up to the correct level to match the road speed for the lower gear

Fig. 13-19. Heel-toe downshifting takes careful coordination of throttle, brake, clutch, and gearshift.

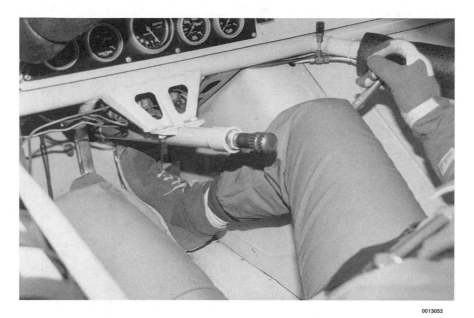

0013052

5. When the revs reach their peak, and as the revs begin to drop, the clutch pedal is released with the left foot. If the timing was accurate, the transition to the next lower gear is smooth

6. During this entire process, brake pedal pressure remains nearly constant, except for minor modulation to maintain maximum deceleration without wheel lock-up

7. If needed, the process is repeated for additional gear changes

8. At the appropriate time, the brake pedal is released, and the ball of the right foot is moved back to the throttle pedal

If you drive a non-synchro car, the procedure is the same, but with double clutching added to each clutch step. In other words, instead of shifting from a higher gear to a lower gear, an extra step is added by shifting into neutral first, then the lower gear. Or, learn to shift without the clutch.

IMPORTANT TIPS FOR TOE-HEEL DOWNSHIFTING. Practice the process without braking. Get the timing and throttle pressure dialed-in before trying during limit braking.

It is much better to make shifts farther into the braking zone, when engine revs will be lower. It is both smoother and quicker, and over-revving is less likely.

It is much better to release the clutch pedal as the revs are dropping instead of climbing. It is like serving a tennis ball. It is easier to hit when it stops at the top of the toss than when moving. It is also easier to hit on the way down vs. on the way up.

Timing is easier and shifts smoother if the heel of the left foot is off the floor during the process.

If timing problems are difficult to overcome, practice while the car is stationary, but with the engine running.

The most common cause of difficulties is leaving the heel of the right foot on the floor while attempting to shift, brake, and blip the throttle.

If you have problems positioning the right foot to use both pedals, the height of one pedal may be mismatched, requiring modification. The dis-

Fig. 13-20. The marked area shows the braking zone and areas where a downshift could be made. Shifts later in area are better, since engine revs are lower.

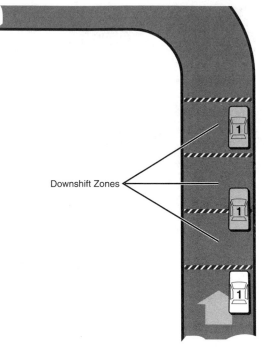

Downshift Zones

0013053

Fig. 13-21. It is more difficult to make a smooth heel-toe downshift when you rest the heel of your right foot on the floor.

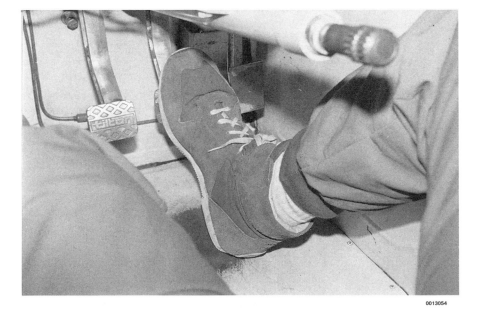

0013054

tance between the brake and throttle pedals may also be too great. The ideal separation is as close as possible without hitting both the brake and throttle at the same time when you are trying to brake or use the throttle only. The optimum separation is different for each individual driver.

CLUTCHLESS SHIFTING. Many modern race cars feature transmissions using straight cut gears and dog rings. This type of transmission is designed to shift without the use of a clutch. The clutch is used only to exit the pit lane. To upshift, light pressure is applied to the gear lever in the direction of the next gear. When the throttle is released, the shifter lever will move, sliding into the next higher gear when engine revs drop the required amount. Upshifts are usually very quick and smooth with this type of transmission.

Downshifts use the same technique, but with the addition of a throttle blip while the transmission is in neutral to raise the revs to match the road speed of the vehicle for the next *lower* gear. Light pressure will move the gear lever to neutral, and a blip of the throttle will increase engine revs. Light pressure towards the next lower gear will let the gear engage as rpm drops to the exact level for the new gear ratio.

The advantage of clutchless shifting is reduced shifting time and, while downshifting, two feet have only two pedals to manipulate. The left foot is free to brake. This allows more precise braking and reduced foot transition time.

Coping with Changing Track Conditions

One of the most difficult jobs for you is adapting to changing track conditions. The important factors for you are traction sampling and monitoring vehicle speed in order to stay at or near the limits of traction. Additionally, in many instances, finding more traction is a major priority.

SLIPPERY CONDITIONS, DRY TRACK. The most common change to track conditions is reduced traction caused by oil, gravel, sand, and water. The key to minimizing the effect of slippery conditions is to recognize their presence. As part of your overall plan, expect a slippery condition at some point in an event, and have a response prepared. Watch for corner workers and their flag signals, cars smoking, minor fluid leaks likely to become major, dust clouds, or any unusual response or condition.

If you spot a potential slippery area, it is wise to reduce speed since you have not had the opportunity to sample the available traction. Once you have sampled traction, and know the exact location of the condition, you can alter your plan to compensate. Less speed and/or alternate lines where more traction is present are the common methods to cope with the changes. Keep monitoring the condition. It is likely to improve with time. Also, watch out for other drivers who were less aware than you. They may be parked in the middle of the track wondering what happened.

SLIPPERY CONDITIONS, WET TRACK. In the rain, or on a rain-soaked track, the slippery conditions are usually more consistent. Driving in the rain, or in any low-traction situation, requires special skills. In reality, driving on a slippery track is no different than a dry or high-traction track surface. Exactly the same principles apply and you must categorize and plan the same priorities. What will change on a slippery track is the traction, and less traction means that you spend more time at the limits of adhesion. The horsepower/traction ratio increases dramatically. And the actual traction from place to place on the track, or from lap to lap, can vary considerably. Traction sampling takes on greater importance.

DRIVING STYLE. With traction reduced, you must reduce speed into and through corners; braking efficiency is reduced, vehicle responsiveness is reduced; wheelspin exiting corners is more likely; data inputs to the driver are more subtle. All of this affects vehicle path around the track. In areas of the track where traction is crucial, i.e., corners, braking zones, and acceleration zones, search the entire racing surface for areas offering greater levels of traction.

Even if a new path is far from ideal, the increase in traction may be more important. Nine times out of ten, areas of better traction will allow quicker lap times than the so-called "perfect lines." Trying alternative paths and evaluating their effectiveness can offer huge advantages. Experiment, sample, and change as needed.

Since vehicle responsiveness will change as traction reduces, it becomes even more important to make your steering, brake, and throttle applications as smooth and precise as possible.

VISIBILITY IN THE RAIN. As if the slippery conditions weren't enough, rain will hamper visibility. Spray from other cars, rain itself, and fog on helmet visor all contribute to impaired visibility. Most drivers hate the rain, not due to reduced traction, but because of poor visibility. There is little advice for improving visibility in the rain, but a few points can help:

- Use an anti-fog compound on helmet visors
- Use distinctive Visual Reference Points where possible
- Keep your visual field moving
- Relax by breathing deeply
- Be certain to have windshield wipers ready (on closed cars) if rain is likely
- Trust your own judgement in the rain

It is very easy in adverse conditions to second-guess your own ability, and follow others. A friend was racing a GTP Lights car at Sebring in 1991. His stint was at night in a torrential downpour—not exactly prime visibility time. Being an airport circuit, Sebring lacks distinctive features in many spots. The fast 180° turn leading onto the pit straight is one such area. A large portion of concrete runway continues on from the entry of the turn, with only small course markers delineating the edges of the race track.

This driver was being lapped by a GTP car entering the turn. The lapping car kept going straight at a point where the Lights driver was certain the turn-in point should be. For a moment, the Lights driver was tempted to follow the faster car. At the last instant, the Lights driver chose to follow his own course. As he turned into the 180, he saw the headlights of the GTP car, then the tail lights, then the headlights again. The GTP driver spun well off the racing surface; the Lights driver made the corner with no problem.

Had the Lights driver decided to follow the GTP car, his race would probably have ended there. Trusting his own judgement paid off, as it usually does. Second-guessing yourself is nothing more than a guess. Your initial judgement is usually based on better data. The same principles apply in any situation where vision is impaired.

CAR SET-UP. With advanced warning, you can alter car set-up to minimize the effects of slippery conditions. The key to wet weather set-ups is traction. Less traction means less cornering force, less braking, and less acceleration. All of these factors reduce *weight transfer*, so car set-up should be changed to accommodate this. The following will help in the wet:

- Soften springs and antiroll bars. Bars are often disconnected. Less traction means less roll
- Set wings and spoilers for maximum downforce. In the rain, drag is very high anyway, and traction at a premium
- Use rain tires

- Soften shock settings. The car does not need to be as responsive, so softer shocks help
- Use less front brake bias. Less weight transfers forward under braking, so the rears can do more work
- If you can, establish wet settings on a wet test day. It's a giant pain, but pays great dividends

Qualifying in an Open Session

Many of the criteria are similar to single car qualifying. The major differences give you additional time to find the groove, but force you to deal with traffic, which can play a major role in qualifying in this circumstance. This alone makes this more difficult than single car qualifying. Traffic takes a large portion of attention, and I need most of my attention to turn a really quick lap time. The level of frustration is also very high when a slower car interferes with you. But there are ways to minimize traffic effects. The key is to anticipate traffic patterns, and leave the pits when a break occurs, taking one full lap to heat the tires, then two or three flyers.

DEALING WITH SLOWER DRIVERS. The worst situation during qualifying is when a slow driver blocks the fast line, and is unaware of it. If you are slowing before or after qualifying laps, or not up to speed for any other reason, it is simply courteous to watch your mirrors and make the job of overtaking as easy as possible for drivers on their qualifying laps.

When you are blocked on a qualifying attempt, what can you do? Two options exist. The first is to take additional risks making a difficult pass or passes. The second is to back off, exercise patience, and try again.

This situations calls for risk management. What is at stake and what risks are you willing to take? If you have a shot at the pole, and the track layout makes passing difficult, the risk level would be viewed differently than if you were shooting for 20th on the grid. It is important to make that decision prior to encountering the situation on the track. The decision requires more thought than the few milliseconds you will have during a qualifying lap.

Part of the decision making process should include an honest assessment of your abilities to anticipate and pass slower traffic. If you have shown good skills in this area, and are comfortable with the instantaneous decision making process, your risk level will be lower than the driver who is less experienced or less skilled in lapping slower cars.

Additionally, the driver of the slower car is a factor, as is the type of car. Sedans are easier to see, especially for the driver being overtaken. Enclosed GTP sports cars have poor rearward visibility, making the overtaking driver's task more difficult and risky.

If you decide to take the increased risks of passing slower traffic during qualifying runs, rehearse and visualize possible situations, and mentally take what you believe to be the appropriate action. This will increase your chances of effecting the pass safely, and reduce the time needed to make the pass.

There will be times when you must abort a hot lap, due to a slower driver blocking, a mechanical problem, or an improper set-up. When full attention is being used to run a quick lap, it can be very difficult to shift gears back to a lower speed mode, where watching the mirrors and dealing with other drivers on their fast laps requires extra attention. It is helpful to have a plan of action that allows for this change in pace. This will keep you from fouling the fast lap of another driver, and will help you to stay focused on your current job. And when you are ready to go back onto the track, it will be easier to get into the groove when your plan allows you to shift gears mentally.

Standing Starts

The unusual situation of the standing start requires a different focus for success. Regardless of position on the grid, your first priority is to launch the car at the maximum rate of acceleration. To do this requires knowledge of the engine characteristics and the way a tire makes peak traction. Autocrossing and drag racing are both excellent training grounds for the standing start. If you are unable to participate in these types of events in the car you are racing, you should still practice several starts prior to a race. Additionally, if you will be making pit stops, especially without imposed pit lane speed limits, the practice for a standing start is more important.

Fig. 13-22. This autocrosser executes the perfect start launch. Note the slight haze from the left rear tire. Perfect!

0013055

The key to a good standing start is to rev the engine to just over peak torque before releasing the clutch. Release the clutch quickly, but smoothly. Too quickly without enough power application and the engine will bog, or even stall. Release too slowly, and the clutch can burn up rapidly. Talk to someone who races the same type of car concerning the best way to release the clutch for a standing start.

The next priority is wheelspin. Peak acceleration requires some wheelspin. Too much or too little will cause a loss of traction. There is only one ideal amount of tire spin. This is technically called "percent slip." Percent slip refers to the amount of slippage of the tire compared to the distance traveled by the tire.

For example, if a tire has a circumference of six feet, the distance traveled by that tire in one revolution at zero percent slip is six feet. At 50 percent slip, the same tire will travel only three feet in a single revolution. Most race tires develop peak traction for acceleration at between 5 percent and 10 percent slip. How can you tell? It's mostly seat-of-the-pants feel. No tire spin is very obvious, as is excessive spin. Within that range, it really is up to your ability to sense acceleration.

Once all the cars are under way from a standing start, the same criteria apply as for a rolling start. But up to that point, a standing start is very chaotic. You want to avoid collisions, so look for stalled cars, poor starts, or other drivers jockeying for position.

Finally, you want to improve your position if possible, so look for holes and opportunities. Be careful, however, since another driver may be seeking the same piece of real estate.

RACING ON SPEEDWAYS

Priorities for Fast Laps

For fast laps on a speedway, the priorities are different than on a short track. As speeds increase, drag, aerodynamic and otherwise, increases, making the rate of acceleration much lower. The higher the speed, the lower the rate of acceleration. Momentum becomes very important. This is especially true on a high bank track or with a car with high downforce.

Lost speed is difficult to regain. In a stock car at tracks like Daytona or Talledega where restrictor plate engines are mandated, it can take a full lap to regain lost speed due to lifting off the gas or adding steering lock to avoid another car. Time loss can be dramatic.

The key here is to minimize time spent off the gas and to minimize steering outputs. More than ever, turning the steering wheel is like putting on the brakes. The driver who turns the steering the least will be the fastest, given that all else is equal. Maintaining momentum and reducing tire scrub are everything in turns where speed reductions are not necessary.

On a flatter track where speed reduction is required to negotiate the corner, reduce speed no more than absolutely needed, get on full power as

Fig. 13-23. Speedways offer some of the closest racing in motorsports. Create your plan, look ahead as far as possible, and drive smoothly. If you turn the steering more than necessary, you will scrub off speed and overheat the tires. Brake delicately. On the other hand, throttle applications are not much of a problem since wheelspin while exiting turns is not likely. Several grooves allow good speed to be carried into a turn, especially when the track is only slightly banked.

0013056

Fig. 13-24. If you get too far out of the groove on the start, you can get into trouble, losing traction in the marbles. Plan ahead to where you want to be, going into Turn 1.

0013057

quickly as possible, and unwind the steering at corner exits. This is the fast way to drive. When speed reductions are needed, use as much of the track as possible to drive through the turns on the largest radius possible. This allows more speed to be carried through the turn and also reduces tire scrub through the corners and at the all-important corner exit.

Fastest Lines

On a high-bank track, line is not very important since the radius of curvature between the low groove and the high groove is very small. On flatter tracks where braking is required to make the corner, using all of the track is important. The fast line around a turn is the largest radius turn. Where corner exit acceleration is possible, a line allowing the earliest throttle application is fastest. Where the corner is flat out, the largest radius is fastest since the largest radius turn requires the least steering wheel movement and minimizes tire scrub.

Corner Segments

In flat-out situations where full throttle is used, it does not matter what the segment is. Minimize tire scrub. Where speed is reduced, the segment priorities are the same as for any other corner.

Fig. 13-25. On most speedways, passing low is the easiest pass. If your car is working, you can make high passes, but be aware of what the other driver is doing. If he doesn't see you to the outside, he could force you into the wall.

0013058

Fig. 13-26. The start on a speedway can be dangerous. The best place to be is at the front. It is important to have several escape routes planned if you are deep in the pack.

0013059

Fig. 13-27. Speedways have wide, sweeping turns. When you need to brake to negotiate a corner, it is usually pretty easy to pass under braking going into the corner. On superspeedways, where you run flat out, passing is much easier coming off the turns or on the straights by drafting.

0013060

Finding Traction

Traction is rarely a problem on a speedway due to wheelspin at the corner exit. Finding cornering traction requires the same priorities as any other type of racing. Sense the grip and watch the track surface for changing conditions. Watch for spilled fluids.

Braking Techniques

Abrupt applications of the brake pedal can cause lockup just as easily on a speedway as any other track, but the stakes are much higher. A smooth application *and* release of the brake pedal is important. Lock the brakes at speed on a speedway and you'll be in the fence *now*.

Visual Priorities

At speedway speeds, you must keep the visual far down the race track. At 200 mph, it can take a quarter of a mile to stop. Keep looking as far down the track as possible.

On high-bank tracks, it can be difficult to look down the track in an enclosed car. On the banking, you look more out the top of the windshield than to the side. Spotters in radio communications are valuable in these circumstances, but you must still keep your eyes up and your field of vision broad and distant.

Alternate Lines

Alternate lines are about the same on a banked track. If you want to run the high groove on a high-bank track, you must watch for rubber chunks in the higher groove, but the steep banking angle keeps the track cleaner. Be-

Fig. 13-28. When you get into a group of cars on a speedway, watch out for cars running really high. If they get into the marbles, they could be headed for a spin or trip into the wall. Be ready.

0013061

Fig. 13-29. Working underneath a car ahead can take several laps. The inside car will scrub the tires more since it is running on a tighter radius. This could overheat the tires. Conversely, it's usually easier to pass slower traffic to the high side. This allows you to carry more speed and not scrub the tires as much.

0013062

fore you venture out of the groove on any type of track, make sure it is somewhat clean; adjust speed for reduced traction.

Banking Angle

More banking angle means more speed, but there is a downside. When a car gets loose on banking (rear tires lose traction, causing a slide), the natural reaction is to countersteer by applying opposite steering lock to overcome the slide. This has a serious consequence, not just on speedways, but on all high banking tracks.

When you countersteer on banking, the front tires are now pointing at the wall. The change in steering angle will cause the rear tires to move *down* the banking. As the rear tires lose traction in the opposite direction, the car steers more towards the wall. Often the car will hit the wall nearly head-on when this occurs.

The higher the cornering speeds, the faster this all occurs and the more difficult it becomes to recover. At tracks like Daytona, it is very difficult if not impossible to "save it" once this happens. To correct a slide caused by a loose condition on a banked track, *do not* steer into the slide, but *roll off the gas gently* to reduce speed. An abrupt lift of the throttle will cause a spin. It is also preferable to let the car spin down the banking rather than to attempt a steering correction. The spin to the inside gives you a chance to avoid the wall, or to scrub off some speed before impact.

Since an abrupt lift off the throttle and countersteering are both natural reactions, you will have to work at developing your reaction to this situation. Skid pad practice is helpful, but the most effective method is mental rehearsal or visualization, which is discussed elsewhere in this book.

Basic Car Set-up The biggest difference in set-up between a short track, or low-speed cornering situation, and a speedway is how handling balance is achieved. The effects of aerodynamic downforce play a much larger role in establishing handling balance as speeds increase. Wings, spoilers, chassis rake, and air dams are the big factors on a speedway.

14 CREATING YOUR PLAN

So far in this book, I have explored many ideas, theories, concepts, and techniques. My goal has been singular: to pose the questions and offer knowledge and insight which will allow you to develop your *own plan*. No one in the world is in as good a position as you to create a plan for your success in motorsports. Needless to say, your plan will likely include many elements. This chapter is intended to pull together those elements in a way that will be meaningful and simple.

Goals

Everyone has goals, spoken or unspoken, attainable or purely fantasy. I have found it helpful to look at goals in two distinct categories. The first of those is Internal Goals. An internal goal is one which we have complete control over. The second category is External Goals. An external goal is one over which we have less than complete control (usually little or no control) over the outcome. I believe that this distinction is very important. To better understand, here is an illustration.

Fig. 14-1. It is important to set lofty goals in racing, but your plan must have internal goals along the way which you reach effectively.

0013065

Mike, at an early age, decided he wanted to pursue a career as a writer, in such a way that he could earn a very comfortable income. Mike has always been interested in science fiction, and decided that being a science fiction writer would be the most rewarding path to follow.

Being a writer is a broad goal, since it encompasses many niches. It is also an internal goal, since Mike has complete control over becoming a writer. He can accomplish this by reading, taking classes, practicing the skills needed by a writer, gaining a broad range of knowledge, etc. All he must do to become a writer is do the work to become a writer.

The specialty of writing science fiction for pay is an external goal, since Mike does not have complete control over the outcome. He may find that his style is not desired by publishers; or that too many writers have flooded the science fiction market and no place is open for new science fiction writers. Mike's ability as a science fiction writer is not even a consideration.

If Mike had chosen a more specific goal, like writing science fiction for a specific publishing house, he would have even less control over this external goal. Maybe the acquisitions editor at this specific publisher dislikes the school Mike attended. Or the color of his hair. Or was in a bad mood when he read Mike's query letter.

Does this mean external goals are bad? Of course not! But external goals must be understood, and the reality of the real world situation accepted, or the results can have a devastating effect.

If Mike had his heart set on writing science fiction for a given publisher to the exclusion of all others, and was coldly rejected by that publisher, the effect would be pretty difficult to take. But if Mike saw that publisher only as his first choice among dozens of possibilities, the rejection, while not pleasant, would simply become part of the search for a science fiction publisher.

On the other hand, if Mike was open to being a writer, not just a science fiction writer, and his efforts to get science fiction published were fruitless, he would be open to pursuing many other avenues open to writers. In this way, he would be much more likely to achieve his internal goal of earning a living as a writer.

To become a paid writer requires that Mike create a plan which allows him to develop the skills and find employment, then make a commitment to undertake and complete the plan. But even then, Mike must face life's biggest paradox. To achieve the goal and not be totally consumed by reaching the goal, Mike must accept the fact that he may never reach his goal. Who knows? By the time Mike develops his writing skills, the world may be too busy watching TV or playing video games to ever read.

INTERNAL GOALS

In motorsports, a driver has the same control of internal goals as in any other pursuit. The physical, mental, and emotional skills needed to drive a race car are internal goals within the reach of anyone willing to make the commitment to develop them. Without the development of these skills, external goals are, in reality, only pipe dreams.

To reach the external goals of fame and fortune in motorsports requires the planning of specific internal goals and the commitment to reach them.

Fig. 14-2. There are many lower classes of racing that offer drivers opportunities to achieve success and gain experience on the road to the top.

0013064

Only by focusing attention on the internal goals, and setting aside the external goals, can one reach the elusive gold ring of success.

Driving Skills

The physical skills required to drive a race car must become internal goals. They are the most obvious ones needed to reach your external goals. Many of the necessary skills can be acquired away from the seat of a race car, though seat time is still an important factor.

The first step required in the process is to determine the external goal that you would like to shoot for. The second step is to take a hard look at reality. Several questions must be answered to lay the initial groundwork.

- Where are you right now in relation to the driving skills needed to reach your external goals?
- What skills need work?
- What funds are required to implement the development of the needed skills?
- How much time will be needed to develop the skills, both short-term on a daily basis, as well as long-term over a period of several years?
- How do you plan to set aside the time needed?
- How will the time and financial requirements impact other areas of your life like job, family, and relationships?
- Is reaching the external goal worth the price you must pay in time, money, and other sacrifices?
- Are you willing to make the commitment to pay the price, and how long will you do it before you follow other options?

Whether your aspirations are to race a street stock on the local short tracks, or to become the World Driving Champion in Formula One, the same questions should be asked, because they will be factors at all levels. Especially if you answered no to #7 above, reconsider your external goal. Possibly a less ambitious racing program will allow you to answer yes, since the commitment will require less time and money.

By undertaking this process, as difficult as it is, you will possess a firm grip on reality, and be in a position to move forward towards a goal that you know is manageable and achievable. Herein lies a very satisfying journey. Ignoring the process leads to frustration, anxiety, and little chance for success.

The most important factor is the clear understanding of your desires, and what is needed to reach your goals. Then you will know if the ride is worth the price of admission.

Mental Skills

In addition to the development of physical skills, time and energy should be spent on the development of mental skills. Like physical skills, mental skills development requires a plan of action and commitment to implement the plan.

Emotions

Emotions are signs telling us how we are doing, and what consequences we may face by doing something. Emotions are easily distorted in our quest to survive and thrive, especially as children. Emotions can be easily hidden or ignored, which leads to inappropriate responses.

It is difficult to achieve success in life when you ignore or hide emotions. It is even more difficult to become a top-notch race driver under these circumstances. Learning to recognize emotions, and take appropriate action based on a conscious choice, is a key element to success on and off the race track. The inability to "feel" feelings and make effective, reality-based decisions about them leads to the creation of unattainable external goals, with little attention being focused on the internal goals needed for success.

While it is relatively simple to pinpoint physical and mental skills that need development, it is much more elusive to recognize emotional dysfunction and choose to make changes. It takes great courage, much more so than strapping yourself into a race car. When necessary, seek the guidance of a mental health professional. Assuming that you can work through your own problems alone is usually a mistake.

Other Controllable Factors

Several other factors come under individual control. Physical conditioning, diet, and rest fit into this category.

One of the most important areas of individual control is the quality of the cars, preparation, and teams that you choose. Based on finances, you select a level of racing. At that level it is important to drive a car that is in good condition and well-prepared, even if you must run fewer events, or select a less expensive class. It is difficult to determine your own level of skill if you race second-rate equipment or poorly prepared cars. While the temptation is often irresistible to drive a faster car in a more prestigious class, it is usually a mistake to do so if the chance of running competitively is reduced. Patience and discipline are needed to make sound choices when confronted with difficult decisions such as this.

Additionally, selecting a team, whether to prepare your car or as a rental-ride driver, requires careful consideration. It is usually a mistake to select a team whose commitment and goals do not match your own. The potential for wasted time and excessive frustration is very high.

The key in situations requiring a major decision is to establish your own set of standards before contacting teams or purchasing a car. Then exercise the discipline needed to uphold your standards. And when evaluating a situation, trust your instincts to tell you if the decision is in your best interests. At some level you will know the answer if you are willing to "listen."

EXTERNAL GOALS

External goals can be long-term, like winning a World Championship someday, short-term, such as finding a sponsor for this season or winning a race next week, or even instantaneous, like making a pass in the next corner. While the situations are vastly different, the dynamics required to reach each of these goals are identical. You must establish internal goals, create a plan to implement those goals, and execute the plan. Let's look at a few examples of external goals and the dynamics involved.

Winning a Race

Since the point of automobile racing is winning, winning a given race is a worthwhile external goal. To accomplish this external goal requires that you establish and achieve the internal goals discussed above. But even if you reach each of your internal goals and you are in a position to win the race, because it is an external goal, outside factors may make reaching the goal of winning impossible. Failed components or other drivers' errors may intervene. Or possibly another driver/car combination was more up to the task on that given day.

Now, if your goal was to win this specific event, you will swallow a bitter pill, for looking ahead to the next race will become difficult. But if your goal was simply to win one race out of 10 this season, then you can still achieve the goal, especially if you look at the possible weaknesses in your plan and make adjustments.

Getting to the "Top"

Getting to the top, however you may define it, is an external goal very difficult to achieve because so many outside factors can play large roles. This is a very long-term goal requiring tremendous commitment. To achieve lofty goals like this, part of your plan must include reality checks on a continuing basis. These checks will tell you how well you are progressing towards your goal, will indicate possible changes to the plan, and most important, may let you know whether the goal is still one you can achieve and want to continue pursuing.

Finding Sponsor Funding

This requires playing the odds as well as the above characteristics. Playing the odds simply means that you stand a better chance of finding a sponsor (or ride) by contacting 100 possible resources, than by contacting one or two. If you find your approach ineffective, try altering the plan.

Fig. 14-3. You may have the goal of winning seven Winston Cup Championships like Dale Earnhardt, but that is an external goal. If your goal is to be mentally prepared for every race you enter, you have a better chance of reaching your lofty dream.

Making a Pass
Making a pass is an instantaneous, or at least very short-term, external goal. This is an external goal since the other driver may not cooperate. To achieve this goal requires a quiet evaluation of the reality of the situation, plus all of the skills developed by the establishment of your internal goals.

ESTABLISH YOUR PRIORITIES

Once you have established external goals based upon your desires and the reality of your personal situation, you can create internal goals. Internal goals take time, money, and commitment, and since each of these is most likely limited, it is important to establish priorities so you use available resources to best effect.

Establishing priorities is like planning a cross-country trip. You begin with a destination in mind, determine the mode of transit, lay out a route, and set out on the journey. The highest priorities are those which get you to your destination safely and on time. Naturally, each step must be reality-based. If you need to cross the country in two days, driving would not be a "real" mode of transportation.

By the same token, if your destination is to race at the Indy 500 this year, but you have never driven a race car, chances are slim that you will reach the destination on time because it is not based on reality. The first element of this reality is where you are right now. Where are you as a driver? Where are you with funding for a racing effort?

Priorities should be based on reality *and* on those parameters over which you, or the team, have control. A driver and team have control over car set-up, preparation, training, and creating strategies; they have no control over what the competition does, the weather, etc. Focusing on the areas within one's realm of control allows progress.

A second consideration for establishing priorities is time vs. need. Only so much time is available. Certain jobs are more important to complete than others, and they should be higher on the priority list. Considerable time can be spent on low-priority tasks which yield little or no benefit. Two examples happen so often that it shocks me at times.

I have often seen drivers on test days spend session after session driving around the track. They are not going quickly, and they never change the car set-up. When queried, they indicate they are practicing. When asked what they are practicing, the most common reply is "driving, of course." From my perspective, they are practicing making mistakes, and they prove that practice pays off, since they are very good at making mistakes.

The second example is a team phenomenon. Most race tracks offer less than clean, comfortable environments. Yet I constantly see teams pay large sums in testing fees and then use the time to prepare cars at the track on a test day. When you arrive at the track at 8:00 AM, but work on the car until 1:00 PM before going on the track, what's the point?

Establishing Priorities for an Event
When you approach an event, whether an autocross or a 24-hour endurance race, you must establish specific priorities, leading up to and during the event. To "wing it" is to ensure chaos; to create a plan is to give yourself the best shot at success. The priority list covers two general areas.

Fig. 14-4. For many racers, dirt track racing is the ultimate goal. To be successful at any level requires a plan. External goals like winning races or championships are important, but without internal goals which are under your total control, you will have a much more difficult time reaching the big goals.

The first is car preparation leading up to the event. This is a time-management exercise where the man-hours available are compared to the work required. If too few hours are available, the jobs must be prioritized to assure that the most important work gets accomplished.

The second list covers car set-up priorities, which are usually different from qualifying to the race. As we have explored elsewhere, many decisions must be made to establish effective priorities.

Mental Preparation

For the driver, most priority setting falls into three categories. The first is mental preparation for the event, which is covered in Chapter 3. Next is the creation of a strategic plan based upon many factors and usually created with the team manager or crew chief. Finally, you must create a tactical plan to address on-track situations. While specific tactical moves are difficult to plan in advance, it is important to plan reactions to specific situations in advance so that response is automatic. Often opportunities are lost because a driver did not have a planned response in a situation.

The "Fluid" Game Plan

As I have mentioned several times, it is important when creating a plan to allow for unexpected situations. Regardless of the situation, expecting the unexpected allows you to solve problems more quickly and to grab opportunities on the spot. The lack of a fluid game plan can paralyze you or the team, which can have disastrous results, even if it lasts only a few seconds.

CONCLUSION

As you come to the end of *Think to Win*, now is the time for you to create *Your Plan*! Success in motorsports is a long, difficult road. Everything presented within these pages is offered to help you create a plan and achieve success in this great sport. What has been presented here is simply my personal opinion or interpretation of the elements I believe to be important for success. Whether you agree or disagree is immaterial. What is important is that you understand the issues, problems, and skills required to be successful in auto racing, and then form your own ideas and opinions. It is from that base that you can create your own plan for success. Here, then, are some final ideas and thoughts.

Making the Commitment

A commitment is the bridge connecting a dream to reality. Without a commitment, dreams remain, but have no chance for becoming real. The more grandiose the dream, the larger the bridge that you must commit to building. But with adequate commitment, any dream, within the confines of reality, is achievable. The key is to understand what the commitment entails, and then make the commitment to pursue the dream. The plans for the bridge, the tools to build it, and the courage to do it will all present themselves once the commitment is truly made.

If you find the plans fuzzy, the tools out of reach, or the courage wavering, look to your commitment for the reason.

Going with the Flow

When creating any plan, allow for change. Often, new opportunities will present themselves. Be ready for any possibility.

Creating Your Own "Road Map"

Your plan to achieve success, whatever that may be, is like a road map. You have a destination, with many alternate routes and means of transportation. Planning your route requires making many decisions. Knowledge and understanding are the tools that will allow you to make the best decisions for yourself.

However you design your own road map, it should contain these elements.

- A destination, with an estimated time of arrival
- A mode of transport; this is the financial part of the plan
- A route. What path will you follow to reach your destination? What stops along the route will best serve your purpose?
- Luggage. What do you need to take along on your journey? This includes knowledge, skills, and all of the other elements we have explored within these pages
- Courage. The first step is the toughest. It takes courage to make that first step, and to face reality as the journey progresses

I have spent most of my adult life teaching about racing, both as a writer and instructor. But I have spent all of my life as a student. In the course of studying philosophy, I encountered a set of principles which I feel make the journey smoother and more enjoyable. You may find they offer you the same insight.

The Principles of Yoga

Silence, so that thoughts can enter.
Listening, so that we can learn.
Remembering, so that we can consider.
Understanding, so that it will have meaning.
Action.

When I first embarked upon my auto racing trek over 30 years ago, a sage old wizard offered this wisdom: "The satisfaction is in reaching the destination, but life's joy is found in the journey!" It has taken me a long time to realize how true that is. I have also found that taking myself too seriously leaves little room to experience the joy of the journey.

Enjoy Your Trip!

Index

ART CREDITS

Art Courtesy of David Allio
2-2

Art Courtesy of Audi of America
2-10

Art Courtesy of W. Barney
1-4, 4-5, 12-3, 13-8, 14-4

Art Courtesy of Robert Bentley, Inc.
3-6

Art Courtesy of Brad Bernstein
4-6, 4-15, 4-16, 4-22, 4-23, 4-24, 5-2, 5-3, 5-4, 5-5, 5-6, 5-7, 5-8, 5-9, 5-10, 5-11, 5-13, 5-14, 13-17, 13-18, 13-19, 13-21

Art Courtesy of Michael C. Brown
1-1

Art Courtesy of Bob Carpenter
3-1, 4-25, 8-1

Art Courtesy of Bob Eckhardt
page v

Art Courtesy of Christie Helm
2-3, 2-12, 11-12

Art Courtesy of Alan Huber
2-6, 2-8, 2-11, 2-13, 2-16, 4-1, 4-2, 4-4, 4-8, 4-9, 4-10, 4-12, 6-8, 7-2, 7-3, 7-4, 7-5, 7-6, 7-7, 7-10, 7-11, 9-4, 9-5, 9-6, 9-8, 9-10, 9-12, 9-13, 10-2, 11-3, 11-4, 11-5, 11-6, 11-7, 11-8, 11-9, 11-10, 11-11, 11-12, 11-13, 11-14, 11-15, 11-16, 11-17, 11-18, 11-19, 11-20, 11-21, 11-22, 11-23, 11-24, 11-25, 11-26, 11-27, 11-28, 11-29, 13-20

Art Courtesy of Kenny Kane
page vi

Art Courtesy of Tom MacLaren
14-2

Art Courtesy of Ron McQueeny
1-3

Art Courtesy of Dozier Mobley
13-16

Art Courtesy of Photos by Pereza
8-3

Art Courtesy of David Ryan
8-2, 12-1, 12-2, 14-2

Art Courtesy of Bob Ryder
page vii

Art Courtesy of Jeff Sandt
2-1, 2-7, 3-2, 3-7, 4-21

Art Courtesy of Sutton Photographic
1-2

Art Courtesy of Earl Yamagami
8-4

All other pictures are by the author

ACKNOWLEDGMENTS

Over a 30-year period, many people contribute to a career. Most notable are all of the students I have had an opportunity to work with over the years. Thanks to each and every one of you.

A special thank you to Dan Gurney, who took time to offer advice early in my career which forever altered my outlook on driving race cars effectively. Also a special thanks to Richard Boren, the founder of DRIVETECH, who gave me the opportunity to create the finest, most hard-core race training program in the country. His comments on this work are greatly appreciated.

I have worked with many instructors; each has taught me. Thanks to the following: Terry Hall, Wally Ward, Ric Paronelli, Jim Hawes, Danny McKeever, Bill Shubert, Craig Stanton, Shane Lewis, Terry Herman, Bill Follmer, Larry Pond, John Green. A special thanks to the instructors and crew involved with the creation of DRIVETECH: Rick Titus, Bob Eckhardt, Gerry Kane, Ron Esau, Kenny Hendrick, Mac DeMere, Christie Alexander, Greg Scheidecker, Norm Breedlove, Charles Wilson, Eddie Wirth, Rich Crites, John Pentelei-Molnar, Steve Anderson, Bobby Morse, Jeff Klein, Brett Mulford, Connie White, Bob Ryder and the rest of the hard-working DRIVETECH staff. Together, we created a helluva program.

Thanks to my trainer and friend, Dr. Jeff Spencer, for all his guidance and encouragement.

Ronn Langford of Master Drive teaches a remarkable class which helped to gel many of my own thoughts.

Rick Titus has been instrumental in my development as a writer and driver. He has also been a great friend. Thanks for everything. I would also like to thank the following for their help and support along the way: Bill Huth and the staff at Willow Springs International Raceway; Jeff Cheechov, Suspension Techniques; Bob Carpenter, Circle Track Magazine; Glen Grissom, Circle Track Magazine; Athene Karis, BF Goodrich Tires; Joe Ruggles, Rugglescales; Chris Willis, Racing Collectibles for the great model cars used in some of the photos; Brad Bernstein for his excellent photography.

Without good publisher support, a book like this would be rubble. Thanks to David Bull, John Kittredge, Michael Bentley, and the staff at Robert Bentley for an outstanding job and the courage to break new ground.

And thanks for the support, encouragement, and help from my wife, Christie.

ABOUT THE AUTHOR

Don Alexander has been involved in cars and racing in one way or another for over 30 years. His driving career began in 1960, with go-carts. After a brief stint in drag racing, Don moved to sports cars and road racing, driving in such diverse classes as production cars, Formula cars, GT cars, and Trans-Am. He has raced in several showroom stock categories including the Firestone Firehawk series, and has won endurance titles. In a parallel driving career, Don has worked as a test driver for major tire manufacturers, for suspension companies, and for magazines.

Don has been teaching race driving since 1970, when he started working for Bob Bondurant. He has operated his own high performance driving school, and was Chief Instructor for the Willow Springs International Racing School. He has worked independently as a consultant with many drivers and schools, most recently for the EVOC Training Center of the San Bernadino County Sheriff's Department.

As an author, Don has ten books and hundreds of magazine articles to his credit. His *Formula Car Technology* won Book Of The Year from the American Automobile Racing Writer's Broadcaster Association. He is currently Editor of *Circle Track* magazine.

NOTE

If you are a racer who would like to improve your skills through one-on-one driver coaching, Don is available for private consulting. Please call him at (818) 441-4181 or contact him at:

Don Alexander
1012 Fair Oaks Ave., Suite 392
South Pasadena, CA 91030

Automotive Books from Robert Bentley

AUTOMOBILE BOOKS

Jeep Owner's Bible™ *Moses Ludel*
ISBN 0-8376-0154-1

Ford F-Series Pickup Owner's Bible™
Moses Ludel ISBN 0-8376-0152-5

Chevy C/K Series Pickup Owner's Bible™ *Moses Ludel*
ISBN 0-8376-0157-6

Chevrolet by the Numbers™: 1955-1959
Alan Colvin ISBN 0-8376-0875-9

Chevrolet by the Numbers™: 1960-1964
Alan Colvin ISBN 0-8376-0936-4

Chevrolet by the Numbers™: 1965-1969
Alan Colvin ISBN 0-8376-0956-9

Chevrolet by the Numbers™: 1970-1975
Alan Colvin ISBN 0-8376-0927-5

Alfa Romeo Owner's Bible™ *Pat Braden with foreword by Don Black*
ISBN 0-8376-0707-9

Sports Car and Competition Driving
Paul Frère with foreword by Phil Hill ISBN 0-8376-0202-5

The Technique of Motor Racing *Piero Taruffi with foreword by Juan Manuel Fangio*
ISBN 0-8376-0228-9

The Design and Tuning of Competition Engines *Philip H. Smith, 6th edition revised by David N. Wenner* ISBN 0-8376-0140-1

New Directions in Suspension Design: Making the Fast Car Faster *Colin Campbell* ISBN 0-8376-0150-9

The Scientific Design of Exhaust and Intake Systems *Philip H. Smith and John C. Morrison* ISBN 0-8376-0309-9

Vintage Racing British Sports Cars *Terry Jackson with foreword by Stirling Moss*
ISBN 0-8376-0153-3

FUEL INJECTION

Ford Fuel Injection and Electronic Engine Control: 1980-1987 *Charles O. Probst, SAE* ISBN 0-8376-0302-1

Ford Fuel Injection and Electronic Engine Control: 1988-1993 *Charles O. Probst, SAE* ISBN 0-8376-0301-3

Bosch Fuel Injection and Engine Management *Charles O. Probst, SAE*
ISBN 0-8376-0300-5

BMW SERVICE MANUALS

BMW 5-Series Service Manual: 1982-1988 528e, 533i, 535i, 535is *Robert Bentley*
ISBN 0-8376-0318-8

BMW 3-Series Service Manual: 1984-1990 318i, 325, 325e(es), 325i(is), and 325i Convertible *Robert Bentley*
ISBN 0-8376-0325-0

VOLKSWAGEN OFFICIAL SERVICE MANUALS

GTI, Golf, and Jetta Service Manual: 1985-1992 Gasoline, Diesel, and Turbo Diesel, including 16V *Robert Bentley*
ISBN 0-8376-0342-0

Corrado Official Factory Repair Manual: 1990-1994 *Volkswagen United States*
ISBN 0-8376-0387-0

Passat Official Factory Repair Manual: 1990-1992, including Wagon *Volkswagen United States* ISBN 0-8376-0377-3

Cabriolet and Scirocco Service Manual: 1985-1993, including 16V *Robert Bentley*
ISBN 0-8376-0362-5

Volkswagen Fox Service Manual: 1987-1993, including GL, GL Sport and Wagon *Robert Bentley* ISBN 0-8376-0340-4

Vanagon Official Factory Repair Manual: 1980-1991 including Diesel Engine, Syncro, and Camper *Volkswagen United States* ISBN 0-8376-0336-6

Rabbit, Scirocco, Jetta Service Manual: 1980-1984 Gasoline Models, including Pickup Truck, Convertible, and GTI *Robert Bentley* ISBN 0-8376-0183-5

Rabbit, Jetta Service Manual: 1977-1984 Diesel Models, including Pickup Truck and Turbo Diesel *Robert Bentley*
ISBN 0-8376-0184-3

Rabbit, Scirocco Service Manual: 1975-1979 Gasoline Models *Robert Bentley*
ISBN 0-8376-0107-X

Dasher Service Manual: 1974-1981 including Diesel *Robert Bentley*
ISBN 0-8376-0083-9

Super Beetle, Beetle and Karmann Ghia Official Service Manual Type 1: 1970-1979 *Volkswagen United States*
ISBN 0-8376-0096-0

Beetle and Karmann Ghia Official Service Manual Type 1: 1966-1969
Volkswagen United States
ISBN 0-8376-0416-8

Station Wagon/Bus Official Service Manual Type 2: 1968-1979 *Volkswagen United States* ISBN 0-8376-0094-4

Fastback and Squareback Official Service Manual Type 3: 1968-1973
Volkswagen United States
ISBN 0-8376-0057-X

AUDI OFFICIAL SERVICE MANUALS

Audi 5000S, 5000CS Official Factory Repair Manual: 1984-1988 Gasoline, Turbo, and Turbo Diesel, including Wagon and Quattro *Audi of America*
ISBN 0-8376-0370-6

AUDI OFFICIAL SERVICE MANUALS (CONT'D)

Audi 100, 200 Official Factory Repair Manual: 1988-1991 *Audi of America*
ISBN 0-8376-0372-2

Audi 80, 90, Coupe Quattro Official Factory Repair Manual: 1988-1991 including 80 Quattro, 90 Quattro and 20-valve models *Audi of America*
ISBN 0-8376-0367-6

Audi 5000, 5000S Official Factory Repair Manual: 1977-1983 Gasoline and Turbo Gasoline, Diesel and Turbo Diesel *Audi of America* ISBN 0-8376-0352-8

Audi 80, 90, Coupe Quattro Electrical Troubleshooting Manual: 1988-1992
Robert Bentley ISBN 0-8376-0375-7

Audi 4000S, 4000CS, and Coupe GT Official Factory Repair Manual: 1984-1987 including Quattro and Quattro Turbo *Audi of America*
ISBN 0-8376-0373-0

Audi 4000, Coupe Official Factory Repair Manual: 1980-1983 Gasoline, Diesel, and Turbo Diesel *Audi of America*
ISBN 0-8376-0349-8

SAAB OFFICIAL SERVICE MANUALS

Saab 900 16 Valve Official Service Manual: 1985-1993 *Robert Bentley*
ISBN 0-8376-0312-9

Saab 900 8 Valve Official Service Manual: 1981-1988 *Robert Bentley*
ISBN 0-8376-0310-2

Saab 9000 Official Service Manual: 1987-1992 *Robert Bentley* ISBN 0-8376-0314-5

VOLVO SERVICE MANUALS

Volvo 240 Service Manual: 1983-1993 DL, GL, Turbo, 240 DL, 240 GL, 240 SE *Robert Bentley* ISBN 0-8376-0285-8

RB ROBERT BENTLEY, INC. | AUTOMOTIVE PUBLISHERS

Robert Bentley has published service manuals and automobile books since 1950. Please write Robert Bentley, Inc., Publishers, at 1033 Massachusetts Avenue, Cambridge, MA 02138 or call 1-800-423-4595 for a complete listing of current automotive literature, including titles and service manuals for **Jaguar, Triumph, Austin-Healey, MG,** and other cars.